The Librarian's Guide to Homelessness

The Librarian's Guide to
HOMELESSNESS

An EMPATHY-DRIVEN
APPROACH *to*
SOLVING PROBLEMS,
PREVENTING CONFLICT,
and
SERVING EVERYONE

R Y A N   D O W D

ALA
Editions   CHICAGO | 2018

Ryan Dowd has spent most of his career as executive director of a large homeless shelter near Chicago. In addition, he trains organizations around the globe (libraries, homeless shelters, security guards, hospitals, police departments, businesses, etc.) on how to use empathy-driven enforcement with homeless individuals. He is a licensed attorney and has a master's degree in public administration. Dowd is ecstatically married to his soulmate—Krissie—and has two amazing children—Cameron and Hailey. For more information, go to www.homelesslibrary.com.

© 2018 by the American Library Association

Extensive effort has gone into ensuring the reliability of the information in this book; however, the publisher makes no warranty, express or implied, with respect to the material contained herein.

ISBN: 978-0-8389-1626-1 (paper)

Library of Congress Cataloging in Publication Control Number: 2017052410

Cover design by Alejandra Diaz. Book design and composition in the Chaparral Pro and Sagona typefaces by Mayfly Design.

♾ This paper meets the requirements of ANSI/NISO Z39.48–1992 (Permanence of Paper). Printed in the United States of America

22 21 20 19 18   5 4 3 2 1

K,

Thank you for never asking me to be anyone else.

R

Contents

Acknowledgments

This book would not have been possible without a lot of people, particularly:

- Jamie Santoro (and the whole ALA Editions team): You were awesome, even when I was a pain in the butt.
- Aurora Public Library: Thank you for being the guinea pig for the early iterations of the concepts in this book. And thank you for changing your approach with homeless patrons from Hesed House. Oh, and thank you for letting me check out books!
- The staff, volunteers, guests, and residents of Hesed House: I learned how to "do hesed" from you all. You changed my world.
- To my parents: Thank you for letting me hide in your basement to write this book (and for giving me life and love, too, of course!).
- Krissie, Cameron, and Hailey: Thank you for giving me the enormous amount of time (and support) it took to write this book. You are my world.

Introduction

Who Am I? Who Are You?

All Librarians are Secret Masters of Severe Magic. [It] goes with the territory.
—CATHERYNNE M. VALENTE[1]

It was a cold December night in Illinois. Snow flurries swirled around the parking lot outside the homeless shelter (a large brick building that used to be a municipal incinerator) in mini-cyclones.

Inside, the shelter was relatively quiet. At 10:30 p.m., most of the residents had gone to bed in order to get a restless night of sleep before getting up early for work.

I was twenty-one years old. I had been working in the shelter for a week and this was my first shift "flying solo." My training had consisted of "Here are your keys. There is the bathroom. Try to do what the other staff do." The brevity of training was spectacularly effective at weeding out people who didn't belong (and some who did).

The night had been a little crazy (I still didn't know what I was doing), but everyone had survived. By 10:30, things had finally calmed down enough that I could get dinner. I went back to the industrial kitchen and got a tray of food—pulled pork sandwich, peas, and a Styrofoam cup of cherry Kool-Aid. I ate standing up so I could watch the room.

A short gentleman with a scraggly mustache approached me agitated, and a bit defiant. I squared my body off at him and straightened my shoulders to show him I was not intimidated. He got loud, but I was able to match his volume every time he got louder. He was rude with me, but I was rude back, lest he think he could get his way through bullying. I was determined not to be perceived as weak and to "teach him a thing or two."

Just as a pot of water eventually boils over when enough heat is applied, the small man with the scraggly mustache exploded. He lunged at me. His open palm came up, making contact with my tray of food. Like a sprinter coming out of the blocks, the tray exploded upwards. The cherry Kool-Aid splattered to my right in big red droplets and the peas went left as if ejected from a shotgun. The pulled pork sandwich went straight up.

The pulled pork separated from its bun and then came back down, landing on the top of my head with a noise that was somewhere between a "splat" and a "shpwack." Satisfied with the outcome, the small man with the scraggly mustache stormed past me and out the door.

I was stunned by what had happened, standing dumb and mute. A 400-pound African American man called "Big Ride" strolled over casually and started to pick pulled pork out of my hair. I asked him what had happened. Big Ride broke into a big friendly grin and said, "Welcome to Hesed House."

· · ·

Who I Am and What I Believe

This book comes out my life's work of caring for homeless families and individuals. I started volunteering at my local homeless shelter—Hesed House—when I was thirteen years old. It just felt right to be there. I continued volunteering in junior high, high school, and then in college. In my senior year of college—when I was twenty-one years old—I got a part-time job in that shelter. I worked there through graduate school and law school. After I took the bar exam (and passed!), I became executive director of Hesed House.

In the last two decades, I have met tens of thousands of homeless individuals. I have talked to individuals on the day they became homeless and the day they moved into their own apartments. I have sat with women who had just returned to the shelter after being raped. I have laughed with some homeless individuals and cried with others. I have broken up more fights than I can count and had a knife pulled on me (only once, thankfully).

This book comes out of that experience, but it is also philosophically rooted in what I believe in the deepest—most intimate—parts of my soul. Consequently, it is worth quickly sharing those beliefs:

1. I believe that *every* human being is worthy of basic human dignity (without exception).
2. I believe that people are basically good, and—when treated with respect and care—*most* people *most* of the time will respond in kind.
3. I believe that compassion and empathy are not weakness. In fact, compassion and empathy are the most powerful tools for creating a more just world.

4. I believe that compassion and empathy are not enough. We also need skills and practice to make compassion as effective as it can be. We need "practical compassion" in order to change the world.

While this book is about all four of these beliefs, it really focuses on belief number 4. I have spent the entirety of my career learning—and teaching—the art of "practical compassion." It really is the key to changing the world. If we have compassion for the most vulnerable, but we are too afraid of them to have a conversation with them, our compassion isn't worth much. The revolution is in the relationship. Sometimes, though, the relationship requires a little effort and understanding, and a few practical skills. The essence of this book is a specific practical skill: "empathy-driven enforcement."

Empathy-driven enforcement is a system for getting people to follow your rules without having to threaten them with punishment. It is in contrast to the typical "punishment-driven enforcement" approach that is the dominant model in most places. In fact, punishment-driven enforcement is so prevalent that we often mistakenly believe that our only other option is to not enforce the rules. Many staff—thinking they have no other choice—feel like they have to choose between compassion and enforcing the rules. They don't. There is another way!

Empathy-driven enforcement leverages research in psychology, neuroscience, and social science to obtain voluntary compliance with the rules. It is substantially more effective than punishment-driven enforcement. Libraries that have switched to using empathy-driven enforcement report that

- Problems with homeless patrons are reduced by 80 percent
- Staff are happier and more confident
- Non-homeless patrons feel safer
- Homeless patrons feel more welcome and dignified

Empathy-driven enforcement is not a panacea for all of your woes. It won't help you pass that referendum for additional tax revenue (though it will help people feel safer in your libraries, which can't hurt your ballot initiative). It is a very effective system, though, for reducing problems with homeless patrons while still fulfilling your library's mission of serving the whole community.

What Problems Do You Face?

I have spoken to library groups all around the country. I begin every training by asking the attendees what problems they face with homeless patrons. I always get different versions of the same answers:

1. Sleeping/snoring in the library
2. Strong odor
3. Bringing in multiple bags
4. Drunk or high
5. Monopolizing space
6. Arguing with staff
7. Arguing with each other
8. Bathing in the bathroom
9. Panhandling
10. Taking shoes off
11. Bringing in pets
12. Sitting, but not reading
13. Talking to self
14. Pacing

A Quick Note about Language

Throughout this book, I will refer to "homeless individuals" and "homeless people." This violates the principles of people-first language, which say that instead we should say "people experiencing homelessness."

I am sympathetic to the idea that language shapes our perception of others. In fact, I was trained to never say "the homeless" (which removes "people" entirely).

I have chosen not to use the term "people experiencing homelessness" for three reasons:

1. It is a very cumbersome phrase. Given the number of times I need to refer to "people experiencing homelessness" in this book, it would be nearly unreadable if I used the preferable language.
2. I have been doing this as my full-time profession for a long time and I simply have been unable to retrain my brain away from phrases I have said hundreds of thousands of times. Please forgive this old dog who is unable to learn a new trick.
3. Homeless people don't care how they are referred to (at least not the tens of thousands I have talked to). If it isn't their crusade, I'm not going to make it mine. Language does matter, but we cannot allow "right words" to be a substitute for "right actions." Instead of focusing on how we describe homeless people, I'm going to save my energy for what truly does matter to them: being treated with basic human dignity.

If you disagree with my choice, I still totally respect you. I would ask the same.

Does this list sound familiar? You're not alone. Libraries all around the country (around the world, actually) are trying to come to terms with what it means to be "public" in an era of widespread homelessness. In this book, we will go over how to handle these predicaments you face.

Is This Book for You?

Are you the type of person who wants to serve every member of your community, even those who have been cast aside?

This book might be for you.

Do you sometimes get frustrated when homeless patrons break the rules and cause trouble?

This book might be for you.

Do you wish your library had a system for creating a calm, safe library that did not require you to kick people out?

This book is definitely for you.

What You Will Learn in This Book

It took me two decades to learn the art and science of empathy-driven enforcement. This book is the distillation of what I have learned, of making a lot of mistakes along the way and doing a lot of research.

- In part I, you will learn some deep (and non-obvious) lessons about homelessness, as well as the science behind empathy.
- In part II, you will learn specific tools of empathy-driven enforcement.
- In part III, you will learn how to handle particular predicaments, like sleeping patrons or how to deal with individuals struggling with mental illness.
- In part IV, you will learn how to lead your team in empathy-driven enforcement and how your library can best assist your homeless patrons.

Grab a cup of coffee. Kick up your feet. Clean your glasses. It is time to learn some cool stuff that just happens to be dang practical!

Note

1. Catherynne M. Valente, *The Girl Who Soared over Fairyland and Cut the Moon in Two* (New York: Feiwel & Friends, 2013).

Part I

Homelessness and Empathy

Top Ten Homeless Myths

I could no longer pull wands, potions, and light sabers out of books, but when it came to research, give me a well-stocked library and I was a goddamned Merlin.

—Jim C. Hines[1]

Everyone sat around the donated conference room table—oblong and scratched—waiting for me to speak first. There were six of "them" and me.

There was the older white woman—with long, stringy grey hair—her body too thin for her bone structure. The wire-frame cart she pulled was tidier than most, but the contents—plastic bags and yellowed tabloid magazines mostly—retained the appearance of a stereotypical *bag lady*. Since college, she had always drank a little too much, but in the way that makes middle-class women likable at dinner parties. But then her son died. He was two. He would have been in his mid-thirties now. For three decades she had filled a toddler-sized hole in her soul with vodka, mostly from 50-milliliter plastic single-serving bottles like the airlines serve ("nips" some people call them, or "miniatures").

There was the large black man who laughed most of the day—every day—with a booming laugh that made everyone smile upon hearing its impact. The shelter volunteers loved him because gratitude is an art and he was a master artist, able to paint over the awkwardness one feels while serving another who cannot repay the kindness. He called me "Ryan's Hope," after some defunct soap opera that I've never seen. He had been shot once—in the shoulder, he showed me the wound—walking home from work at the factory (apparently the teenage boy a few yards behind him was wearing the wrong colors for that part of town). For work, he had done just about everything: landscaping, retail, McDonald's, shoveling snow—but his real passion was fixing cars ("My pappy taught me to take an engine apart and put it back together again").

There was the eighteen-year-old white girl with pink hair and fresh tattoos, barely old enough to live in a shelter without a parent. Had she arrived a few months earlier we would have had to call the Department of Children and Family

Services to come get her. But a few months ago—when she was still legally a child—she was living in a crack house—the only place that would take her. She left after the second time she was raped, wishing she had left after the first time. A few months before that, her parents had given her two hours to pack her stuff. Women aren't supposed to love women, not in *that way,* and her parents were not about to allow an abomination in their house. She was very pretty—which is a significant handicap when you are trying not to be noticed by certain types of men.

There was the middle-aged man with the middle-sized midsection. His grey goatee was always neatly trimmed and he ironed everything before he wore it. He seemed like a straight-shooter—as the expression goes—but one day he told me that he had been a Secret Service agent assigned to the presidential detail in the 1990s. He didn't seem to be a liar or mentally ill. He reached into his back pocket and pulled out an old photograph. In the center of the picture was Bill Clinton looking vibrant and strong and confident (before Monica, *obviously*). Standing slightly to one side and back a few feet was a younger version of the man in front of me. He was wearing a black suit, a starched white shirt, and a dark, unspectacular tie. His face was completely blank and his gaze was wide and over the crowd, with an earpiece just like in the movies. I never did find out for sure what precipitated his remarkable tumble from presidential escort to homeless shelter resident, but based on a few cryptic comments he made over the months, I suspected it had something to do with a woman.

There was the heavy woman with one large breast. The surgeon had tricked her and cut off the other for absolutely no medical reason, though the medical exam board dismissed her complaint quickly ("the whole medical profession is corrupt"). She never did find out why he had taken half her womanhood, but she was pretty sure that J. K. Rowling was behind it. Ever since that bitch had stolen her manuscripts about the young wizard, she had been persecuted by strangers who had no other obvious reason to hurt her. She liked me, though, because I hadn't taken it personally when she wrote the Board of Directors a letter, warning them that I was using the shelter to embezzle drug money that I kept buried on an island in the river. I—apparently—was more forgiving than her family, who had long ago tired of her delusions.

There was the "sometimes single" father, who looked a little like a young Michael Jackson, but much smaller and not as handsome. His smile was slight, but genuine, and the crow's feet around his eyes were honestly earned. His wife would appear occasionally and then disappear for weeks at a time. He had the particularly tragic curse of loving a woman who was indifferent to both his affection and the weight of the burden he carried trying to be a good father to two young boys in a large homeless shelter. I liked him.

This motley crew was a focus group I was leading in our homeless shelter. We needed to pick a new legislative advocacy goal for the volunteers and we wanted the opinion of the residents.

I had prepared a list of issues for them to pick from:

1. Mental health services
2. Police harassment
3. Affordable housing
4. Sexual assault
5. Health care

I quickly lost control of the conversation, though. There was one injustice that they kept coming back to, no matter how often I tried to talk about my list of topics.

They wanted library cards.

I didn't really understand. *Were they not allowed in the library?* No, they were allowed in the library. *Were they not able to use the computers for job searches?* No, they were able to use the computers. *Why were library cards so important, then?*

The woman with one breast and a grudge against J. K. Rowling looked at me like I was crazy. "Because," she said slowly, as if she was talking to a toddler, "without a library card you cannot check out books."

"It's like this, Ryan," the single father who looked like Michael Jackson said. "I was born in this town. I have lived here my whole life, but I can't get a library card. Some guy who just moved to town yesterday can get a card, but I can't. I mean, did I stop being a member of this community when I got evicted?"

The room was silent as everyone nodded along.

And for the first time in my life, I fully understood libraries. Libraries are at the center of community in a way that no other modern institution is. Libraries are indifferent to race, creed, color, religion, political affiliation, or socioeconomic status. A library card is one of the few attributes that fully defines who is a member of the community. Every single inhabitant in your community can use the library.

Except sometimes homeless people.

Note: I am happy to report that the local library did change its policies, allowing homeless individuals to get cards and check out books.

• • •

Ten (Plus One) Homeless Myths

There are a lot of myths out there about homeless people. I'm not going to try to dispel all of them. But I do want to address some of the ones that affect how your library works with homeless patrons:

- Myth 1: People are homeless for a long time.
- Myth 2: Most homeless people are mentally ill.
- Myth 3: Most homeless people are addicts.
- Myth 4: Most homeless people are unemployed.
- Myth 5: Most homeless people are old men with long beards.
- Myth 6: Most homeless people are stupid and/or uneducated.
- Myth 7: Homelessness can happen to anyone.
- Myth 8: Homeless people know they are homeless.
- Myth 9: Homeless people like libraries because libraries are warm and dry.
- Myth 10: Homeless people are nothing like you and me.
- Bonus Myth: Homeless people are just like you and me.

Myth 1: People Are Homeless for a Long Time

There are multiple "types" of homelessness. Experts disagree on exactly how many types there are—and exactly what to call them—so I will simplify it. For our purposes, there are three types:

- *Short-Term.* Individuals experiencing short-term homelessness aren't homeless for very long. At Hesed House, 50 percent of the people who come to our shelter are out again within two weeks. They typically have no major issues. Some sort of financial crisis bumped them out of housing and they scramble quickly to get back in.

- *Medium-Term.* Individuals experiencing medium-term homelessness are homeless for up to one year. This subgroup typically has one— but only one—major issue (e.g., mental illness, substance abuse, health problems, legal problems, etc.). It takes about a year to work through a major life challenge. This subgroup accounts for 42 percent of the residents at Hesed House.

- *Chronic.* Individuals experiencing chronic homelessness are homeless for more than one year (and often much more). This subgroup has multiple major issues (e.g., mental illness *and* substance abuse *and* health problems *and* legal problems, etc.). It can take years (or forever) to work through multiple serious life challenges. This subgroup comprises 8 percent of the residents at Hesed House in any given year. The federal government estimates that the chronically homeless account for 10 percent of all homeless people nationally.

When most people—including librarians—talk about homeless individuals, they are actually talking about chronically homeless individuals. Most homeless individuals simply don't fit our stereotypes: long beards, dirty clothing, talking to themselves, panhandling. In fact, I guarantee you that you see homeless individuals all the time and have absolutely no idea that they are homeless. They simply don't "look homeless." We had a guy at our shelter who ironed his clothing every night so he could go to work the next day as a paralegal at one of the biggest law firms in Chicago. I'm sure that no one outside of the shelter ever realized he was homeless.

The chronically homeless (8–10 percent of the total homeless population) are much more likely to fit the stereotypes we have about homelessness. They often struggle with mental illness and addiction, which can really take a toll on a person's physical appearance over time.

When library staff express concern over their homeless patrons, what they usually really mean is that they are having problems with their chronically homeless patrons. Consequently, this book is intended primarily to help you have more confidence in working with your chronically homeless patrons.

Myth 2: Most Homeless People Are Mentally Ill

National estimates are that about 20–25 percent of homeless individuals struggle with mental illness. Yes, that is much higher than the general population (6 percent), but it is hardly "most."[2]

What is worth noting, though, is that—in my opinion—mental illness, and particularly severe mental illness—is increasing. As governments continue to cut funding from the public mental health system, more and more individuals with mental health needs are left to fend for themselves. This has had a profound impact on shelters around the country (and libraries, too). The hardest part for shelters and libraries is not so much the breadth of mental illness, but the depth. A patron with paranoid schizophrenia can be a very difficult challenge for unequipped staff.

For a slightly deeper dive into mental illness, turn to chapter 10.

Myth 3: Most Homeless People Are Addicts

National estimates are that 38 percent of homeless individuals struggle with alcohol abuse and 26 percent struggle with other drugs.[3] *Note:* Many people struggle with both, so you can't add them up to get the "total" addiction rate. Yes, that is higher than the general population (6.6 percent for alcohol and 9 percent for drugs).[4] No, that is hardly "most" homeless people being addicted.

As Forrest Gump would say, "And that is all I have to say about that." Actually, that's not true. I'll say a lot more in chapter 11.

Myth 4: Most Homeless People Are Unemployed

This myth becomes less true every year. I have worked in homelessness since 1999, and every year a larger and larger percentage of our residents are employed. While a few decades ago the majority of homeless individuals were unemployed, an increasingly large percentage are now "underemployed."

At Hesed House, about 50 percent of our residents head off to a job in the morning. The reason is simple: wages have remained relatively stagnant for the last several decades while housing prices have increased dramatically. Since 1960, wages have increased (adjusting for inflation) by only about 20 percent, whereas rental prices have increased by 60 percent during the same time period (adjusted for inflation).[5]

You might be thinking that the Great Recession helped by pushing down housing prices. You would be wrong, though. While the Great Recession decimated home values, it actually increased rental prices in most communities. After people's homes were foreclosed on, they joined the rental market, thereby increasing demand (and raising prices).

Myth 5: Most Homeless People Are Old Men with Long Beards

We all have an image in our mind of what a homeless person looks like. He is male. He is middle-aged or older. He has a long, untrimmed beard. Yes, some homeless people do fit this stereotype, but not most.

The U.S. Department of Housing and Urban Development (HUD) requires communities to do periodic "point in time" counts. We count everyone in the shelter, and then we run around in the dark at night trying to find people living under bridges and in abandoned buildings. It is a heck of a lot of fun! (No, seriously, it actually is.) Anyhow, in 2016 (the most recent year with available data) on a single night there were 549,928 homeless individuals in the United States.[6] This includes some startling statistics:

- 22 percent were children
- 40 percent were women
- 35 percent were part of a family

Every year, women and children become a larger percentage of the homeless population. The first time Hesed House had a child in the shelter for a single night, it was on the front page of the newspaper. Now we average 40 children per night (and have had as many as 80). Similarly, we used to have a small room for women and children. We have steadily increased room for women and children. Soon we will be creating a second shelter for families, just to handle their numbers.

Myth 6: Most Homeless People Are Stupid and/or Uneducated

Many people mistakenly believe that homeless individuals are stupid or uneducated. It just isn't true. A few years ago, I was eating at the shelter—meat loaf, if you were wondering—when the guy across the table started telling me all about the Brazilian economy during the 1980s. When he was done, I asked him how he knew so much about such an obscure topic. "I did my master's thesis on it," he replied. Apparently, he had a master's degree from Georgetown University. That was before the voices started to tell him to focus his efforts elsewhere.

I once did an informal poll of residents at Hesed House about their educational level. While some had not graduated high school, many had college degrees, a few had master's degrees (one guy had two), and one woman had a medical degree (I looked her up . . . she had—in fact—been a doctor).

When you talk to homeless patrons as if they are stupid and uneducated, they feel like you are being disrespectful. Do you know why? Because you *are* being disrespectful. People who feel disrespected are unpredictable (which is bad for you).

Myth 7: Homelessness Can Happen to Anyone

Homelessness can happen to anyone. *Wrong.*

We're all just one paycheck away from homelessness. *Not true.*

Both of these statements (incorrectly) assume that homelessness is just extreme poverty. Yes, homelessness is an extreme form of poverty, but it is not *just* the most extreme version of poverty. Homelessness is a very unique (and, fortunately, relatively rare) form of poverty.

Imagine that your landlord or mortgage company showed up at your door today with the sheriff demanding that you leave your house immediately. Would you go to a homeless shelter? Would you sleep in your car? Would you sleep outside or in an abandoned building? Probably not. You would most likely go stay with a relative or friend. In fact, take a second and make a quick mental list of people who would let you stay in a spare bedroom or on a couch. I can think of over twenty people that I know—for certain—would let me stay with them. I suspect that with a little begging, there are probably fifty different people who would let my family stay with them temporarily.

Money is not the only resource that matters. Relationships are a resource too. You don't need money if you have friends or family willing to help. Conversely, you don't need friends or family if you have money (at least not for survival).

When I was still in college, my girlfriend became pregnant. I was able to finish college and go to law school because my parents allowed me, my girlfriend, and our son to live in their finished basement for five years. Had I not had parents with the resources (and willingness) to help us, the trajectory of my life would have been *very* different. Spoiler alert: that college girlfriend is now my wife!

As I said, homelessness is a very particular type of poverty. It is a poverty of both money *and* relationships. Most people who are poor will never be homeless because they have friends or family who will prevent that. In 2015, the U.S. Census Bureau reported that 43.1 million Americans were living below the poverty line.[7] During the "point in time count" for 2015, HUD reported there were 564,708 homeless individuals.[8] In other words, only 1.31 percent of individuals who were poor were also homeless. Homelessness is relatively rare—even among individuals below the poverty line—because most people have sufficient relationships to give them shelter.

The only people who live outside or in a shelter are those who don't have sufficient relationship resources. There can be many reasons for this. Some people simply don't have family (e.g., foster kids). Some people have family, but that family is living on the edge already (e.g., in public housing, and they will be evicted if they take more people in). Others have family, but they have burned those bridges because of addiction or mental illness.

Unfortunately, as society changes to be more individualistic, families feel less and less responsibility for one another. The result is homelessness.

Myth 8: Homeless People Know They Are Homeless

I guess, "technically," most homeless people know they are homeless. They just don't think of themselves in that way.

Think about it this way: What are the labels you use to define yourself? What aspects of you make up your self-identity? If you are like most people, you probably define yourself around four dimensions:

- *Profession*—Librarian, security guard, and so on.
- *Relationships*—Mother, sister, brother, husband, and so on.
- *Hobbies*—Reader, fisherman, and so on.
- *Physical traits*—Tall, Asian, athletic, and so on.

Where does your housing status fit into your identity? If you meet someone at a party, do you say, "Hi, I'm Ryan. I live in a duplex with two bedrooms and two baths?" Of course not. That would be absurd. People don't use their housing as a key element of their identity. Guess what? Homeless individuals don't either. They don't introduce themselves as, "Hi, I'm Gary. I'm homeless." They don't even think about themselves as "homeless." It simply isn't an element of their self-identity. It is only non-homeless people who think in these terms.

Remember this when you are interacting with homeless individuals. If you see someone as a one-dimensional "homeless guy" and he sees himself as an "out-of-work mechanic with two children and a passion for old Ford Mustangs," you two will have a hard time truly communicating.

I once went to the funeral of a thirty-year-old man who had lived in our shelter. I had only known him in the context of his homelessness. In fact, I had never even spoken to him anywhere but at the shelter. At his funeral, the family had lots of pictures of him around the room on cork boards. It turned out that this "homeless guy" was a Chicago Cubs fan who loved to water ski. He looked as awkward in his high school prom photos as I did in my own. He liked to play Monopoly with his nephews and nieces. He had been a professional welder, though he had delivered pizza in high school. He had a mother and a father and siblings and friends who loved him. Homelessness did not define his life. In fact, homelessness wasn't even a footnote at his funeral (my presence was the only thing to give it away).

Myth 9: Homeless People Like Libraries Because Libraries Are Warm and Dry

Yes, homeless people do like the fact that libraries are warm and dry. There are also a lot of other reasons why homeless people enjoy being in libraries so much. Basically, if you were to make a list of all of the negative aspects of homelessness, a library is the antithesis of most of them.

Homelessness	Libraries
Crowded—Homeless shelters are inherently crowded places where people are forced to sit and sleep right next to each other.	**Spacious**—Even a very busy library has ample space for everyone to carve out a little space of his or her own.
Loud—Homeless shelters are loud.	**Quiet**—Even the children's section on a Saturday is quieter than a homeless shelter on its quietest day.
Chaotic—Homeless shelters have a lot of people, and many are struggling with substance abuse and mental illness. This makes for a pretty crazy environment.	**Calm**—Again, even on its craziest day, the library is going to be far calmer than a shelter on its best day.
Boring—Homelessness is very boring, without a lot of stimulation. Imagine sitting around for hours every day with nothing to do…	**Stimulating**—Libraries have a nearly infinite supply of free entertainment (books, magazines, computers, etc.).

continued on next page

continued from previous page

Homelessness	Libraries
Depressing—Being homeless is really bad for one's self-esteem.	**Escapism**—What better way to escape a rough life than to spend some time looking at the world through the eyes of Jay Gatsby or Clarice Starling or Jon Snow or Lucy Pevensie?[9]
Police-"Saturated"—Most anywhere homeless people go (e.g., public parks, walking around, etc.), they are hassled by police to move along.	**Police-"Free"**—Police tend to not go looking for homeless people in libraries, so it is a great place to go to "just be."
Excluded—Most everywhere that homeless people go, they are separated out from the rest of the community in a form of economic apartheid. They are forced out of the public eye.	**Inclusive**—Libraries are the heart of the community in many places, allowing homeless people a rare opportunity to be a part of the wider community.

The public library may, in fact, be the last truly democratic institution. Homeless individuals know—and appreciate—that.

Myth 10: Homeless People Are Nothing like You and Me

I once took an ignorant politician through our shelter at 10:00 p.m. It was a really crowded night and we had forty or fifty people sleeping in our dining room. His eyes were huge, never having really seen poverty up close. After we left the shelter, he was flabbergasted by what he had seen. He just kept saying, "Those people don't look homeless!"

I think he partially subscribed to *Myth 5: Most Homeless People Are Old Men with Long Beards*, but that wasn't all. He also had come to believe that homeless people are almost a different race of human beings. I think he would have been less surprised to find someone with two heads or purple horns.

I don't think ignorant politicians are the only ones who fall into this trap. It is easy to think of homeless individuals as "wholly other" than us. This is one of the reasons why I am a huge advocate of getting children to volunteer in homeless shelters as young as possible. Adults have preconceived notions and stereotypes firmly cemented in their brains. When kids start volunteering young enough—while they still just see "people" instead of "homeless people"—they often never develop the stereotypes.

Try this: next time you see some ragged soul with a cardboard sign panhandling on the side of the road, remember:

- He has (or had) parents that loved him, just like you.
- He played with toys when he was a child, just like you.

- He has had crushes on people and (hopefully) been in love, just like you.
- He has pains and hopes and dreams and disappointments, just like you.
- If you prick him with a pin, he will bleed. If you tickle him, he will laugh. If you poison him, he will die. Just like you (and William Shakespeare).

Thinking that homeless people are totally different than you is wrong and dangerous.

Bonus Myth: Homeless People Are Just Like You and Me

Thinking that homeless people are exactly like you is also wrong and dangerous. A homeless person's life and experience are very different from yours.

Have you ever

- Been evicted or foreclosed on?
- Eaten out of a dumpster?
- Gone longer than forty-eight hours without eating?
- Been forced to panhandle to survive?
- Slept outside in the winter without a tent or sleeping bag?
- Been mugged?
- Been arrested?
- Been sexually assaulted?
- Gone more than a week without access to a shower?
- Had to go to the bathroom (no. 2) outside in a city?
- Worn the same clothes for more than two weeks straight?
- Grown up poor?
- Been ticketed for jaywalking?
- Had something thrown at you out of a moving car?
- Slept in a bed with bedbugs?
- Lost all hope?

Many of you will be able to answer "yes" to some of these (I have experienced three of them). Unless you have been homeless, though, you probably have not experienced most of these things.

Someone with these very different experiences looks at the world differently than you do.

It is helpful to understand and appreciate the very real ways that a homeless person is different from you. In fact, understanding those differences is at the root of empathy.

Q & A

Question: How is rural homelessness different from urban or suburban homelessness?

Answer: Rural homelessness is much more complicated than urban or suburban homelessness for two reasons:

1. There are far fewer services. Cities tend to have far more nonprofit organizations than the country.
2. There are fewer forms of public transportation. Someone without a car is at a significant disadvantage.

In a rural area, the public library may be one of the few public institutions available for homeless individuals. It is especially important for your library to network with any other organizations (private or governmental) that do exist in your community.

Conclusion

There is a lot of misunderstanding around homelessness. So, next time you hear someone spouting off one of these myths about homelessness that have just been debunked, you can correct them.

Notes

1. Jim C. Hines, *Unbound* (New York: DAW, 2016).
2. National Coalition for the Homeless, "Mental Illness and Homelessness," www.national homeless.org/factsheets/Mental_Illness.pdf.
3. National Coalition for the Homeless, "Substance Abuse and Homelessness," www.national homeless.org/factsheets/addiction.html.
4. National Institute on Drug Abuse, "Nationwide Trends," https://www.drugabuse.gov/publications/drugfacts/nationwide-trends.
5. Andrew Woo, *How Have Rents Changed Since 1960?* https://www.apartmentlist.com/rentonomics/rent-growth-since-1960/.
6. U.S. Department of Housing and Urban Development, "The 2016 Annual Homeless Assessment Report (AHAR) to Congress," https://www.hudexchange.info/resources/documents/2016-AHAR-Part-1.pdf.
7. United States Census Bureau, "Income and Poverty in the United States: 2015," https://www.census.gov/library/publications/2016/demo/p60-256.html.

8. U.S. Department of Housing and Urban Development, "The 2015 Annual Homeless Assessment Report (AHAR) to Congress," https://www.hudexchange.info/resources/documents/2015-AHAR-Part-1.pdf.

9. One of our residents was once in a coma for a week. When he woke up, he told me: "Ryan, when I was in a coma I thought I was a pilot for American Airlines. It was so real. I had a great job and a family and a home. People respected me. And then I woke up, and I was just a drunk."

Homeless People Are (Not) Just Like You

Lance could be trusted with your life. Librarians are like that.
—Victoria Abbott[1]

I was thirteen years old, sitting in Sunday school class, when someone handed me a clipboard. I hadn't been paying attention, so I wasn't sure what the sign-up sheet was for. I noticed a strange pattern, though: every single girl in class had signed up and none of the boys. I liked those odds. Even a scrawny, nerdy guy like me could be a ladies' man if there was no competition. I scribbled my name at the bottom of the sheet and asked the girl next to me what I had just signed up for. She said, "Hesed House. It's a homeless shelter. We're going to volunteer there to serve dinner." "Cool," I said.

And that, folks, is how I accidentally discovered my calling and life's work. Yes, I went to a homeless shelter for the first time in an attempt to get a date (even as the only guy in the group, I still was unsuccessful). A few years ago, we were on the *Rosie O'Donnell Show* and Rosie asked me how I got started. My wife begged me to make something up, but I told Rosie the truth on national television. Awkward. Very awkward. But I digress . . . .

On the actual night, I arrived at Hesed House with my harem of pubescent girls and a few adults. We brought with us trays of ham slices covered in little pineapple cubes and a few cherries. (Ironically, my church still brings ham slices with pineapples/cherries nearly thirty years later.)

The homeless shelter was unlike anything I had ever experienced in my thirteen years of suburban life. Not everyone had all of their teeth. Some people smelled like my school's locker room. A few guys walked unsteadily the way my uncles did towards the end of a family Christmas party.

I will never forget one middle-aged woman in an oversized men's winter coat. The other residents sang "Happy Birthday" to her and gave her a present. *Homeless people have birthdays? Huh.* I had never thought about that. When she opened

17

the present, it was a box of "Japanese Cherry Blossom" scented feminine douche. The women all laughed and I made a mental note to ask my mom what douche is. *Homeless people laugh? Huh.* I had never thought about that.

I had completely forgotten about the reason I had come—the girls in my Sunday school class. This place captivated me more than any mere girl. It was exotic and different. It was unlike anywhere else in the world. I didn't know why—that would take years to understand—but I felt completely at home in the shelter. All I knew was that I liked it here and I liked these toothless, smelly, funny homeless people. They were absolutely nothing like me and yet—paradoxically—they were exactly like me. And—somehow—they showed me who I am.

Decades later, I understand myself better and I understand homelessness better. I have come to appreciate that homeless individuals are mostly like everyone else, but that there are some important differences. Understanding those differences has made all the difference for me in my career of working at a homeless shelter.

• • •

Knowing Is Half the Battle

"A man who is warm cannot understand one who is freezing," wrote Aleksandr Solzhenitsyn of life in a Soviet forced-labor camp.[2] I think the same is true of people who have never been homeless. Those of us who have never been homeless cannot understand someone who has been homeless for decades. But there is hope! As they say: "Knowing is half the battle!" If we begin with the premise that we don't fully understand the life of someone who is homeless, we can begin the path to true empathy.

Homeless people experience so many things that are outside the mainstream that their world is different from yours in significant ways. There are twenty differences that will help you run your library better. Specifically, homeless individuals

1. Grew up poor
2. Speak differently than you
3. Have a smaller vocabulary than you
4. Pay more attention to nonverbal cues than you
5. Argue differently than you
6. View respect differently than you
7. Look at time differently than you
8. Value relationships more than you
9. Value their possessions more than you

10. Look at space differently than you
11. Are funnier than you
12. Have experienced more trauma than you
13. Are in more danger than you
14. Want to look scary
15. Have had their IQs lowered
16. Are "habituated to punishment"
17. Have less self-worth than you
18. Are treated like crap more than you
19. Trust people less than you
20. Value fairness more than you

1: Most Homeless Individuals Grew Up Poor

Most homeless individuals grew up poor (not all, but most). I'm sure this does not come as a big surprise to you. After all, intergenerational poverty traps many families in cycles of poverty. This fact, though, is *very* important for your ability to work effectively with homeless patrons.

The main reason is that you probably did not grow up poor. When I do live trainings, there is always someone who is offended by my assumption that most library staff came from middle-class homes, but statistically it is true. I am not saying that *all* library staff grew up middle class, but most did. And if you grew up middle class, you have a very different worldview than someone who grew up poor.

There is a theory about the "culture of poverty" that is very useful for helping you to understand your homeless patrons. The basic premise is that individuals who grew up in a culture of poverty learned different norms, expectations, values, and ways of seeing the world than individuals who were raised in the middle class. Similarly, individuals who were raised in wealth learned different norms, expectations, values, and ways of seeing the world than individuals who were raised middle class or poor.

If you ever have the opportunity to take a Bridges Out of Poverty training based on the work of Ruby Payne (www.ahaprocess.com), I highly recommend it. One of the things they do in the training is have you take a quiz to see how well you would do in poverty, middle class, and wealth. The poverty quiz asks you questions like:

- "Do you know how to move in half a day?"
- "Could you get by without a car?"
- "Do you know which grocery store garbage bins can be accessed for food?"

The middle-class quiz asks questions like:

- "Do you know how to get your children into Little League?"
- "Do you talk to your children about going to college?"
- "Do you know the difference between principal, interest, and escrow on a house payment?"

The wealth quiz asks questions like:

- "Do you know how to ensure confidentiality from domestic staff?"
- "Do you know the hidden rules of the Junior League?"

Does This Book Stereotype Homeless People?

Some people have asked me if I am stereotyping homeless individuals (and library staff, too). They (correctly) point out that not every homeless person is the same. Similarly, not every library staff member is the same. A few people have even asked whether my emphasis on how homeless individuals are different than housed individuals is divisive of the human community.

I am sympathetic to these concerns. But…

The key to empathy is putting yourself in someone else's shoes. Empathy is easy with people who are just like you. Empathy is much harder, though, with people whose lives are very different than yours. You need to make a little extra effort to understand how their life is different than yours, how their worldview is different than yours, how their expectations are different than yours, and so on.

Of course, not every homeless individual is alike. Some are young. Others are old. Some are highly educated. Some are illiterate. Some struggle with mental illness, others don't. I obviously cannot paint a picture of a group of people that is true 100 percent of the time for 100 percent of the people.

I'm not trying to create a universally true model of homelessness (that is a fool's errand). I am trying to highlight the way that homeless individuals are *very often* different from their housed neighbors. It would be a massive disservice to homeless individuals to ignore some very real differences in worldview because we want to pretend that all human beings are exactly alike.

So, please, as you are reading the next few chapters, if you find yourself thinking, "But I know a homeless person who did not fit this description," do not immediately discount what I am saying.

- "Do you know how to enroll your children in an elite private school?"

Every time I take the quizzes, I score 100 percent on middle class and close to 0 percent on poverty and wealth. I am solidly middle class and I know it. You probably are too.

What the "culture of poverty" concept teaches us is that you and your homeless patrons have some very important differences, which we will visit in this chapter.

Disclaimer

The "culture of poverty" concept is not without its ardent detractors. In fact, I have been criticized for including it in my trainings. I am sure I will be criticized for including it in this book. The chief arguments against the culture of poverty include:

- It draws attention away from systemic causes of poverty and injustice.
- It can be used to blame victims (e.g., "you are poor because you don't think correctly").
- It ignores the differences between different cultures, pretending that all poor individuals are the same (e.g., Appalachian poverty is very different from inner-city poverty).
- It is can be misused as a code word for "black culture."

There is some validity to all of these concerns. The concepts in the "culture of poverty" theory can be misused for inappropriate purposes (especially by politicians). I have chosen to include this theory for one simple reason: it is—by far—the most effective tool I have found for helping middle-class Americans to break out of their own worldview and realize that their way of seeing the world is not the only valid one.

I think that we do a huge disservice when we pretend that "everyone is exactly the same." If everyone is exactly like me, then I don't need to try to put myself in their shoes. I don't need to try to understand them. I don't need empathy.

It is the differences between people that make humanity such a rich tapestry. If we can't talk about our differences for fear that someone will manipulate the idea, then we miss opportunities for genuine understanding.

In the United States, the dominant worldview is that of the middle-class culture, so it is easy to think of its norms and expectations as the "correct" ones, but this is very unhealthy. A middle-class worldview is not inherently better or worse than a poor worldview or a wealthy worldview, but they are very different. These differences leave a lot of room for miscommunication that we will be discussing throughout this book.

2: Homeless Individuals Speak Differently Than You

According to linguists, there are five levels of formality with which humans talk. Each of these levels is called a "register." For our purposes, only two matter:

1. *Formal register*—This is how you talk during a job interview or when you are pulled over by a police officer. It is very proper and does not use slang or swearwords.
2. *Casual register*—This is how you talk to family and friends. It is very informal and includes slang and the occasional swearword.

According to the "culture of poverty" theory, middle-class (and wealthy) parents teach their children about the two different registers and when to use each. Of course, middle-class parents don't realize that this is what they are doing. When my son was five years old he watched a lot of Bugs Bunny. We were meeting a new doctor and my son asked, "What's up, doc?" because he thought it was funny (which it is, kind of). I quickly corrected him, "No, Cameron, we don't talk to a doctor that way. We call her 'doctor' or 'ma'am.'"

During this exchange, I was unconsciously teaching my son the difference between formal and casual register and telling him that he should use formal register when talking to doctors. Of course, I didn't realize what I was doing. I thought I was just teaching him the "proper" way to talk.

According to the "culture of poverty" theory, poor families do not teach their children the difference between casual and formal register. In fact, they don't teach their children formal register at all. Consequently, many individuals raised in poverty use casual register all the time, in every conversation, even when middle-class etiquette demands otherwise.

It is important to note that there is nothing inherently correct about the middle-class use of two registers. Similarly, there is nothing inherently incorrect with individuals raised in poverty using only casual register. Unfortunately, because middle-class culture completely dominates American culture, we take it for granted that the "proper" way to speak to a stranger is in formal register. This leaves a lot of room for misunderstanding.

Consider this scenario: you are working the circulation desk when an unfamiliar patron approaches. You ask him if you can help him and he says, "Damn right you can. I can't find Harry Potter. Where that s--t at?" You will be surprised by the way he is talking. You will probably even be a little offended. You take the way he is talking to you—a member of the respected library profession—as disrespect. You wouldn't dream of talking to a stranger (especially a professional one) that way. But you are operating with middle-class rules of language. He is not. He is probably not trying to offend you. He is simply using casual register, the register he uses when he talks to everyone.

So, next time you are surprised by how someone is talking to you, stop and consider whether they are simply using casual register when you were expecting formal register.

3: Homeless Individuals Have a Smaller Vocabulary Than You

Individuals who grow up in poverty typically have a smaller vocabulary than individuals who grow up in wealth. By the age of three, a child from a professional home has heard 30 million more words spoken than a three-year-old in poverty.[3] In fact, a three-year-old in a professional household has a larger vocabulary than an adult in a welfare household.[4] In particular, individuals raised in poverty have a shortage of prepositions (e.g., "astride," "toward," "upon") and adverbs (e.g., "boldly," "solemnly," "zealously").

Let's pause here for a moment and clarify what I am *not* saying. I am not saying that homeless individuals (or other poor individuals) are stupid. Having a smaller vocabulary is not the equivalent of being stupid.

I was talking to a friend recently about his decision to go back to college as an adult. He said, "I want more words. There are times when I can't say what I want to say. I'm sure there is a word for what I'm thinking, but I don't know what it is. I want more words." If you have an expansive vocabulary, you probably take for granted that the word "expansive" means more than just "large."

Think about the problem of having a smaller vocabulary with this little thought experiment. Take thirty seconds and think of every word you know that means "problem." How many can you list? Without the aid of Google, I could think of nearly ten. My good buddy Google came up with this list: bind, bother, can of worms, catastrophe, complication, crunch, dilemma, dispute, headache, hitch, impasse, issue, jam, mess, morass, obstacle, perplexity, pickle, plight, predicament, puzzle, quandary, standoff, and trouble. Each of these is a synonym for "problem," but with a slightly different nuance and meaning.

4: Homeless Individuals Pay More Attention to Nonverbal Cues Than You

Obviously, everyone pays attention to nonverbal cues. That is why it can be so difficult to communicate by e-mail and text (have you ever accidentally insulted someone via text or e-mail?). In fact, nonverbal cues are so important to communication that we have even invented ways to convey body language and volume with only the written word. I CAN SHOUT AT YOU WITHOUT MOVING MY LIPS.

So, yes, everyone uses nonverbal cues. Individuals raised in poverty, though, pay *much* more attention to nonverbal cues than you do. (I apologize for shouting at you, but I feel very passionate about this topic.) Because of their smaller vocabulary, homeless individuals have to rely on nonverbal cues more to convey meaning. Specifically, they pay more attention to

1. Body language
2. Vocal inflection
3. Volume

The reason is simple: if you don't have different words to convey nuanced meaning, you need other ways to do it. Homeless people compensate for an absence in nuance in the words used by adding more nuance in body language. If I don't know the words "impasse" or "standoff," I use the word "problem" and try to convey the rest with my body and face.

The practical implication of this is that you need to be acutely aware of your body language, vocal inflection, and volume when talking to a homeless patron. They are listening more to what your body says than what your words say. When a homeless patron approaches you, if your body tenses up, your lips might be saying, "How may I help you?" but your body is saying, "I don't want you here because I'm afraid."

5: Homeless Individuals Argue Differently Than You

Homeless individuals also argue differently than you. In order to understand the difference, you need to understand something I call the "volume-to-anger ratio." The idea is to ascertain how loud someone is at different anger levels.

So, for example, how loud would you talk if you were mildly annoyed with a stranger? You would probably be relatively quiet (if you were raised in a typical middle-class home). What if the stranger said something that genuinely upset you? How loud would you be then? If you are a typical middle-class person, you will still speak at a normal level. Your tone might get sharper, but your volume wouldn't go up much.

So, how mad would you have to be to shout at a stranger? If you are like most middle-class people, you wouldn't shout at a stranger unless you were absolutely furious and had completely lost your temper. I call this "pull-out-a-bazooka-and-shoot-you-in-the-face" mad. This is the level of anger where you would hit someone.

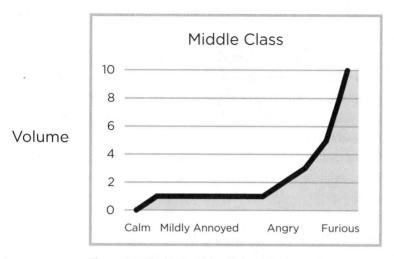

Figure 2.1: Chart of middle-class "volume-to-anger" ratio

This is how middle-class people argue: "I'm annoyed and I'm quiet. I'm upset and I'm quiet. I'm mad and I'm still quiet. OKAY, NOW I'M SHOUTING AND I'M GOING TO PUNCH YOU IN THE FACE!"

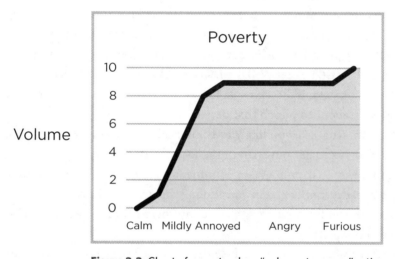

Figure 2.2: Chart of poverty-class "volume-to-anger" ratio

But this is not how individuals raised in a culture of poverty argue. Their "volume-to-anger ratio" is very different. Individuals raised in poverty get much louder much quicker. When they are only mildly annoyed, they may already be shouting. When they are furious, the volume goes up slightly (from a level 9 to a level 10). A middle-class individual cannot tell the difference between a level 9 "I'm annoyed" and a level 10 "I'm about to punch you!" Another individual raised in poverty—who is more attuned to body language, vocal inflection, and volume because of a smaller vocabulary—can tell the difference and knows when it is wise to back down. I am so middle class that I still can't tell the difference between the volume level for "mildly annoyed" and "I'm going to punch you!" On a weekly basis, I go running towards two people shouting at each other (I'm thinking World War III is about to erupt), only to get quizzical looks from people who aren't even mad at each other.

The much greater use of volume makes sense when you consider that poverty is inherently loud. If you live in a small apartment with eight other family members talking simultaneously (and the TV in the background), you need to be loud to be heard.

Neither of these approaches to communication is inherently right and neither is inherently wrong. As long as everyone knows the rules, everything is okay. Two individuals raised in poverty who are shouting at each other know that the other is only mildly annoyed. The problem arises in places where the two cultures intersect . . . places like libraries.

Imagine that you are working the circulation desk when a homeless patron approaches. He wants to get a library card and you ask to see his photo ID. He explains that he doesn't have an ID. You tell him that when he remembers to bring his ID, you can help him get a library card. He begins to get loud, barking that he didn't forget his ID; he doesn't have one. In your calmest librarian voice, you explain that you cannot issue a library card without a photo ID. At this point he explodes, "I CAN'T GET A NEW ID! I DON'T HAVE THE TEN DOLLARS!" You—being a prototypical middle-class person—wouldn't shout at someone like that unless you were about to punch that person in the face.

In this situation, what are you likely to think is about to happen next? Yup, you think you are about to get punched in the face. Consequently, you are likely to talk to him in a way that only makes him madder. If this cycle goes on long enough, it will almost certainly end in your calling the police. Unfortunately, you didn't need to call the police because he wasn't anywhere near mad enough to hit you. He was only annoyed.

I had this exact thing happen to me recently. I was talking to two individuals in my office. A woman—a resident of the shelter—became upset. The other person in my office asked, "Why are you so mad? Why are you shouting?" She turned to him and screamed "I'M NOT MAD AND I'M NOT SHOUTING!!" She actually wasn't mad, just merely upset. In her mind, her volume was perfectly appropriate for how upset she was. She was using a poverty "volume-to-anger ratio" and the guy was using a middle-class "volume-to-anger ratio."

The first Gulf War was started because of a similar cultural misunderstanding. When Saddam Hussein was preparing to invade Kuwait, he first met with the

American ambassador to Iraq. She expressed "concern" (American diplomats talk in very calm, measured tones, even when expressing something grave). Saddam Hussein, though, came from a culture where people shout and throw shoes. He took her mere "concern" as a signal that the United States would only issue a verbal condemnation of him if he invaded his neighbor. If the United States was willing to go to war, surely their ambassador would have shouted at him. So he invaded Kuwait…and America ejected him from Kuwait and invaded Iraq…and lots of people died. After the fact, the ambassador to Saudi Arabia intimated that a more effective message would have been to say, "Mr. President, if you really are considering invading Kuwait, by God, we'll bring down the wrath of God on your palaces, and on your country, and you'll be destroyed."[5] He also suggested that no American diplomat would talk like that.

6: Homeless Individuals View Respect Differently Than You

What did your parents teach you about respect? When you meet a stranger, should you show them respect immediately or do they need to earn it?

If you were raised in a middle-class home, your parents probably taught you to automatically grant respect to strangers when you first meet them. You can always withdraw that respect if it is warranted, but you start with it.

Individuals who were raised in a culture of poverty were often taught the exact opposite. They were taught that respect must be earned. To show respect to someone who has not yet earned it is to be a "chump." To show respect to someone who has not yet earned it is to be the dog that immediately rolls over when the larger alpha dog approaches. It is a sign of submission to someone else's dominance and superiority.

Neither of these approaches is inherently right or wrong, but there is a lot of room for misunderstanding when these two cultures interact. As a middle-class librarian, you expect to be treated according to middle-class mores, which includes being granted automatic respect. When the new homeless patron does not show you respect automatically, you probably view it as an attempt to be disrespectful. It isn't. You simply have not earned his respect yet, and if he grants you respect before you have earned it, he will feel inferior to you.

7: Homeless Individuals Look at Time Differently Than You

According to "culture of poverty" theorists, the three socioeconomic groups view time differently:

- *Poverty = Present*

  Individuals raised in poverty focus on the present because survival requires prioritizing immediate needs.

- *Middle Class = Future*

  Middle-class individuals focus on the future because their prioritization of achievement requires long-term goal-setting.

- *Wealth = Past*

  Wealthy individuals focus on the past because tradition is an important source of power. Don't believe me? Queen Elizabeth is only queen of England because her father was king (as was his father and his father's father). Queen Elizabeth's power is explicitly grounded in history.

Homeless individuals don't just focus on the present more than you. They also have a "shortened time horizon." A time horizon is how far out into the future you can see and think about. Think about the normal horizon for a skyline, how far you can physically see. When standing on the plains of Illinois on a sunny day, you can see for mile after mile. When standing in the middle of a thick forest or dense fog, you can't see very far. Time horizon is like that.

How often do you think about retirement? I think about it at least weekly (mostly to worry about whether I am saving enough to retire). How often do you think about next year? Most people think about next year frequently. How often do you think about next month? Next week?

Conversely, how often do you think about 250 years from now? Probably never. Me too. 250 years from now is simply beyond our time horizon.

For most middle-class individuals, their time horizon is somewhere between one year and as long as they expect to live.

For most homeless individuals, though, their time horizon is about twenty-four hours. That is as far out as they regularly think. Ten years from now is irrelevant. A year from now is not a priority. Even next week is not something regularly thought about. The reason for this is that most homeless individuals are in *crisis mode,* where the pressing survival needs of the next two days take priority.

Imagine that you don't know where you will sleep tonight, or whether it will even be indoors. Imagine that you don't know when you will get your next meal (or whether it will even be today or tomorrow). Imagine that there is a warrant out for your arrest (for a jaywalking ticket that you ignored) and you could go to jail at any moment. If this was your reality, would you think about retirement? Would you think about next month? How about next week? It is easy to think "Well, I would make long-range plans to better my situation," but you probably haven't gone thirty-five hours since your last meal. Hunger and fear change everything.

Having a time horizon of only twenty-four hours hurts homeless individuals in two very important ways:

1. It is really hard to get back on your feet again without the ability to make plans for more than one day out. Getting a job requires days or weeks of preparation (making a résumé, applying for a job, preparing interview clothing, arranging transportation to arrive for an interview on time, etc.). This shortened time horizon means that many good starts (e.g., applying for a job) are ruined when a new crisis hits and diverts attention away from them.

2. Any punishment that will occur more than one day from now isn't all that relevant. Any punishment that will last more than one day isn't any worse than a punishment that lasts only one day.

This last point is very important for library staff to understand. If you threaten a homeless individual with something that will happen next week, it is the same as if you were threatening him with something that will happen in the year 2250. Similarly, threatening to kick someone out of the library for one month is not that different from threatening to kick someone out for one day. This is especially important to remember when you are "escalating" punishment. If you say, "You are out for one week, but if you don't leave immediately it will be one month," the threat of additional time is meaningless. It is the equivalent of the court system giving a prisoner multiple life sentences (once you have one life sentence, the additional life sentences don't have much deterrent effect).

8: Homeless Individuals Value Relationships More Than You

According to the "culture of poverty" theory, relationships are more important to poor people than to their middle-class and wealthy counterparts. I am not saying that your friends and family don't mean much to you if you are middle class. What I mean is that relationships are more necessary for individuals in poverty. People with money can solve most of their problems by throwing cash at them. People without money don't have this option, so they have to use relational currency to solve their problems. This plays out in two specific ways:

1. It is a matter of survival. If you have two hot dogs and I have none, the strength of our relationship determines whether I will eat today or go hungry. If you and I are sleeping under a bridge and someone attacks me, the strength of our relationship might determine whether I survive the attack or not.

2. Friends are free entertainment. If you cannot afford a TV or a movie ticket, talking to friends is a great way to curb boredom (and—as will be discussed in chapter 13—homelessness is boring).

Don't be surprised if other homeless patrons come to the defense of their comrade you are punishing. Think about it this way: if you had to live on the streets and your buddy didn't even have your back with an irate librarian, would you trust him to protect you from a mugger? Probably not.

9: Homeless Individuals Value Their Possessions More Than You

Let's do a little thought exercise together: I want you to imagine that you woke up this morning knowing that you would be evicted today. Think about how you woke up *this* morning.

Now, if you were being evicted today, the first thing you would need to do is pick a bag to carry your belongings. Different people use different strategies. Some people pick backpacks because of the convenience (but they're small). Some people pick suitcases or duffel bags because they're large (but they're hard to lug around). Take a moment and think through all of the bags you own and mentally select one to become homeless with. Do you know which one you would take? Good.

Okay, now I want you to think through all of your belongings and decide which ones you are going to take with you. The catch, though, is that you can only take as much as will fit into this one bag. Which of your clothing makes the cut? Which of your photo albums? What about the Christmas ornament your daughter made for you in fifth grade? Don't forget your birth certificate; you'll need that. Do you have your bag mentally packed? Good, now mentally throw away the rest. It all ends up on the curb, picked through by neighbors before the garbage truck arrives. You will never see any of it again. Ever.

Now I want you to think about that single bag which carries every single physical possession that you have left: the pictures of your kids when they were little and of your deceased parents ... the only copy of your high school or college diploma ... your favorite T-shirt from that concert you went to when you were twenty-one ... the cookbook your grandmother passed down to you that had been her grandmother's ...

How much emotional attachment would you have to that bag? You would care about that bag more than any bag you have ever owned—or will ever own—in your entire life.

10: Homeless Individuals Look at Space Differently Than You

According to the "culture of poverty" theory, individuals raised in poverty view space differently than wealthier individuals do. Individuals raised in poverty do not attach as much importance to the "purpose" of different rooms. The ability to have specialized rooms is a luxury of the middle class. If you live in a three-room apartment with ten individuals, every room is used for every purpose. People sleep in the living room. People eat in every room. I knew a family with twelve children. They had four beds in every single room in their apartment. In fact, at Hesed House, at 9:00 p.m. we clear the tables out of the dining room and put out sleeping mats to turn the dining room into a barracks.

Consequently, do not be surprised when a homeless individual doesn't share your same regard for the varied purposes of different rooms in your library (eat here, study quietly there, etc.).

Homeless individuals have an even greater disadvantage with space than other individuals who are "merely poor." Let's do another thought experiment. This one is a little harder to grasp than the last one, but stick with me:

> When you have had a long hard day, where do you go to unwind and
> calm down? Is it your bedroom? The couch in your living room?
> Your office or study? Maybe your bathtub?

> Okay, now imagine that you can't go there anymore. If that place simply
> no longer existed, where would you go now to be alone? What is
> your second choice? Do you have your Plan B picked?

> Good, now I want you to imagine that it doesn't exist anymore either.
> Neither does your third choice or fourth. In fact, I want you to imag-
> ine that there is absolutely nowhere in the world that is uniquely
> "yours." There is exactly zero square feet in all the entirety of the
> universe where you can go to be alone and no one else can interrupt
> you.

Can you imagine that? I know. It is hard. I struggle too. I completely take my home and my bedroom for granted. I am a raging introvert, and after a long day of schmoozing with volunteers, donors, and staff, I need to be alone to decompress. When I get home and I need more space than my wife and children want to grant me, I simply go to the bathroom for a long while. I am sure that my family thinks I have a medical condition.

Homeless individuals have absolutely nowhere in the world where they can be alone. There is nowhere in the world that is "theirs." Shelters are really crowded places. Police chase homeless people out of parks. Even a public port-a-potty will eventually have someone else knocking at the door.

We tend to think of a home in very utilitarian terms: it is somewhere to go to be warm and store your stuff. But a home is much more than that. It is also a place to "be." I think those of us who have always had a place of our own cannot possibly comprehend what it is like to have nowhere in the entire universe where we can go to "be."

11: Homeless Individuals Are Funnier Than You

What happens when you cross a librarian and a lawyer? You get all the information you want, but you can't understand it.

Yeah, I didn't think that was funny, either. But I'm a lawyer, so . . .

Okay, the heading for this section is a little sensationalist. It isn't that homeless people are necessarily funnier than you (though they might be). They do, though—according to the "culture of poverty"—value humor more than you do. The reason is simple: if someone lacks the money to purchase entertainment (e.g., movie theater, bowling alley, dance club), they look for free forms of entertainment. One of the oldest forms of entertainment is telling jokes. Homeless individuals spend a lot of time talking to each other (sharing jokes, stories, etc.) because it is free.

This has practical implications for you:

- Learn a joke or two that you can tell patrons (they'll love you for it).
- Appreciate the humor of homeless patrons (they'll love you for that too).

12: Homeless Individuals Have Experienced More Trauma Than You

Most homeless individuals have experienced substantially more trauma than you:

- *Physical abuse*—It is *very* common for homeless individuals to have experienced physical abuse as children.[6]
- *Sexual abuse*—As many as half of homeless women were sexually abused as children.[7]
- *Eviction*—Imagine how traumatic it would be to lose your home, or be kicked out of your apartment.
- *Abandonment*—Someone only ends up on the streets after *every* friend and relative has refused them a place to sleep.
- *Physical violence*—Up to two-thirds of homeless women have been physically assaulted as an adult.[8]
- *Traumatic brain injury*—In one study, 45 percent of homeless men had had at least one traumatic brain injury event in their lives.[9]
- *More . . .*—I could go on and on (e.g., job loss, arrests, etc.), but you get the point.

In fact, homeless people's lives are so traumatic that they die much younger than housed individuals. The average life expectancy in the United States is 78 years old, but it is 42–52 for homeless individuals.[10]

13: Homeless Individuals Are in More Danger Than You

It is incredibly dangerous to be homeless. Homeless individuals are constantly being preyed upon by others. Any man who is homeless for more than a year or two has likely been attacked. Any woman who has been homeless for more than a few years has likely been sexually assaulted.

In my first month on the job at Hesed House, a woman was dropped off at the shelter by some guy who found her wandering on the side of a busy road on a wet winter night. She was dirty, but not in the typical "homeless way" (if there is such a thing). The mud on her clothing was fresh, still mixed with slush. It took me a while to get her talking, but eventually she confided in me that a strange man had grabbed her and pulled her into a large storm drain. He had raped her and then left her lying in the muddy snow. Apparently, it had all happened twenty minutes before she was dropped off at the shelter. She was in shock, asking repeatedly if she could take a shower and change clothes.

While this was my first experience with extreme violence against homeless individuals, it was not my last. We regularly have to bandage wounds (physical, mental, spiritual) for men and women who have been attacked.

This constant threat of violence makes many homeless people (understandably) very skittish. I would say it is a form of post-traumatic stress disorder (PTSD) except that it isn't a "form" of PTSD. It *is* PTSD. Just assume that anyone who has been homeless for a year or longer has PTSD. It won't be true 100 percent of the time, but it is close enough that it is a safe assumption.

While all homeless individuals are in constant danger, most homeless individuals are not dangerous. One of the great ironies is that—statistically speaking—homeless individuals have a much greater reason to fear the non-homeless than vice versa.

I have spent most of my career working with homeless individuals, and I can count on the fingers of one hand the number of times I have been afraid. Most homeless individuals are simply no more dangerous than anyone else.

And this includes those struggling with mental illness. Hollywood has taught us to fear those struggling with mental illness with movies like *Psycho, Halloween, Friday the 13th,* and *The Shining*. Halloween (the pseudo-holiday, not the movie) reinforces the link between mental illness and violence because of its strange costumes. (As an aside, can you imagine the public outcry if people dressed up as cancer patients or Alzheimer's patients for Halloween?) Reality just doesn't support this belief that the mentally ill are dangerous.

A recent study concluded that one in four people with mental illness will experience violence in a given year.[11] This is in contrast to the 1 percent of individuals with mental illness who commit acts of violence. In fact, 95–97 percent of violent acts are committed by individuals who are not struggling with a mental illness.[12] Statistically speaking, you are far more likely to be injured by someone who is *not* mentally ill.

14: Homeless Individuals Want to Look Scary

When you combine these two facts—it is dangerous to be homeless, but homeless people are not dangerous—you get a very interesting phenomenon. Many homeless people try to look dangerous on purpose (even though they aren't). The reasoning goes something like this: there are bad people out there who want to hurt me. I am not a bad person. If the bad people think I am a bad person, though, they will leave me alone.

In fact, many of the residents have tried to teach me this skill. They know that I am an activist who goes to marches and protests. (I have been arrested, but never in the United States.) After one protest, a few of the residents sat me down and taught me what to do if I end up in jail. The conversation went something like this:

Homeless guy: When you get to jail, immediately find the biggest, toughest, scariest-looking guy you can find.

Ryan: Got it! And then I offer to pay him for protection?

Homeless guy: No. You punch him in the nose when he isn't looking.

Ryan: But isn't there a chance he will beat me up?

Homeless guy: Oh, there isn't a chance. It is a certainty. He will beat the living hell out of you.

Ryan: Okay. So, why do I want to do this, then?

Homeless guy: Because everyone else in jail will think you are crazy and they will stay away from you.

I laughed at his advice, but he didn't offer it as a joke. He was serious.

I'm not a violent guy, and so I don't know if I could sucker punch a stranger (especially a big one). That said, if I thought it would keep me from getting jumped in the shower later on, I would probably do it.

Fortunately, most homeless people don't walk around sucker-punching big guys. They do often use a similar tactic, though, to have the same effect. Many homeless individuals purposely cultivate a scary image in order to keep the bad guys away. Crazy hair, an unkempt beard, a big coat with lots of places to hide weapons, and a dirty face all send a message. And that message is fairly effective at keeping bad guys away.

The problem, though, is that the "scary guy" image can't be turned off. If I make myself look dangerous to keep the bad guys away on the streets, when I walk into a library I can't suddenly be clean and well-groomed. I still look scary.

You have probably experienced this. Have you ever looked up from your desk to see a scary guy walking towards you and thought, "I thought Charles Manson died?" Your heart races and your mouth gets dry. Then Charles Manson asks you where he can find a book on Japanese horticulture. You are puzzled, but you answer his question. He says, "Thank you kindly, ma'am," and walks off toward the 635 stacks.

The Charles Manson-Botanist may be trying to look scary, just not for you. It is cliché, but the saying "don't judge a book by its cover" is *very* applicable when dealing with homeless patrons.

15: Homeless Individuals Have Had Their IQs Lowered

Being poor lowers your IQ. In fact, it lowers it by about thirteen points, the same as losing an entire night's sleep. How do I know that? Princeton researchers studied sugarcane farmers in India.[13]

Sugarcane is harvested and sold once per year, so the farmers are relatively wealthy right after the harvest and quite poor before it (because the money from the prior year would have been exhausted). They measured the farmers' IQ before and after the harvest, finding a huge change.

So, while homeless individuals are not inherently less intelligent than you, the fact that they are poor has lowered their IQ dramatically.

16: Homeless Individuals Are "Habituated to Punishment"

Most homeless individuals are what psychologists call "habituated to punishment." What this means is that they have experienced so much punishment that the threat of punishment no longer serves as a significant deterrent to breaking rules.

Imagine that in the last year the following has happened to you:

- Your boss fired you because you were late to work when your car broke down.
- Your spouse divorced you because you lost your job.
- Your children, parents, and siblings rejected you because you started drinking to calm down after the divorce.

- Your landlord evicted you even though you promised to pay him as soon as you could.
- The police arrested you for falling asleep in a public park.

Now imagine that you go to the library and the security guard is following you around. You would probably expect to be kicked out of the library (or at least treated poorly) no matter what you did. Experience has taught you that no matter what you do, you get punished by life. If the library security guard told you that he would kick you out if you fall asleep, would you really be afraid of being kicked out of the library after the year you have been having?

This is what it means to be "habituated to punishment." A person can become so desensitized to punishment that the threat of punishment becomes less effective (or completely ineffective) as a method for changing behavior.

Think about this the next time you are threatening a homeless patron. In the grand scheme of his or her life experiences, is your threat really that bad?

17: Homeless Individuals Have Less Self-Worth Than You

Homelessness is very bad for one's self-esteem. This is really obvious once you think about it, but it is easy to forget. There are multiple reasons for this:

- The road to homelessness is pretty bumpy and filled with personal failure. By the time someone becomes homeless, they have usually been fired, been divorced, been evicted, and been rejected by all of their family and friends.

- All homeless women are treated like prostitutes. At Hesed House, we frequently have to chase strange men off the property who think that a homeless shelter is a natural place to look for someone desperate enough to sell sex. In fact, every month or so, one of our female staff is propositioned in the parking lot by some creep who is not homeless. Can you imagine how you would feel if every day of your life someone offered to purchase the use of your body?

- All homeless men are treated like violent psychopaths (and pedophiles). Because of the massive misunderstanding of the link between mental illness and violence (see chapter 10), people think that (a) all mentally ill people are dangerous, and (b) all homeless people are mentally ill. Thus, by logical conclusion, they assume that all homeless people are dangerous. This irrational fear gets exacerbated when children are around. Imagine what would happen to your self-esteem if you were constantly treated like a monster and a pervert.

- Most people either avoid eye contact with homeless individuals or stare at them. These are equally bad. One makes you feel like you don't even exist. The other makes you feel like a circus freak show. We periodically do "poverty simulators" where we put college students through a 24-hour period of homelessness. They are always amazed at how people either stare at them or completely ignore them.

Imagine that you are desperate enough to go panhandling. You finally give up your last shred of dignity and go begging for money. You sit on the sidewalk with an outstretched cup, hoping people will throw some change into it. As pedestrians walk by, they are—literally—looking down on you all day. Most people avoid eye contact, choosing instead to step around you the way they would a pile of litter or dog poop. Children point at you, while their anxious parents grasp their hands tightly and whisk them away. A few people mutter things to themselves, like "pathetic" or "get a job." The few people who give you money talk to you like you are a child or stupid. How much dignity would you have left after one hour of this?

As I said, homelessness is really bad for one's self-esteem. A respected activist at the National Coalition for the Homeless once told me that he estimated that after six months of homelessness, no one had any sense of self-worth left.

This is significant for you, though. Because homeless people feel so bad about themselves, even the smallest compliment will be treated like a glass of ice water in the desert. Even something as simple as appreciating a homeless patron's sense of humor can win you a lifetime fan.

18: Homeless Individuals Are Treated Like Crap More Than You

Just about everywhere that homeless individuals go, they are treated poorly. The reason is simple: people can be rude and mean to homeless people with total impunity. There are no social consequences for mistreating the weak and vulnerable. Consider this:

- Businesses are constantly chasing them away. A few winters ago, I put on clothing from our clothes closet and spent the day walking around town to get a sense of what it would be like to live on the streets for a day. I vividly remember walking into a business about a half-mile from the shelter. The owner—who previously had been sitting idly in a chair—stood up and followed me around the tiny store. After a minute or two, I was so uncomfortable that I left.

- Overzealous police harass homeless individuals. It is amazing how laws that don't apply to anyone else suddenly become relevant when the person is homeless. Everyone jaywalks, but only homeless people get ticketed for it. Everyone just hangs out in public parks (that is what they are created for, after all), but only homeless individuals get chased away for "loitering." Homeless individuals get five days in jail for public intoxication, while tailgaters at a football game get a high-five.

- Strangers shout and jeer at homeless people. One of our male staff members at the shelter has long hair. When he crosses the street between our two buildings, passing cars frequently roll down their windows and shout "get a job!" It is somewhat amusing to him because he is literally doing his job while they are shouting at him, but imagine how that feels to someone who is not an employee.

- Some people attack homeless people for sport. One of our residents was once awakened by teenagers shooting him with BB guns. A few years ago, there was a series of videos called "bum fights" where the producers would pay homeless people to fight each other while they filmed it. California is currently experiencing a rash of teenagers lighting homeless people on fire. Hesed House and other activists around the country have been trying for years to get homelessness added as a criterion for a hate crime. So far we have been unsuccessful.

At Hesed House we have always been a bit zealous about treating our residents with dignity, but something that happened to me a few years ago really solidified my resolve. I had to get a contract signed at the local Department of Human Services (DHS) office. It happened to be the same office where people apply for food stamps. I arrived at a time of day when they weren't accepting applications, so there was no one sitting at the front desk. I rang the little bell and waited. About a minute later a woman approached me, scowling. She hissed, "We aren't open until 4:00! You come back then!" It is hard to fully describe the venom in her voice. The only time I have seen someone talk like that was in the movie *Lord of the Rings*, when someone tried to take the ring away from Gollum. Shocked, I explained that I worked at Hesed House and was there to see the director. Instantly the woman's whole demeanor changed. "Oh, I'm sorry, precious. I thought you were here to apply for food stamps. Have a seat and I'll go get her. Would you like a bottle of water while you wait?"

I try to imagine what it would have felt like if I really had been there to apply for food stamps. If I had lost my job. If I had sold my belongings. If I had skipped meals. If I had watched my wife and children go hungry. If I had finally swallowed my pride and decided to get food stamps so that my family could eat. Never having needed food stamps before, I wouldn't have known there was a specific time to apply. Walking up to the building, I would have left my self-worth out on the street as I accepted that I needed welfare. When I finally got inside, I would be shouted at and told to come back later. And, worse yet, I couldn't even complain to anyone; not if I really needed those food stamps for my children's bellies.

Ironically, about a month after I visited the DHS office, I got a survey in the mail from the state of Illinois asking me to rate the local DHS office. I let them have it! A few months after that, the state fired all of the employees in that office. I don't think it happened because of my single survey, but I like to think that I helped. Of course, I only had the power to hold them accountable because I am not homeless or poor.

The fact that homeless people are constantly treated poorly is important for you. Showing a homeless patron even the simplest kindness or courtesy can be like giving a man a Double Quarter-Pounder with Cheese Extra Value Meal (Super Sized, of course!).

19: Homeless Individuals Trust People Less Than You

Homeless individuals have learned—from experience—not to trust people. As I said earlier in this book, most people who get evicted do not end up on the street or in a homeless shelter. A friend or relative lets them "couch surf" until they are able to get back on their feet.

So, if you did end up on the street, think about all the people who have had to abandon you first:

- Your employer
- Your landlord
- Your neighbors
- Your brothers
- Your sisters
- Your mother
- Your father
- Your grandparents
- Your children
- Your aunts and uncles
- Your cousins
- Your coworkers
- Your best friend
- Your other friends
- Nonprofits that were helping you

You only end up in a shelter when every single person you know has given up on you. You only end up on the street when every social service agency has failed to help you. You only become homeless when *everyone* you have ever trusted has failed you.

That is a lot of rejection and misplaced trust. So, don't be surprised when your homeless patrons don't expect you to follow through on your promises. Don't take it personally—a lot of other people have let them down. Of course, there is an opportunity here: when you actually do keep a promise, you have the ability to help restore a little of that patron's faith in humanity (and win an ardent fan at the same time).

20: Homeless Individuals Value Fairness More Than You

Homeless individuals are constantly singled out and harassed or punished for doing things that you and I do every day. Let me prove it to you:

- Have you ever jaywalked? Almost certainly. Have you been ticketed for jaywalking? Almost certainly not.
- Have you ever gone into a fast-food restaurant to use the bathroom without buying anything? Of course you have. Have you ever been chased out of the restaurant by management? Of course you haven't.
- Have you ever gone to a public park and just sat around? Most likely you have. Have the police ever told you to "move along"? Most likely they have not.

I have personally trained thousands of librarians and I always ask them these questions. Out of those thousands of people, exactly one person got a ticket for jaywalking, exactly one person had been chased out of a restaurant, and exactly one person had been chased out of a public park. And all three happened to the same guy! And he "looked homeless"!

That is the experience of library staff. If I conducted the same poll in a homeless shelter, most of the residents would have experienced at least one of these forms of discrimination (and some would have experienced all three).

Most homeless individuals have developed a complex about being singled out. Do you know why? *Because they are singled out!* Consequently, most homeless individuals absolutely crave fairness. They want to be treated like everyone else. I am frequently told by residents of Hesed House, "I don't mind being treated poorly, as long as *everyone* is treated poorly." Think about that for a minute. It isn't the poor treatment that bothers them. It is the fact that they have to endure "special" poor treatment that bothers them.

To hear homeless individuals explain what it is like to be singled out, go to www.homelesslibrary.com/fairness.

Conclusion

Homeless individuals are not completely and utterly different than you. Nor are they exactly like you. In order to fully empathize with them, you need to understand the differences. Most homeless individuals:

1. Grew up poor
2. Speak differently than you
3. Have a smaller vocabulary than you
4. Pay more attention to nonverbal cues than you
5. Argue differently than you
6. View respect differently than you
7. Look at time differently than you
8. Value relationships more than you
9. Value their possessions more than you
10. Look at space differently than you
11. Are funnier than you
12. Have experienced more trauma than you
13. Are in more danger than you
14. Want to look scary
15. Have had their IQs lowered
16. Are "habituated to punishment"
17. Have less self-worth than you
18. Are treated like crap more than you
19. Trust people less than you
20. Value fairness more than you

Notes

1. Victoria Abbott, *The Christie Curse* (New York: Berkley, 2013).
2. Aleksandr Solzhenitsyn, *One Day in the Life of Ivan Denisovich* (Santa Barbara, CA: Praeger, 1963).
3. Ruby Payne, *A Framework for Understanding Poverty*, 4th edition (Highlands, TX: aha Process, 2005).
4. Payne, *Framework for Understanding Poverty*.
5. PBS Frontline, "An Interview with James Akins," www.pbs.org/wgbh/pages/frontline/shows/saddam/interviews/akins.html.
6. Elizabeth K. Hopper, Ellen L. Bussuk, and Jeffrey Olivet, "Shelter from the Storm: Trauma-Informed Care in Homelessness Services Settings," *The Open Health Services and Policy Journal* 2 (2009): 131–51, available at www.traumacenter.org/products/pdf_files/shelter_from_storm.pdf.
7. American Institutes for Research, "Service and Housing Interventions for Families in Transition (SHIFT) Study – Final Report," www.air.org/resource/service-and-housing-interventions-families-transition-shift-study-final-report.

8. American Institutes for Research, "Service and Housing Interventions," www.air.org/resource/service-and-housing-interventions-families-transition-shift-study-final-report.

9. Anna Almendrala, "The Disturbing Link between Brain Injury and Homelessness," www.huffingtonpost.com/2014/04/29/traumatic-brain-injury-homelessness_n_5227637.html.

10. National Coalition for the Homeless, "Health Care and Homelessness," www.nationalhomeless.org/factsheets/health.html.

11. Karen Hughes et al., "Prevalence and Risk of Violence against Adults with Disabilities: A Systematic Review and Meta-Analysis of Observational Studies," *The Lancet* 379, no. 9826 (2012): 1621–29, available at http://thelancet.com/journals/lancet/article/PIIS0140-6736(11)61851-5/abstract?rss=yes.

12. U.S. Department of Health and Human Services, "Mental Health Myths and Facts," https://www.mentalhealth.gov/basics/myths-facts/.

13. Morgan Kelly, "Poor Concentration: Poverty Reduces Brainpower Needed for Navigating Other Areas of Life," https://www.princeton.edu/news/2013/08/29/poor-concentration-poverty-reduces-brainpower-needed-navigating-other-areas-life.

Empathy

The Psychological, Neurological, and Social Bases for It

Books are only half our job; the other half is human nature.
—MARY VIRGINIA PROVINES[1]

She lived with her family in a fancy suburban subdivision. She was pretty and thin and wearing designer clothes whose names I cannot pronounce. I think she was 16 or 17 years old, with the rest of her life ahead of her.

He lived at Hesed House with a couple hundred other "homeless people." He was a middle-aged African American man with clothing from the local clothes closet. I think he drank too much, and he also had the rest of his life ahead of him.

She was volunteering at Hesed House as part of an experimental program that brings teenagers with anorexia to a shelter to help them gain a new orientation to food. The hope is that by planning a meal, purchasing the food, cooking it, and finally serving it, they can stop viewing food as the enemy.

He was at Hesed House because he didn't have anywhere else to go.

She was serving homemade double-fudge brownies (with nuts)—which must be the worst thing in the world if you are struggling with anorexia—when he casually walked up to her and started talking. The entirety of their exchange went something like this:

Him: You are capable of greatness, whether you realize it now or not.

Her: (Startled, but curious look)

Him: Don't believe people when they say that you can't. Don't believe
     yourself when you say that you can't.

Her: (meekly) Thank you.

Him: We are not defined by our wounds.

(*He shakes her hand, she gives him a brownie, and he goes back to his table.*)

When I heard about this conversation, I asked him how he knew that an eating disorder group was volunteering that night. He said he didn't know anything about the group, but that he could spot self-doubt from across the room. He could tell that she was in pain, and needed to be reminded of her potential.

I never asked him how he knew all that. I suppose his own pain, self-doubt, and need for encouragement made him acutely aware of the pain of others. In her wounds, he saw his own.

He was right, of course. We are *not* defined by our wounds. I am not defined by mine, and I hope that you don't define yourself by the scars on your soul.

• • •

It Is All about Empathy

Interestingly, the word "empathy" is barely 100 years old (it was introduced by the psychologist Edward Titchener in 1909 as a translation of the German word *Einfühlung*, or "feeling into").[2] Since 1909, we have learned a lot about empathy, and where it comes from. In particular, science has taught us many concepts that help us use empathy as a guiding principle for getting people to follow rules without punishment. Among these concepts are

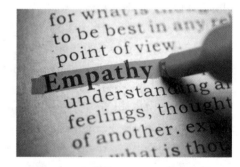

Figure 3.1: "Empathy"

- Emotional contagion
- Psychology of conflict
- Psychology of relationship
- Psychology of likability
- Reciprocity
- Psychological inertia
- Social proof
- Neurochemistry of aggression and empathy
- Legitimacy

> **Empathy** [**em**-*puh*-thee]
>   Noun
>   The ability to understand and share the feelings of another.*
>
> *Oxford Dictionaries, "Empathy," https://en.oxforddictionaries.com/definition/empathy

Emotional Contagion

The first principle of empathy-driven enforcement is the concept of emotional contagion. With it, we can control our own emotions, and also influence the emotions of others. A person in the right emotional state (calm, non-defensive) is much more likely to comply voluntarily with our rules.

The idea is that our emotions are contagious. This isn't a metaphor. They are *literally* contagious. Let me give you the science behind it.

Researchers at the University of Parma in Italy discovered that we have these things in our brains called "mirror neurons." These mirror neurons fire when you experience an emotion or when you witness someone else experiencing that emotion. What this means is that when you feel sad, a specific neuron in your brain fires. When you see someone else sad, though, the same neuron fires. Thus, you can become sad.

This—according to many people smarter than me—is the neurological basis for empathy. I don't just imagine what it must feel like to be you; I actually experience what it is like to be you! Our brain is literally hard-wired to transmit our emotions to others, and receive emotions from them.

Emotional contagion is so strong that human beings begin to "catch" the emotions of others before they have even reached their first birthday. Interestingly—but not surprisingly—women apparently have a greater capacity for emotional contagion than men.

The concept of emotional contagion has several practical implications for you:

a. You are susceptible to catching the moods of others. When your patrons are angry and aggressive, you need to guard against catching it.

b. You can influence the emotional state of others by simply being in the state you want them to be in. If you are pleasant and calm, the pleasant and calm mirror neurons in the patron's brain will start firing and he is more likely to calm down too.

c. We can influence our coworkers' mood—and level of aggressive-
    ness—by modeling the behavior we want from them and getting
    the correct mirror neurons to fire in their brain.

Psychology of Conflict

The second principle of empathy-driven enforcement is the psychology behind
conflict. A lot of training (including this one) includes conflict de-escalation techniques. This is because conflict itself creates additional problems beyond whatever problem created the conflict. Here's why.

Emotional conflict reduces our ability for abstract thought.[3] While this may
not sound like a big deal, it is actually a huge problem. Abstract thinking is essential for:

1. *Problem-solving*—When our minds revert to concrete thinking, we
    see everything in binary terms (winning or losing). We lose the
    creative ability to envision new solutions.
2. *Empathy*—Empathy requires imagining what it would be like to
    be someone else. In order to imagine yourself as someone else you
    must think abstractly.

It is in *your* best interest to be aware of the emotional conflict that your homeless
patrons are experiencing. When they experience conflict, they lose the capacity
for abstract thought (and thus, problem-solving skills and empathy). This is bad
for you!

It is also in *your* best interest to be aware of your own emotional conflict. You,
too, may have lost abstract thinking, problem-solving skills, and empathy. This
is bad for you!

There are many techniques for de-escalating emotional conflict that you will
learn in part II of this book.

Psychology of Relationship

The third principle of empathy-driven enforcement is relationships. People are
more likely to comply voluntarily with requests when there is a relationship. I
don't mean you have to marry your patrons in order to get them to comply with
the rules. Any step above "stranger" is a step in the right direction of relationship.

It turns out that we know a lot about how relationships function. We know
what makes them healthy and what destroys them. There are three specific aspects of relationship theory that are helpful for an empathy-driven enforcement
approach:

1. *The 5:1 ratio*—Dr. John Gottman has studied the ultimate relationship, marriages. His principles apply to less intimate relationships too, though. Gottman discovered that in order for a relationship to remain healthy, the ratio of good to bad interactions must stay above 5:1. In other words, for every one bad interaction you have with someone, you need to have at least five good interactions. If you are going to offer a criticism, you better have offered at least five compliments already. The higher the ratio, the better, but 5:1 is the minimum. Anything below that and the relationship implodes on itself (which usually leads to divorce in a marriage). Applying this to a library, if you want to maintain a healthy relationship with your patrons, you should maintain a ratio of at least five good interactions for every one negative one. Since you never know when you will have to have a negative interaction (like enforcing a rule), you want to "store up" positive interactions preemptively.

2. *The three building blocks of relationships*—So it turns out that there are three things that build relationship:

   a. *Words*, specifically *compliments* and *questions*. Obviously, compliments build relationship, but why questions? Questions show interest in another person. When I ask you how your day is going or where you are from, I am showing that I care enough to be interested in you. That builds relationship.

   b. *Deeds*. Doing something helpful for someone else builds relationship. It doesn't have to be big. Even the act of smiling at someone is a deed that creates relationship. So when you are trying to build relationship with your homeless patrons, consider smiling at them (one), saying good morning (two), shaking their hand (three), offering your name (four), and asking their name (five). Now you have built up the requisite five positive interactions in order to offset a later negative interaction.

   c. *Touch*. In a library context you have fewer touch options than in a marital context. You do still have the handshake, which is very powerful for creating relationship. Think about this: human beings started shaking hands thousands of years ago as a means of showing each other that they didn't have a weapon in their right hand. That original purpose has long since passed (most of us don't walk around with a dagger anymore) and yet we still keep doing it. Why? Because it creates relationship. In fact, researchers have even discovered that shaking hands serves as a form of "chemosignaling" where we transfer social chemicals between people. Apparently, there is a tendency to unconsciously sniff your hand after you have shaken someone's hand. All of this creates relationship.

3. *The four destroyers of relationship*—Gottman—who discovered the 5:1 ratio rule—also identified four specific actions that destroy relationship (and lead to divorce). He calls them "the Four Horsemen":

    a. *Criticism*—Obviously, criticizing someone does not endear you to them.

    b. *Defensiveness*—Getting defensive destroys relationship equity. Think about this in the context of when you feel criticized.

    c. *Stonewalling*—Refusing to communicate or cooperate is a huge destroyer of relationship. Think about this the next time you walk away from an ornery patron.

    d. *Contempt*—Contempt is described as a mixture of disgust and anger. It is the number-one predictor of divorce and the number-one destroyer of relationship. Contempt includes "hostile humor, name-calling, mimicking and/or body language such as eye-rolling and sneering."[4] Next time you are tempted to roll your eyes, don't!

Psychology of Likability

The fourth principle of empathy-driven enforcement is likability. The reason is simple: people who like us are more cooperative. We don't need to threaten people when we can get them to comply voluntarily because we are just so darn likable.

Research has demonstrated this. It has also shown what makes someone likable:

- *We like people who are similar to us.* We tend to like people the more similar they are to us. You can't suddenly make yourself a 60-year-old homeless man in order to be similar. You can, though, call attention to other similarities. If you are both from Tennessee, highlight that. If you both like Stephen King, focus on that. And so on.

- *We like people who compliment us.* This is not rocket science. Everyone likes a little bit of sincere appreciation from time to time.

- *We like people whom we have helped.* Obviously, we help people we have liked, but we also like people we have helped. It appears that the mere act of assisting someone (even in a small way) increases their likability in our eyes. It is almost like we say, "I helped John, so I must like him because I wouldn't have helped someone I didn't like." Professional fund-raisers are trained to ask donors for things other than money. This helpfulness cements the relationship and makes the person more likely to write a check. In a library setting, simple requests will help a lot: "Will you keep an eye out for problems?" or "Will you put the magazines back when you're done?"

- *We like people who share a common crisis.* The easiest way to get rid of "us" and "them" thinking is to combine the groups against a common enemy. That common enemy need not be another group of people, though. You see the same effect after a hurricane. We like people who share a common struggle. That common struggle can be to keep an area clean or keep viruses off the computer, or whatever.

- *We like people who like us.* My dog Sahara taught me the most important lesson I know about how to be likable. Sahara is part dachshund and part jerk. She really is an unpleasant animal. But Sahara has one huge redeeming trait. When I have been away for a few days on a work trip, she gets really excited when I come home. In fact, Sahara gets so excited, that she pees when she first sees me. I like Sahara—despite her numerous flaws—because she likes me. It is really that simple. This is why 36.5 percent of American households have a pet dog but only 3.1 percent have a pet bird, despite the fact that birds cost substantially less. We like dogs because dogs like us.

  It also works for car salesmen. Joe Girard—who holds the Guinness World Record for car sales—had a simple habit of sending every customer a greeting card every month. Each card had the same simple message inside: "I like you." That's it. It may sound cheesy, but it worked so well that it enabled him to sell a trainload of cars and cement his place in history.

  This is the most powerful way to get people to like you. It is also the easiest. Smiling when you see someone makes them like you. Greeting someone happily makes them like you. Inquiring about how someone is doing today makes them like you. Remembering someone's name makes them like you. I think this principle is doubly true for homeless individuals because so many people dislike them. If everyone else all day has looked annoyed upon their arrival, if you look pleased to see them, you will have won a true ally.

- *We like (and trust) people who argue against their own self-interest.* In one research study, researchers found that letters of reference on behalf of job applicants were far more effective if the letter included one negative about the candidate. When we are willing to admit a weakness, flaw, or mistake, it makes us more likable and more credible.

- *We don't like people who deliver bad news.* The research tells us that if we have to deliver bad news—even if it isn't our fault—it damages our likability. Plutarch (the Roman historian from 2,000 years ago) wrote how Tigranes the Great had a messenger's head cut off after the man informed him of an advancing army. He really didn't like that guy. You probably won't get your head cut off for delivering bad news, but it does damage your likability (and make it harder to get voluntary compliance). The lessons for this are twofold: (1) use punishment-driven enforcement as infrequently as possible because it damages your likability and future compliance efforts, and (2) make sure you have stored up a lot of likability points in advance of enforcing a rule, so that you are still likable afterwards.

Reciprocity

The fifth principle of empathy-driven enforcement is the concept—drawn from social science—of reciprocity. The concept behind reciprocity is that people should repay in-kind what another has done for them. This is a form of Reverse Golden Rule: Do unto others as they have done unto you. Imagine you are at a bar with work colleagues and one of them buys you a beer. Would you feel a sense of obligation to buy that person a beer either that night or later? The psychological debt that you would experience is the psychological principle of reciprocity. Has a coworker ever covered a shift for you or helped with a big project and you felt obligated later to repay the favor? That is the principle of reciprocity.

Human beings are hard-wired for reciprocity. It creates a psychological debt that we feel obligated to repay. In fact, it is so strong in human beings that researchers have identified it in children as young as two. Actually, it isn't just you, me, and toddlers. Researchers at the Yerkes National Primate Research Center at

Emory University have found that brown capuchin monkeys have a strong sense of reciprocity.

It works both ways, though. When someone does something kind for us, we feel the need to repay them with kindness. But when someone does something unkind to us, we also feel the need to repay them with unkindness. This is the origin of the phrase "tit-for-tat," which comes from the sixteenth-century phrase "tip for tap," which means "blow for blow."

There are four caveats to the psychological principle of reciprocity:

- *Reciprocity is based on perceived treatment, not actual treatment.* If you do something nice for me and I never know about it, then I won't try to repay it. Conversely, if you are scowling because of the patron before me, but I think you are scowling at me, I am going to repay you in-kind. So, actually, *the Reverse Golden Rule is to do unto others as you perceive they have done unto you.*

- *The desire to repay kindness seems to fade with time,* especially for the person who received the kindness. Over time, you will feel less and less psychological debt to repay your colleague who bought you a beer. Your colleague's sense of being owed, though, will not fade as quickly.

- *You have to let people pay you back.* People who don't repay kindness with kindness are viewed as moochers and are punished by society (usually by not receiving any more favors). This is not very surprising. What is surprising, though, is that society also punishes people who do not allow others to repay the kindness. It seems that human beings prefer to move back towards an equilibrium of being psychologically debt-free. Think about that the next time a poor person tries to repay your kindness with a token gift or favor. If you refuse it out of a mistaken desire to help them, you hurt them psychologically.

- *The negative is stronger than the positive.* If you do one nice thing for me, I feel obligated to do one nice thing for you. But, if you do one nasty thing to me, I feel obliged to do five nasty things to you. In fact, many people hypothesize that this human inclination for escalated revenge is the origin of the biblical concept of "an eye for an eye." In modern times we think of it as a barbaric concept that leaves the whole world blind, but several millennia ago, it would have been very progressive. If you poke out my eye, my human nature would be to take your eye, your goats, your home, and your life (oh, and slaughter your whole village while I'm at it). By comparison, eye for an eye is progress.

The principle of reciprocity is so strong that it even overpowers the principle of likability. In one study, researchers found that people would repay the kindness of another, even if they didn't like the person.

Psychological Inertia

In physics, inertia is an object's resistance to change in speed and/or direction. Remember Newton's First Law of Motion from physics class ("An object in motion . . .")? It isn't just physical objects that have inertia. Human beings' brains have it too. Once we are moving in a certain direction psychologically, we tend to keep moving in that direction. It takes some other significant force to change that direction. This is both good and bad:

> Once we have established a pattern of healthy behavior, we tend to keep doing healthy behavior. Psychologists call this "momentum of compliance." Once people have been compliant long enough, they tend to remain compliant.

> Once we are moving in the direction of friction, conflict, and noncompliance, we tend to keep going in that direction.

It isn't that we can't change directions, psychologically. We can. It just usually takes something happening to change the direction. You have probably experienced this in your life. There was someone you liked (maybe even married) who did something to hurt you, but you didn't automatically cut them out of your life entirely. There was enough psychological inertia built up for you to maintain the relationship. Similarly, you have probably had other individuals in your life (perhaps your in-laws) where the negative trajectory of the relationship exacerbated every interaction.

In the context of the library, your goal is to get your patrons (homeless and housed) to psychologically move in the right direction as early as possible. Once healthy patterns are established, they are easier to maintain. If you greet patrons with a smile every morning, they are much more likely to behave well later because you have used the principle of psychological inertia to your benefit. Unfortunately, the reverse is also true. If a homeless man walks into your library for the first time and is greeted by a hostile security guard, the psychological inertia of that patron is already going in the wrong direction. It will take a lot of effort on your part to turn that ship around.

This is why it matters what your coworkers do. Even if you yourself follow the principles of empathy-driven enforcement, if your fellow library staff are all about punishment, it will be very hard for you to overcome the negative inertia they create. You should probably rush out and buy a copy of this book for each of your colleagues (or at least get them to sign up for the e-mail list at www.home lesslibrary.com)!

There are two specific mechanisms of psychological inertia:

1. *Commitment.* The basic idea behind commitment is that once we have committed to a course of action, we feel a psychological need to stick to it. Breaking a commitment causes psychological discomfort. Have you ever stuck with something you didn't want to do simply because you had committed to do it? Maybe you finished reading a book even though it was lousy. Maybe you stayed in an unhealthy relationship longer than you should have. Maybe you stayed in a bad job. The psychological inertia of commitment is what kept you going on a path that wasn't a very good one. Of course, the opposite is also true. Many marriages have been saved based on the strength of the commitment made when people say "till death do us part."

   Not all commitments are equal, though. Researchers have determined that four factors increase the strength of psychological inertia with a commitment:

   - *Active*—We are more likely to follow through on a commitment if we actively agree to it, rather than if we are simply asked to comply. One research study examined the number of people who made dinner reservations at a restaurant but then failed to show up. If—when making the reservation—they were *told,* "please call if you have to cancel," 30 percent of people were a no-show. If, on the other hand, they were *asked,* "Will you please call if you have to cancel?" the no-show rate dropped to 10 percent (a two-thirds reduction in problem behavior).

   - *Public*—If we never tell anyone our commitment, we are far less likely to stick with it. For example, researchers have deter-mined that when dieters declare their weight-loss goals publicly, they lose much more weight than if they keep their goal to themselves.

   - *Effortful*—If we have to actually do something as part of a com-mitment, we feel more ownership over it. In fact, the harder we have to work in order to fulfill a commitment, the greater our resolve to stick with it. This is the basis of fraternity hazing. Once people have suffered humiliation at the hands of their "frat brothers," commitment to the fraternity increases substantially. Many concert promoters intentionally don't advertise the price, forcing customers to call for the price. This tiny effort (calling to get the price) increases commitment to seeing the concert (and increases sales).

- *Freely chosen*—If we agree to do something under either *threat of punishment or promise of reward*, we don't feel as much psychological need to actually follow through with it. Our brains know that we didn't actually choose it. This is one of the reasons why punishment-driven enforcement doesn't work. While it can sometimes gain compliance as long as someone thinks they might get caught, it doesn't create any psychological inertia of good behavior.

2. *Consistency.* We human beings like to be consistent with our self-image. We feel a psychological discomfort when we are inconsistent. If we view ourselves as "honest," then acting dishonestly causes us more psycholosogical pain than if we don't view ourselves as "honest." There are two opinions in particular with which we want to be consistent:

    1. *Our own opinion*—If we view ourselves as someone who follows the rules, then we tend to follow the rules. This much is not surprising. What is surprising, though, is that we form our opinion of what type of person we are by looking at what we have done. If we sit quietly in a library and behave, then over time we come to view ourselves as the type of person who behaves in a library. Being inconsistent with this self-image breaks our psychological inertia and causes discomfort. Again, this is why you want to establish a healthy relationship early by using empathy-driven tools.

    2. *The opinion of others*—We also feel psychological discomfort when we don't conform to the opinions of others. In one research study, children who are told "you are the kind of student who cares about good handwriting" spent much more of their free time practicing handwriting. Anwar Sadat, president of Egypt from 1970 to 1981, would go into negotiations with other countries' leaders by telling them that they were widely

known to be cooperative and fair. This compliment didn't just flatter the other side; it gave them a reputation to live up to (which benefited Sadat).

Social Proof

Human beings are social animals. We are heavily influenced by the behavior of others. Have you every shopped on Amazon? Have you ever decided to make a purchase (or not) based on the ratings of other users? This is "social proof" in its purest form. We look to our peers for cues on how to believe.

This reliance on social proof is particularly strong when things are unclear or ambiguous. In such times of uncertainty, we look to others to see what to do. What could be more unclear, ambiguous, or uncertain than having nowhere to live and nothing to eat? Homelessness is the very definition of uncertainty.

The result is a specific type of social proof that I call the "homeless information network." Homeless people talk to each other a lot. It isn't just a form of free entertainment (though it is that, too). Homeless individuals talk to each other as a means of survival. If you are hungry and I can tell you which church is handing out leftovers, our conversation will fill your belly. If I have a warrant for my arrest and you know where the cops are patrolling today, our conversation keeps me out of jail.

Homeless individuals are very selfless when it comes to sharing information with each other. They share lots of information:

- Where to find the best free food
- Where to find the best free clothing
- Where to find the best shelter
- Which police officers are fair and which are cruel
- Which library staff won't enforce the rules
- Which library security guards are sadistic and mean

The result is a weird phenomenon where your treatment of one homeless individual can reverberate through the entire homeless community. If you treat one homeless individual unkindly, you may be punished by ten other homeless people who weren't there, but heard about your unkindness. Similarly, treating one homeless patron with respect and dignity can endear you to individuals you have never met (yet).

Think about it: you are homeless and just trying to get by. Everything in your world is in chaos and crisis. Your buddy tells you, though, that Librarian Larry is a good guy who is fair. When Librarian Larry approaches you for the first time, how do you expect him to treat you?

Neurochemistry of Aggression and Empathy

Would you like your patrons to have less aggression/violence and more empathy, relaxation, and impulse control? Then you should do things that impact the chemistry in their brains.

There are three "good" chemicals in the brain that matter to us:

Chemical or Hormone	Effects
Serotonin	• Reduces impulsive behavior • Reduces violence
Dopamine	• Reduces impulsive behavior • Reduces aggression
Oxytocin	• Increases empathy • Increases serotonin

Researchers have determined the effects of these different hormones through a variety of means, including shooting serotonin up the noses of test subjects. You probably can't do that. Instead, you have to resort to methods that are more in your control:

- *Shaking hands*—Shaking someone's hand increases their oxytocin.
- *Trusting someone*—When someone engages in an act of trust (like doing a favor), it increases their oxytocin.
- *Empathizing*—When someone empathizes with us, their brain releases oxytocin, which—in a virtuous cycle—helps them empathize more.
- *Ritual*—Predictable ritual releases serotonin. So, being greeted every morning with the same phrase increases serotonin.
- *Social standing*—Feelings of increased social standing raise our levels of serotonin.

There is also one "bad" chemical that matters to us:

Chemical or Hormone	Effects
Cortisol	• Increases aggression

But how do you affect your patrons' levels of cortisol? Here's how:

- *Stress*—Stress causes an increase in cortisol (the bad chemical that increases aggression), so don't create unnecessary stress/conflict.

Legitimacy

Researchers have studied what factors must be present in order for authorities to be viewed as "legitimate." So, for example, what must a government do in order to be viewed as legitimate? The research around legitimacy applies, though, to other contexts where an authority figure has to enforce rules. For example, the same concepts apply to a school, a homeless shelter, or even a library. In other words, in order for your patrons to view you—and your rules—as legitimate, certain things must be true.

Specifically, three things must be true in order for you, your staff, and your rules to be viewed as legitimate:

Rule 1: People must feel like they will be *listened to*.

Rule 2: The rules have to be *predictable*.

Rule 3: The rule-enforcer has be *fair*.

Let's break each of these down.

Rule 1: People Must Feel Like They Will Be Listened To

Imagine that you start a new job at a new library. And imagine that at this library, they do not have their records computerized; they are still using an old card-catalog system.

Like any good employee, you go to your boss and say, "Hey, have we ever considered using a computerized card-catalog system?"

Now, imagine that your new boss says, "I am the boss. You are the employee. I tell you what to do. You do not tell me what to do. Never, ever ever."

Would you view your boss as legitimate? Of course not!

You wouldn't expect your boss to necessarily jump up and immediately buy a computerized system (there are cost considerations, of course), but you would expect him or her to at least listen to you.

Or imagine that you are driving to work one day, and a cop pulls you over and starts to write you a ticket. You ask what the ticket is for and the cop tells you that if you speak again he will take you to jail. Would you view that police officer as legitimate? Of course not!

In order for an authority to be viewed as legitimate, people must believe that the authority will listen to them. It is important to note, though, that the authority does not necessarily need to act on what is said. For example, in the police example, if you explained that you didn't think you were speeding, but the officer explained that his radar gun said otherwise, you might be annoyed to get a ticket, but you wouldn't view the cop as crooked.

Remember this when a patron—homeless or otherwise—is trying your patience and you are in a rush. It can be tempting to cut someone off when they are protesting a rule or a fine. This undermines your legitimacy in that patron's eyes.

Rule 2: The Rules Have to Be Predictable

In order for an authority figure to be viewed as legitimate, the rules must be predictable. Basically, what this means is that the rules today are the same as the rules yesterday (and tomorrow).

Imagine that you are driving to work (driving at or below the speed limit) when you get pulled over by a police officer. He gives you a speeding ticket and when you protest, he says, "Oh, I decided that for today all speed limits are half of what it says on the posted sign."

What would you think about speeding laws, or your local police force?

Or, imagine that you arrive at work at 8:50 a.m. for your 9:00 a.m. shift. Your boss greets you at the door and hands you a written disciplinary action for "not arriving fifteen minutes early." You protest that you didn't know you were supposed to arrive fifteen minutes early and she tells you that it is a new rule that starts today.

What would you think about your boss? Would this undermine her credibility?

Rule 3: The Rule-Enforcer Has to Be Fair

The third rule for legitimacy is that the rule-enforcer has to be viewed as fair. Basically, this means that the rules apply equally to everyone.

Imagine how you would feel in the following situations:

1. Your library creates a rule that all blond employees must get preapproval before taking a sick day.
2. Your local city council passes an ordinance that all left-handed citizens have to pay an extra tax.
3. Your boss wants to change the rules so that gay patrons can only check out one book at a time.
4. Your local police start handing out tickets for jaywalking, but only to people under six feet tall. Everyone over six feet tall is exempt.

Research on legitimacy—and common sense—would say that the authority figure's legitimacy would be damaged in each of these instances. As stated in chapter 2, homeless individuals are *very* sensitive to being singled out and treated in a discriminatory fashion. Most want to be treated no better and no worse than every other patron.

I need to pause here and clarify something, though. Often, when people hear about this third rule, they think it means they should "be consistent." There is some truth to that, but consistency taken too far is not viewed as fair and actually damages legitimacy. Don't believe me? Let me give you two examples of inappropriate consistency:

- Women and men should be treated consistently. They should be treated the same. So, in order to treat men and women the same, we should eliminate separate men's and women's events in the Olympics and let everyone compete in the same event. No more women's 100-meter race and a separate 100-meter race for men. The top athletes, regardless of gender, compete. In the 2016 Olympics, the gold-winning female, Elaine Thompson of Jamaica, had a time of 10.71 seconds. The qualifying standard for men was 10.16 seconds. In other words, not a single female runner would have qualified for the men's 100-meter race. It would have been consistent, but would it have been fair?

- People with disabilities should be treated like everyone else. They should not be discriminated against by inconsistent treatment. So, in order to treat them consistently, we need to get rid of special parking spaces, wheelchair ramps, and accommodations in the workplace. While we are at it, aren't we treating people with learning disabilities inconsistently when we give them extra assistance? Eliminating all of these items would be consistent, but would it be fair?

These two examples make an important point about the relationship between consistency and fairness. Where people are similarly situated, consistent treatment is fair. Where people are not similarly situated, consistent treatment is not necessarily fair. This lesson is especially important when dealing with mentally ill patrons. Two patrons may be engaging in the same behavior. One does it because he's just a jerk. Another does it because he struggles with mental illness. You don't need to treat them identically in order to be fair.

Pulling the Three Rules of Legitimacy Together

At the risk of getting too political: the current impasse between the Black Lives Matter movement and many police forces is a standoff over perceptions of legitimacy. Basically, the Black Lives Matter movement is saying:

a. African Americans are punished in ways that others aren't (Rule 3)
b. African Americans don't know what rules to expect ("when we get pulled over for speeding, sometimes we get a speeding ticket and sometimes we get shot") (Rule 2)

c. When African Americans try to call attention to perceived discrimination, their concerns are dismissed (Rule 1)

This isn't the place for me to take sides, but it is very clear that many police forces have a "legitimacy problem" within the African American community. They would be well-served to see why they are perceived as violating the three fundamental rules of legitimacy.

Similarly, your library would be well-served to inquire into perceptions about how well it adheres to the three rules. Do your patrons believe that you will listen to their complaints, enforce the rules predictably, and enforce the rules fairly?

It is worth noting what is *not* on the list of rules for legitimacy. The following are *not* required for you to be viewed as a valid authority figure, according to research:

- *Toughness*—Many people mistakenly believe that if they show any signs of weakness or vulnerability (or even humanity), it will undermine their authority.
- *Seriousness*—Other people think that any playfulness or humor will undermine their role as an authority figure. These unpleasant people do not engender respect.
- *Aloofness*—While you don't need to be friends with everyone, being friendly does not undermine your authority (in fact, the opposite is true).

I can personally attest that the above three factors are not required. In the shelter I have never had a problem with being viewed as a legitimate executive director (as far as I know), even though I wear shorts and sandals during the summer, wear a Tinky Winky Teletubby costume every Halloween, tell dumb jokes constantly, and smile at everyone.

The reason is that homeless people use the same three rules for legitimacy as everyone else.

Conclusion

The psychology of most homeless patrons is remarkably similar to the psychology of every other human being. Fortunately, we live in an age where researchers can explain "human nature" more empirically. These insights allow us to use the principles of empathy to get people to follow the rules without resorting to punishment.

Notes

1. Mary Virginia Provines, *Bright Heritage* (London: Longmans, Green, 1946).
2. Stanford Encyclopedia of Philosophy, "Empathy," https://plato.stanford.edu/entries/empathy//.
3. Kenneth B. Gorton, "Attribution Theory & De-Escalation: Transforming Concrete into Abstract as a Method of Conflict Management," www.mediate.com/articles/gortonK1.cfm?nl=74.
4. Gottman Institute, "The Four Horsemen: Contempt," https://www.gottman.com/blog/the-four-horsemen-contempt/.

Part II

Empathy-Driven Enforcement

Empathy vs. Punishment

Librarians are the secret masters of the world.
They control information.
Don't ever piss one off.

—Spider Robinson

We were deep in the bowels of a Chicago winter. It was below zero degrees outside even without the wind, which blew in swirly white gusts. I suspect Jon Snow was nearby, organizing the Wildlings against the White Walkers. I guess what I'm trying to say is that it was cold outside.

Inside the shelter, everyone was relieved to be out of the elements. Our city had gone six years without a homeless person freezing to death, and half that time since anyone had lost any body parts to frostbite. No one wanted to be the schmuck who broke our streak.

"Ryan! Quick! You need to get to the men's bathroom! There's going to be a fight!" I wasn't even sure who had said it, but it didn't matter. I rushed over to the men's bathroom. Mr. Johnson—a lanky guy in his early sixties with a weathered face and a disposition that matched the weather—was shouting obscenities at guys who just wanted to pee. He staggered back and forth, trying to keep his balance, as if he was on a ship in a storm. When he saw me, Mr. Johnson squared off like an old-time gunslinger. The ensuing conversation went like this:

Ryan: Mr. Johnson, what's going on?

Mr. Johnson: These #%$#%# are a bunch of no good @##$%#%@s!

Ryan: That's not very nice.

Mr. Johnson: But it's true!

Ryan: Mr. Johnson, how do we get you to calm down?

Mr. Johnson: Hey! I could kif yer asssss!

Ryan: What?

Mr. Johnson: I said [hiccup] I could kick your ass.

Ryan: Mr. Johnson, you are a very strong man. I believe that you could kick my ass.

Mr. Johnson: Damn right I could! In fact, I could kick two of your asses!

Ryan: Mr. Johnson, you are a very manly man. Two of my asses wouldn't have a chance against you.

Mr. Johnson: Do you want me to leave?

Ryan: No. I want you to stop picking fights.

Mr. Johnson: I don't think I can do that. I'll just leave.

Ryan: It is *really* cold outside. Why don't you just go to bed?

Mr. Johnson: No. I better leave before I do something stupid.

Mr. Johnson then promptly walked out into the winter night. In case you are worried about Mr. Johnson out in the cold, he showed up a few days later with absolutely no recollection of having tried to fight my asses.

• • •

What Is Punishment?

Okay, by now you have a deeper understanding of homeless patrons and the psychological basis of empathy. Now it is time to combine these two concepts into a practical system for enforcing the rules.

Before I teach you a new method, though, we need to talk about the old model: punishment-driven enforcement.

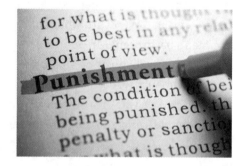

Figure 4.1: "Punishment"

Punishment-Driven Enforcement

Most of our thinking about getting people to follow the rules revolves around coming up with clever threats and punishments. It is pervasive in every area of life:

> **Punishment** [puhn-ish-m*uh* nt]
> Noun
> i.   Suffering, pain, or loss that serves as retribution;
> ii. A penalty inflicted on an offender;
> iii. Rough treatment*
>
> *Merriam-Webster Dictionary, "Punishment," https://www.merriam-webster.com/dictionary/punishment

1. *Law enforcement* = if you drive above the speed limit, we will give you a speeding ticket.
2. *Employment* = if you show up late for work, we will fire you.
3. *Housing* = if you do not pay your rent on time, we will evict you.
4. *School* = if you talk back to the teacher, we will give you a detention.
5. *International affairs* = if you violate a treaty, we will bomb your country.
6. *Parenting* = if you arrive home after curfew, we will ground you.
7. *Library* = if you cause problems in the library, we will kick you out.

The thought process behind punishment-driven enforcement is pretty simple. I don't want a speeding ticket, so I won't speed. I don't want to be fired, so I don't show up late. I don't want to be homeless, so I pay my rent. And so on .... Basically, it assumes that people make a rational calculation, choosing to follow the rules if the cost of noncompliance is too great. Consider this: if a speeding ticket only cost $1, would you speed more often? Probably. Me too! Conversely, if the punishment for speeding was a one-year prison sentence, would you speed less often? Certainly you would. Me too!

Punishment-driven enforcement is common for two reasons:

- *It is very easy to design and implement.* I can make a list of infractions and the punishment for each. Even the most incompetent staff member can follow a simple chart.

- *It is effective—in the short term—for getting compliance from most people.* I don't speed (very much) because I don't want a speeding ticket. The threat of a speeding ticket is very effective at getting me to follow the rules. I don't cheat on my taxes (very much) because I don't want the IRS to show up at my house. The threat of an audit is very effective for getting me to pay my taxes.

There are three massive problems with punishment-driven enforcement, however, and they are implicit within this second reason. It is only effective in gaining *short-term* compliance and it only works with *most* people. In other words, punishment-driven enforcement is ineffective at gaining long-term compliance and it doesn't work with some people. Furthermore, punishment multiplies resentment, which increases noncompliance. Let's explore each of these.

Punishment and Long-Term Compliance

Punishment-driven enforcement only works as long as there is a legitimate threat of actually being punished. If the only reason I drive below the speed limit is a fear of a ticket, how will I behave when there are no police officers around? If the only reason I pay my taxes is fear of the IRS, what will I do when I realize that the statistical odds of the average person (who earns less than $200,000) getting audited are 0.4 percent?[1]

Let's apply this to your library. Suppose your library has a problem with people sticking gum to the bottom of tables. The staff of your library assigns a Special Gum Task Force to examine the problem and propose a solution. Realizing that the punishment for gum-related infractions is only a one-day suspension of library privileges, the Task Force proposes raising that to one year. Faced with the possibility of losing their library card for one full year, certainly people will stop sticking gum to the undersides of tables. The problem, of course, comes with enforcement. As long as you and your colleagues are willing to vigilantly patrol all of the tables, people will comply. But will they still comply when the library staff aren't looking?

What other options could the Gum Task Force have proposed that would get people to comply? Be patient. I'm going to tell you.

Punishment and Certain Types of People

As I said, punishment-driven enforcement works well (in the short term) for most people. The problem, though, is that there are certain types of people who are resistant to punishment. The deterrent effect of punishment is based on people making a mental calculation of the costs of noncompliance. Consequently, punishment-driven enforcement doesn't work well with people who:

1. Struggle with mental illness
2. Are intoxicated or high
3. Are habituated to punishment
4. Have a shortened time horizon
5. Are highly traumatized
6. Are emotionally overwhelmed

Who did I just describe? Yep, I just described a homeless person. If I were to design the prototypical person who is immune to punishment-driven enforcement, it would be a homeless person. This makes total sense, if you think about it. Consider all the steps that have to happen before most people become homeless: losing a job, getting evicted, becoming estranged from all family and friends, and so on. Think of all the threats of punishment that didn't work: I did something to lose my job, even with the threat of termination; I didn't pay my rent, even with the threat of eviction; I alienated my family, even with the threat of estrangement. While this is a gross overgeneralization of homelessness, the basic point still stands: homelessness is often the culmination of repeated punishment failing to change behavior.

In fact, let's take it one step further. With homeless individuals, punishment often has the exact opposite of its intended effect. Instead of getting a person to stop engaging in a bad behavior, the threat of punishment often causes him to do it more (or add other bad behavior).

> **D**o not misunderstand what I am saying here. I am *not* saying "homeless people cause their own homelessness." There are a myriad of factors that have created the modern phenomenon of homelessness in the last forty years: destruction of affordable housing, the failed "war on drugs," inadequate community mental health services after de-institutionalization, and so on.
>
> Some individuals—particularly those struggling with personality disorders and other mental health issues—are resistant to punishment. Many of these individuals become homeless.

Consider this: a homeless patron approaches you in an agitated state. He immediately starts yelling at you about his computer being too slow. Wanting to quiet him down, you say, "Sir, if you don't lower your voice, I will have you removed from the library." Let's pause and listen to the internal mental monologue of the patron at this point:

How dare she talk to me like that? I wasn't even shouting! This is just one more example of an authority figure trying to crush a homeless person. This is just like that police officer who gave me a ticket this morning for jaywalking . . . and the McDonald's manager who wouldn't let me use the bathroom yesterday. Everybody is against me! I feel powerless, again. How can I feel powerful again? How can I show this uppity librarian what a jerk she's being? Hmmm ... well, obviously she doesn't like being yelled at. I'll teach her a thing or two! I'll *really* yell at her.

He starts yelling louder and you have to call the police. Not only did your threat of punishment not work, it had the exact opposite of its intended effect.

So, if punishment-driven enforcement doesn't work for homeless people, what does? I will tell you what works. But first we need to talk a little more about punishment.

Punishment Increases Resentment, Which Increases Noncompliance

There is another—more problematic—reason why punishment-driven enforcement is not very effective in gaining long-term compliance. It multiplies resentment, and resentment is never good for gaining voluntary compliance with the rules. When a teacher gives a student a detention, it might temporarily curb bad behavior. In the long term, though, the student will resent the teacher, which usually manifests itself in other problems.

Using our Gum Task Force example, a one-year ban might prevent people from sticking gum under their table. But do you think those people are going to vote for your referendum to raise more taxes for the library district? Resentful people always find a way to strike back.

So, what do you do instead? I'm going to tell you, in a page or two.

What Is Punishment?

Punishment is much broader than you might think. There are six basic forms of punishment:

1. *Monetary penalty*—When you return your book late, you have to pay a fine.
2. *Extra work*—When you are a teenager and you talk back to your father, you have to mow the lawn as punishment.
3. *Removal of benefit*—When you don't do your chores, you don't get to go to your friend's pool party.
4. *Removal from physical location*—When you get into a fight at the high school football game, you get ejected from the game.
5. *Physical discomfort*—When you cuss, you get a spanking or a mouthful of soap.
6. *Psychological discomfort*—When you aren't home by curfew, your mother yells at you.

Most of these are fairly apparent. The last one, though—psychological discomfort—is less obvious. It is also the most common form of punishment. We employ psychological discomfort all the time without ever realizing it. Anytime our body language or words project a negative emotion (shame, scorn, disapproval, hatred, aggression, etc.) at another person, we are punishing that person through psychological discomfort (remember the concept of emotional contagion and mirror neurons). Common ways of doing it include

- Shouting
- Insulting someone
- Scolding
- Demeaning talk
- Laughing at someone
- Eye-rolling
- Avoiding eye contact
- Glaring
- Frowning
- Smirking
- Pointing fingers
- Aggressive body language

Combine this list with the fact that homeless people are highly attuned to your body language and they feel punished a lot. Such punishment is not very effective at gaining their compliance with the rules, but it does create a lot of resentment. Their resentment is a big problem, *for you*!

Think about it: someone threatened them with job loss, and it did not work. Someone else threatened them with eviction, and it did not work. Many people threatened them with being cut off from family and friends, and it did not work. Do you really think your threats are going to work where these failed? Fortunately, there is another way.

Empathy-Driven Enforcement

There is a better way than punishment-driven enforcement. It is called *empathy-driven enforcement*. It works by using the scientifically based principles of empathy described in chapter 3 (e.g., emotional contagion, reciprocity, psychological inertia, legitimacy, etc.) to get patrons to comply with the rules. Since it doesn't rely on punishment, it works better on homeless, addicted, mentally ill, and other punishment-immune patrons. Some of the tools and methods of empathy-driven enforcement are common to conflict de-escalation and verbal judo methods, but it is broader than either.

Let's look at the differences between empathy-driven enforcement and punishment-driven enforcement:

	Empathy-Driven Enforcement	Punishment-Driven Enforcement
Culture	Rooted in a culture of assistance and cooperation.	Rooted in a culture of domination and legalism.
How It Works	Gains compliance with the rules by minimizing the power imbalance between the rule-enforcer and enforcee.	Gains compliance with the rules by maximizing the power imbalance between the rule-enforcer and enforcee.
Mentality	Creates a "partner" mentality in the patron.	Creates a "victim" mentality in the patron.
Who Decides	Library staff decide the terms of engagement.	Patron decides the terms of engagement.
Benefit	Effective.	Simple.

Empathy-driven enforcement has the same ultimate goal as punishment-driven enforcement (compliance with the rules), but it goes about achieving this goal in the exact opposite way. There are five key concepts you need to understand with empathy-driven enforcement:

1. *You need to accept that your behavior determines 80 percent of patron behavior.*

    I am going to tell you something that might hurt your feelings, but you need to hear it. Are you ready? Here goes: you are the cause of 80 percent of your patrons' misbehavior. Let me put it another—slightly nicer—way: your behavior determines 80 percent of your patrons' behavior. In 80 percent of bad situations, if you had handled the situation differently, the bad situation could have been prevented. Al Gore would call this an inconvenient truth, or at least an uncomfortable truth.

    I know this is true in libraries because it is true in homeless shelters (and because libraries report an 80 percent reduction in problems after their staff take my live or online trainings). At the shelter, when we have a crop of new staff working in the shelter, all hell breaks loose. They are constantly calling the police and kicking people out. A few months later when all those same staff are properly trained and have some experience, they almost never call the cops or kick people out. Eighty percent of the problems resulted because inexperienced and untrained staff didn't know how to handle difficult homeless individuals.

So, the bad news is that it is kind of your fault. That's actually really good news too, though! It means that with training and practice you can prevent 80 percent of problems. We'll come back to that. I need to explain another concept first.

I like to think about difficult patrons on a level system:

- *Level 0*—Patron is calm
- *Level 1*—Patron is annoyed (e.g., muttering under breath)
- *Level 2*—Patron is upset (e.g., sharp words and accusations)
- *Level 3*—Patron is angry (e.g., yelling)
- *Level 4*—Patron is out of control (e.g., knocking over tables)
- *Level 5*—Patron is dangerous (e.g., violence)

I like this spectrum of misbehavior because it helps us understand our goal. Our goal is twofold: (1) keep patrons from moving up the spectrum to worse levels, and (2) move patrons down the spectrum to better levels. If you can keep a Level 1 patron from moving to Level 2, that is good. If you can move a Level 3 patron down to Level 2, that is great!

It is important to recognize, though, that very rarely does a patron start at Level 3 or above. Most patrons start at Levels 0–2. It is only when we mishandle them that they move up the spectrum. Like the story in the beginning of this book when I got the pulled pork sandwich dumped on my head. The resident started at Level 1 and quickly moved to Level 4 as I handled the situation poorly.

After some practice, this becomes a game. When a resident is at a Level 2 or above, I see how quickly I can get him down to a Level 1 or 0. It is very satisfying to help an angry person calm down completely. This realization that we have control over patron behavior 80 percent of the time is very empowering. It means that most of those problems that make you sometimes dread your job are preventable.

I am very careful to say 80 percent because you cannot control patron behavior 100 percent of the time. There are situations that—no matter how well you handle them—will end poorly. Even the most skilled and experienced staff members at Hesed House still have to call the police occasionally. Mental illness, substance abuse, and stress make people unpredictable. They are controllable, though, much more often than we realize. It just isn't 100 percent of the time.

2. *The secret is to lead, not follow.*

    There is an old saying that you can't "push a string." If you try to push a string on a table, it will not do what you want. It will bunch up. If, on the other hand, you pull it on the table, you can make the string do anything you want: make a straight line, a circle, even a triangle.

    People are like a string: if you try to "push" them into compliance, they will often not comply. Like the string, they will stubbornly refuse to do what you want. If, on the other hand, you lead them into the behavior you want, you can gain compliance much more easily.

    Basically, you want to lead your homeless patrons into the behavior you want from them (calm, quiet, respectful) and not follow them into the very behavior you are trying to stop (frantic, loud, rude). This is a very important concept. *Modeling appropriate behavior is a much more effective way of controlling behavior than yelling and threatening.*

    Action movies have taught us that whoever is more violent is more powerful. This might be true in war and riot control (I don't think it is even then, actually), but it is simply not true in most ordinary confrontations. In the type of confrontations that library staff face every day, there is far more power in controlling the tone of the conversation. Whoever controls the tone of the conversation, controls the situation. This is an incredibly important concept and worth saying again:

> Whoever controls the tone of the conversation, controls the situation.

    Picture this: You are having a pleasant day when an angry patron approaches you and yells at you. He is really rude and insulting. Your face becomes flushed and you can feel your blood pressure rising. Pretty soon, you are talking loudly too and being a bit rude yourself. Eventually, you kick the patron out of the library. You "know" that the patron caused it, but you still feel lousy.

Consider this instead: You are having a pleasant day when an angry patron approaches you and yells at you. He is rude and insulting. You take a deep breath and respond with a level of respect and kindness he doesn't deserve. Little by little, he lowers his volume and becomes more rational. Eventually, he goes on his way, partially satisfied with your answers. You go back to your pleasant day.

In the first situation, you might have "shown him a thing or two" by kicking the patron out, but he was in control. He ruined your pleasant day, got you to talk loudly in a library, and forced you to kick him out. In the second situation, you were in control. You were able to get him to do what you wanted (lower his voice and act appropriately).

Never follow the lead of an angry or disrespectful patron. It only empowers and emboldens him to manipulate you further. Instead, lead him into the behavior you want. "Fighting fire with fire" might work in *Die Hard* movies, but it doesn't work in libraries. If you have a fire, don't dump gasoline on it. Use water.

3. *You have tools (lots of 'em!).*

As a librarian, you are a lot like Batman. Besides the obvious similarities, you also both have a utility belt full of tools. You probably don't have grappling hooks or freeze grenades, but you have your own tools. The way you stand has the power to calm someone down. The words you use have the power to get people to leave the library quietly. Your tools may not have names like "Batarang," but they do have names like the "Praying Ninja" and the "Shot Across the Bow." In every difficult situation, you can choose from your tools. You choose *how* to enforce the rules.

Not every tool works on every person, though. This is why it is helpful to imagine yourself as having a whole Batman utility belt full of tools. If a patron is immune to your "Ultrasonic Bat Beacon" tool (according to a nerdy fan site I found, Batman used it in #406 of the comic book series), then you can switch to trying your "Kryptonite Ring" tool (#612). I wish I could teach you the exact words that will pacify every homeless patron every time, but it isn't that simple. I want you to have lots of options—lots of tools—for engaging difficult patrons.

Just like any superhero, you can acquire new tools. In fact, the biggest difference between a seasoned librarian and a novice is that the veteran librarian has more tools and knows how—and when—to use each of them. I am going to give you new tools. This book is my offer to teach you the tools that we use in homeless shelters. My gift to you is a utility belt full of tools that have proven to be effective with homeless patrons.

In order to use your Batman Utility Belt, though, you need to understand that there are two "types" of tools: "fire tools" and "water tools." Fire tools *escalate* the tension and friction by punishing. Water tools *de-escalate* the tension and friction by using empathy. Yes, fire tools are the tools of punishment-driven enforcement, and water tools are the tools of empathy-driven enforcement.

> *Fire Tools* = Punishment-Driven Enforcement
> *Water Tools* = Empathy-Driven Enforcement

4. *Empathy is always first. Punishment is always a last resort.*

Forget Batman for a minute and think about Luke Skywalker from *Star Wars*. Luke—after he became a Jedi master—had two basic tools. He had his lightsaber and he had the Force. His lightsaber was an instrument of violence. He could use it to force people to do things (at the penalty of death). Whenever possible, though, he would use the Force to control people's minds ("Jedi Mind Trick") to get people to do what he wanted.

Fire tools are your lightsaber. You can try them when nothing else is working. Water tools are the Force, your tool of choice whenever possible.

> Always use empathy-driven enforcement first, and punishment-driven enforcement only as a last resort.

Like you, my wife and I are superheroes. Most of our battles are against the cable company. Whenever we have a problem with our connection or our bill, we call the cable company. My wife is a big fan of yelling at the customer-service representative (punishment-driven enforcement). I prefer trying to get the customer-service representative to like me (empathy-driven enforcement). I always go first. Most times, I can get the cable company to give us a credit on our next bill without ever raising my voice. If they won't give me what I want, then I say, "Oh, big mistake, buddy boy! You've done it now! I'm going to hand the phone to my wife!" We couldn't do it the other way, with my wife going first. If she yelled at the customer-service representative and couldn't get a credit on our bill, my charm and empathy wouldn't work because he or she would already be mad at us. Always use empathy-driven enforcement first, and punishment-driven enforcement only as a last resort.

5. *There are three parts to empathy-driven enforcement: your head, your body, and your words.*

    There is an order to the tools I am going to teach you:

    1. Your head tools

        Your head always comes first because it is most important that you approach the problem patron in the right mindset. Honestly, if you are losing your temper and freaking out, you simply won't remember any of the other tools. The first set of tools will teach you how to get the right attitude and mindset.

    2. Your body tools

        After you get your attitude right, the second most important thing is your body. Remember, homeless patrons pay much more attention to body language than you do. It doesn't matter what your mouth says if your body is saying, "You disgust me." The second set of tools will teach you how to position your body.

    3. Your word tools

        After your head and body are right, you need the right words. I'm going to teach you the "six unforgivable" curses that you should never say to a homeless person and how to be like Oprah Winfrey (and a bunch of other tools).

Okay, are you ready to become a Jedi master with a Batman Utility Belt? If you are ready to learn, you are ready.

Figure 4.2: Head, body, words

Leaping Lizards, Batman!

I am going to teach you dozens of tools. Do not try to employ them all at once. Pick a few to practice first. Once you have mastered them, move on to a few others. Otherwise you will get overwhelmed and quit.

Conclusion

We often mistakenly believe that the only way to get people to follow the rules is to threaten them with punishment. This shortsighted (and completely wrong) belief often creates more problems than it solves, especially with homeless patrons. Fortunately, there is another way: empathy-driven enforcement. Next we will learn the specific tools you can use to be a Jedi Librarian.

Note

1. Tony Nitti, "What Are Your Odds of Being Audited by the IRS?" https://www.forbes.com/sites/anthonynitti/2013/03/25/what-are-your-odds-of-being-audited-by-the-irs/.

Step 1: Your Head Tools

But you want murderous feelings?
Hang around librarians...
All that silence. Gives them ideas.

—Louise Penny[1]

It was a Tuesday afternoon and I was buried in paperwork. My phone rang and I considered letting it go to voice mail. The voice on the line said: "Ryan, you need to get outside right now! There is a guy with a knife! The police have already been called!"

I dropped the phone on my desk and ran towards the door, literally shoving someone out of my way. When I got outside, I found two staff members calmly talking to a resident. I was completely confused, having expected to find a chaotic scene. I casually walked up and whispered to one of the staff, "Is this the guy with the knife?" He nodded. Then I asked, "Did we get it from him?" He shook his head.

I took a deep breath.

I reached my hand out to the resident, saying, "Hi, my name is Ryan. I don't think we have met. What is your name?" He told me his name and I asked (in my most super-duper casual voice), "Can I have your knife?"

He pulled a large steak knife out of his pocket and handed it to me. I slid the large knife into my own pocket and relaxed a bit. I was just about to talk about our rules against weapons on the property when I caught movement out of the corner of my eye.

I turned around and saw a police officer sneaking towards us, with his Taser gun drawn. My first thought was, "Uh-oh! They are going to shoot this guy and he doesn't even have the knife anymore." I pulled the knife out of my pocket to show that I had it. The officer pointed his Taser gun at my chest and closed one eye, taking aim. Uh-oh!

I dropped the knife and raised my hands like a bank teller in a robbery. "I'm staff! I'm staff! I'm staff! We have the knife. It is okay!" I used my chin to motion towards my name tag, careful not to lower my hands. The officer froze, perfectly

Figure 5.1: HEAD, body, words

still, deciding whether to shoot me or not. I am sure it only took him a half second, but it felt like minutes.

Eventually the police officer put the Taser gun away and walked over to talk to us. We explained that we had the situation under control. As he was getting ready to leave, I asked him what he was going to do. "I was going to shoot you."

• • •

Get Your Head in the Game

Always start with your own mind. If you aren't in the right mindset, it is much harder to fake everything else. Tools involving your head fall into four categories:

- Your basic orientation and mindset
- How to think about homeless patrons
- How to think in the moment
- How to prepare for problems

Let's take a look at each of them . . .

Your Basic Orientation and Mindset

The first thing that Yoda did was teach Luke Skywalker how to master his own mind.

Do likewise, if Jedi Librarian you want to be.

Tool: The Michael Jordan

I want you to imagine that you are watching Michael Jordan play basketball back in his prime (when he could easily have beaten LeBron James). When Michael got the ball, did he ever throw it at the other team, like he was playing dodgeball? No. What if another player was a jerk? No. What if someone fouled him especially hard? No. He never threw the ball at the other team. He either shot the ball or passed it to a team member.

Why?

Because the goal of basketball is to get the ball through the basket. Ultimately, it is the only thing that matters. Throwing the ball at the other team might have been emotionally satisfying for Michael, but it would not have helped the Chicago Bulls win. In fact, it would have created major problems for the team. Michael Jordan was the best player of all time because he never lost track of the objective.

You need to "be like Mike."

You need to know your goal. Your goal—your *only* goal for difficult patrons—is to get them to follow the rules. That's it. It really is that simple. Here are some examples:

- Getting a patron to stop shouting
- Getting a patron to put her shoes back on
- Getting a patron to stop staring at another patron
- Getting a patron to leave

I know what you are thinking. "Ryan, this is really dumb advice. Of course, we are trying to get difficult patrons to follow the rules. What else would be our goal?" Unfortunately, staff members have all sorts of other goals that have nothing to do with gaining compliance. For example:

- Getting a patron to respect you (or to respect libraries)
- Defending your coworker's honor (or your own)
- Teaching a patron "a thing or two"
- Getting a patron to feel sorry for his actions

Trying to accomplish any of the above is like Michael Jordan throwing the ball at the other team, dodgeball-style: it might be emotionally satisfying, but it is not the goal and it will create problems for your team. You need to know your goal, and your goal needs to be about rule compliance. If you cannot articulate your goal, then you are probably just trying to throw the ball at someone.

The common theme with bad goals is that they are usually more about your own emotional needs than about the patron's behavior. The key is to remember that it is all about patron behavior. You care what a person *does*. You don't care what a person *thinks* or *says*. If a patron is shouting, that is a real problem. If a patron thinks you are a jerk, who cares? If a patron is tearing pages out of a book, that is a real problem. If a patron mutters under his breath, "This library is a joke," who cares?

As long as a patron follow the rules, allow him to think whatever he wants. If a patron follows the rules, allow him to say (quietly and to you) whatever he wants.

It isn't about you. Which brings me to my next point . . .

Tool: The Stick and the Stone

Don't take (or make) anything personal (ever!).

It is *never* about you. I'll prove it to you: Did you work at a library in the year 1930? Do you think in 1930 that some homeless individuals were disrespectful to some librarians? Of course they were. Do you expect to work at a library in the year 2100? Do you think that in 2100, some homeless individuals will be disrespectful to some librarians? Of course they will be. So, some homeless people were rude before you and some will be rude after you. This proves my point that it simply isn't about you. It is just the way the world is. Cats and dogs don't always get along. Homeless individuals and librarians don't always get along.

There are a lot of reasons why a homeless patron might be ornery that have nothing to do with you. Maybe he slept poorly the night before (if he is homeless, this is most likely true). Maybe he was arrested this morning for something he didn't do. Maybe he is detoxing from drugs and trying really hard not to use, but he feels terrible. Maybe he just got into an argument with his wife, or kids, or boss, or parents. None of this has anything to do with you, but it does put people in a bad enough mood to be argumentative with you.

Here is a universal truth: if you take things personally, you will make a mistake. If you think it is about you, you will make matters worse. On the other hand, if you can recognize that the mean thing that a homeless patron said is a reflection of his life—not yours—you will handle it better.

It is like the old saying, "Sticks and stones may break my bones, but words will never hurt me." When you realize that it isn't about you, there is nothing a patron can say to hurt you.

There is one exception to the rule that you shouldn't take it personally. If you share something personal about yourself and someone uses it against you, then that is personal. And it is your fault. I hope this doesn't happen in a library, but it sometimes happens in a shelter. A staff person is working the overnight shift and one of the residents can't sleep. They get to talking, and the resident confides that he thinks his wife is cheating on him. In a moment of genuine human connection, the staff member in turn confides that his wife once cheated on him. The next night the resident is drunk and tells everyone that the staff member's wife cheated on him. That is very personal. And it is the staff member's fault for over-sharing.

Tool: The Cup of Pennies

I need you to remember two concepts from chapter 3 about empathy:

- *Psychology of relationships*—In order to maintain a healthy relationship, you must have at least five positive interactions for every one negative interaction. Relationships are built with compliments, questions, deeds, and touch.
- *Reciprocity*—We feel obligated to repay kindness 1:1. Our vengeful selves want to repay rudeness, though, with more rudeness than we received (e.g., 1:5).

Combining these two concepts, you need to build up lots of "positive" credits in order to avoid having someone try to punish you for a negative interaction. The minimum ratio you should be looking for is 5:1.

It is helpful to imagine that you have an empty cup in your hand. Every time you do something positive for a homeless patron, you add one penny to the cup. Every time you do something negative, you remove five pennies. Anytime you have zero (or fewer) pennies in the cup, you are more likely to have problems with that patron. You want to build up a healthy reserve of pennies that you can use later to solve or prevent problems.

Let's look at an illustration of this in action:

What happens	Pennies added or removed	Total pennies in cup
Patron enters the library.	0	0
You smile as he walks towards you.	+1	1
As he gets nearer, you reach out your hand to shake his hand.	+1	2
You say, "Hello, my name is Ryan."	+1	3
You ask, "What's your name?"	+1	4
You ask, "How may I help you today?"	+1	5
You help him get logged onto a computer.	+1	6
Ten minutes later you have to ask him to stop yelling at other patrons.	-5	1

I guarantee you that enforcing the rule (no yelling at other patrons) will go better if you have done a lot of positive things to put pennies in your cup first. *It will still be uncomfortable and unpleasant, but you will get substantially less resistance.*

There is another way you lose pennies. Anytime you use a fire tool, you lose five pennies. If you roll your eyes, you lose five pennies. If you raise your voice, you lose five pennies. If you point your finger in someone's face, you lose five pennies. Anytime you use punishment (even psychological), you lose pennies. Don't do it. Save your pennies for when you need to ask for compliance with a rule.

We like to pretend that every conversation we have should be judged purely on the merits of that one conversation, but that is not how human beings work. We carry over our past experiences. We keep score (both good and bad). Use it to your advantage!

By the way, this penny analogy works really well in other contexts:

- *Marriage*—If you have read the book *The Five Love Languages* by Gary Chapman, then the cup of pennies is like the analogy of keeping your partner's "love tank" full. If you are married and you haven't read it, you are playing Russian roulette with your marriage.

- *Employment*—You get a penny every time you complete a project on time, save the organization money, help your boss or coworker, excel at something, and so on. You lose five pennies every time you screw something up. In this context, though, your goal is to hoard as many pennies as possible so you can cash them in later for a raise, promotion, work-from-home arrangement, extra vacation, or whatever.

Tool: The Selfie

The next time things have gone south with an ornery patron, this is what I want you to do:

- Pull out your smartphone.
- Hold it out in front of yourself (or use a selfie stick).
- Make your biggest, cheesiest smile.
- Take a selfie picture.
- Pull up the picture on your phone.
- Tell the person in the picture that he or she is responsible for the problem.

Always start with the assumption that the problem with the patron could have been avoided. It isn't always true, but it is usually true. Most problems can be avoided. Ask yourself the following questions:

- Did my words or body language convey hostility, disrespect, anger, disapproval, or any other negative emotion?
- Did I take the time to put pennies in my cup? Did I build up positive interactions (greetings, smiles, etc.) so that when I had to enforce a rule, I stayed at or above the 5:1 ratio for a healthy relationship?

The trick in analyzing what went wrong is to go back before the problem got bad. Usually, the seeds of a problem were sown earlier than you realize. At the shelter, when we analyze what went wrong, staff usually point out everything they did right in the last five minutes of a confrontation. Upon deeper analysis, we help them realize that they made a curt comment earlier in the evening that set off the chain of events. If they had not made the curt comment, the confrontation never would have happened in the first place.

Do not assume that you are the exception (who never does anything wrong), or you will never learn and improve. Assume that there is something you could have done better. Then figure out what it was.

Tool: La Bibliotecaria

In Spanish, the words for male and female librarian are slightly different. A *bibliotecaria* is a female librarian. This brings me to two facts:

- *Fact #1*: There are more female library staff than male library staff.
- *Fact #2*: There are more male homeless individuals than female homeless individuals.

This means that—statistically—most confrontations in a library are between female library staff and male homeless patrons. If you happen to be a female staff member, this fact may make you very uncomfortable.

It shouldn't.

In the shelter at Hesed House, the best staff members are almost always female. Women are at a distinct advantage when using empathy-driven enforcement:

- Because of their smaller size, women learn to use their words rather than trying to rely on physical size for protection.
- Women are less threatening. When male staff argue with male homeless individuals, the homeless individuals sometimes "puff up" to some juvenile machismo showdown.

- Most homeless individuals have a strong sense of chivalry. They might be willing to punch a man, but they would never think of hitting a woman.
- Women generally have higher emotional intelligence than men and tend to have a higher "empathy quotient" score (which lends itself to an empathy-driven enforcement approach).

I will admit that it is a little hypocritical for me to tell women not to worry about being female. I am a six-foot-tall male (with my bald head, I kinda look like a skinhead—but not by choice). But consider this: in two decades of working in Illinois' second largest homeless shelter, I have *never* had to defend myself physically. I have always talked my way out of tough situations. I use empathy-driven enforcement tools that are available to even the tiniest woman (and those tools are taught in this book).

A while ago I interviewed a college student for an internship. She was under five feet tall and weighed less than 100 pounds. To give you a visual image, she was—literally—a waitress at Hooters (I'm not making this up). I hired her for the internship, but assumed that she would be eaten alive in the shelter. I doubted that she would finish the internship. On her first night in the shelter, a large middle-aged man walked up to her and said, "Hey darlin.'" She spun around and in a firm voice said, "If you want my help, you will refer to me as 'Lynne' or 'Ms. Pagni' or 'ma'am.' Do you understand?" The man literally took a step back and stammered, "Yes ma'am, I mean Lynne, I mean Ms. Pagni." No one in the shelter ever called her "darlin'" again. In fact, she finished out the internship and joined the staff after college. She no longer works at Hesed House, but I know for a fact that she doesn't allow anyone to call her darlin' (except maybe my brother, whom she married!).

So, if you are a woman, don't worry about your gender. It isn't a problem unless you make it one. Just practice your water tools and you will do great!

Tool: The Homeless Golden Rule

Homeless Golden Rule

"Thou shalt treat homeless patrons
no better and no worse than any other patron."

If you remember nothing else from this book, remember the Homeless Golden Rule. Inscribe it on the bedrock of your library and write it on your heart. As I said in chapter 2, homelessness is inherently arbitrary, causing people to crave fairness. Individuals will respect your rules and authority much more if they do not feel that they are being singled out. If you follow this rule, it will save you hours of trouble (and just might make you a better person).

How to Think about Homeless Patrons

Tool: The Anti-Judge Judy

Don't judge a homeless person for why (you think) they became homeless or what their life has become. I offer this advice not because it is the right thing to do (although it is), but because your judgment will come across in your body language and how you talk. And that will make your job more difficult. No one likes to be judged (especially by a stranger). If a person can tell that you are judging them, they will not work with you. They will not go out of their way to be helpful, and they may even go out of their way to make your life more difficult.

There are two ways to "not judge." The first is to remember that you have absolutely no idea what brought this person to their current situation. It could be a health issue. It could be a mental break after their child died. You also have no idea who this person is. She could have a doctorate. He could have been a Secret Service agent for a sitting president, or been Eric Clapton's drummer. I have encountered everyone in this paragraph in a homeless shelter.

So, if at all possible, try not to judge the person in front of you. If you can't do that, at least fake it. If you find the person disgusting, hide it. If you find the person's behavior repulsive, hide it. If you think the person's choices are morally bankrupt, hide it.

It would be nice if you could save your judgment until you have "walked a mile in their shoes," but I will settle for your merely hiding your judgment. If the other person can feel you judging him, your job will be harder.

I have two extra tools for how to short-circuit your own judgmentalism:

- The Your Momma
- The Time Machine

Tool: The Your Momma

When faced with a difficult homeless patron, ask yourself, "How would I want people to treat this person if he or she was my relative?" If your mother struggled with alcoholism or delusions, how would you want the world to treat her? If your uncle was a Vietnam vet with PTSD, how would you want him to be treated? If your grandfather lived on the streets, how would you hope people treated him?

It is helpful to remember that—somewhere—this individual has relatives who are hoping you treat their relative with dignity. Give this person the treatment that you would ask for your own relative.

Tool: The Time Machine

I want you to get in your mental time machine and go back to high school. Ignore your friends there for a moment and think back to the kids who struggled. Do you remember

- The kid in learning disability classes who could never quite fit in?
- The kid who came to school with unexplained bruises from his alcoholic father?
- The kid who would miss months of class and then return with scars on her wrists?
- The kid being raised by his grandparents because his parents were both in prison or dead?

Some people have horrible childhood experiences. Because of the trauma, these people are much more likely to become homeless than the quarterback or prom queen. Try this: think back to the kid in high school that you felt most sorry for. Then ask yourself how you would want people to treat that kid after he or she grew up. Treat all homeless patrons that way.

Tool: The Billy Bias

According to the Kirwan Institute for the Study of Race and Ethnicity at Ohio State University, implicit bias is

> the attitudes or stereotypes that affect our understanding, actions, and decisions in an unconscious manner . . . Residing deep in the subconscious, these biases are different from known biases that individuals may choose to conceal for the purposes of social and/or political correctness.[2]

In other words, implicit bias is made up of the prejudices that we unconsciously have towards all sorts of people. Every single person on the planet has them. It is part of the human condition. You can't completely rid yourself of implicit bias.

If you can't get rid of implicit bias, what should you do? Name it. I recommend the name "Billy" because it just has a nice ring to it. I mean, "William Bias" just sounds pretentious.

Yes, I am being silly. You don't need to actually give your implicit biases a name (unless you want to). You would do well, though, to know where you are biased. Once you know, you can steer clear of it. So how do you know where you have an unconscious bias (it is unconscious, after all)?

Harvard University to the rescue! Researchers from Harvard (and some other swell universities) have created an online test that is pretty much impossible to fake. There are a bunch of different tests you can take that test your implicit biases with regard to race, age, religion, gender, disability, and so on. I recommend—at a minimum—that you take the "Race IAT."

The website address is currently https://implicit.harvard.edu/implicit/takeatest.html, but if it has changed by the time you read this, just Google "Harvard Implicit Bias Test."

The last time I took the tests I discovered:

- I have an unconscious bias against African Americans. This is not surprising. Most Americans (even African Americans) have an unconscious bias against African Americans. Jesse Jackson bravely said, "There is nothing more painful to me at this stage in my life than to walk down the street and hear footsteps and start thinking about robbery—then look around and see somebody white and feel relieved."[3]

- I have an unconscious bias in favor of Eastern religions (Buddhism, Hinduism) and against Western religions (Christianity, Islam, Judaism). This one surprised me, since I (and just about everyone I know) fit into the second category!

Once you understand your implicit biases, you can try to be more aware of them and guard against treating people poorly because of your unconscious thought processes.

How to Think in the Moment

Tool: The Marijuana Plant

You want to be calm when talking to homeless patrons. I don't mean "not frantic." That isn't calm enough. Imagine you just got an hour-long massage. That's not calm enough. Imagine you just took a lavender bubble bath with jasmine candles. That's not calm enough. Imagine you just smoked a marijuana plant. Even *that* is not calm enough. I want you to imagine that you *are* the marijuana plant. Now, *that* is calm.

You want to be calm because your discomfort is contagious (through mirror neurons) to the people you talk to. If you are uncomfortable, your patrons will be uncomfortable (and uncomfortable people do dumb things). If you are mellow, though, your patrons will be more mellow. You are the leader. Lead them to mellowness.

If you aren't calm, fake it until you are. There are two specific techniques:

- Take a deep breath. It works for the Zen monks. You can breathe your way into library nirvana. Seriously, though, taking a moment to breathe can lower your heart rate and clear your head. Scientists say that breathing "down regulates arousal," which is just a fancy way of saying it calms you down.

- Stand confidently. The research says that if your posture is confident, your mind becomes confident. Of course, the mind influences the body, but the body also influences the mind. For a fascinating—and worthwhile—21-minute explanation of this phenomenon, find Amy Cuddy's Ted Talk called "Your Body Language Shapes Who You Are." You will never slump again.

Tool: The Big Bird

As stated earlier, according to the "culture of poverty" theory, individuals raised in poverty will not grant respect to someone until he or she has earned it. The good news is that it is really easy to earn someone's respect. You simply "go first." If you show someone else respect, that gives them cultural permission to respect you back.

All you have to do is practice the manners that you learned from Big Bird on *Sesame Street*. When you get yourself in a jam with a homeless patron, simply ask yourself, "What would Big Bird do?"

Try these actions to get you started:

- Smile
- Make eye contact
- Introduce yourself
- Shake a person's hand
- Do not interrupt someone who is talking
- Refer to a person as "sir" or "ma'am"

It is especially important to remember to be respectful when you first meet someone (because it sets the tone for the whole conversation) and when tempers start to flare (because it is easy to lose your manners). If you aren't sure of when you should be respectful, just do it all the time!

Tool: The Nashville Minute

Merriam-Webster defines a "New York minute" as "a very short amount of time; an instant; a flash." Don't do that with homeless patrons. Everyone is always rushing them. Instead, do the Nashville Minute. In Tennessee, the pace is a little slower and people are willing to take the time for pleasantries and small talk. Have you ever been to a Cracker Barrel restaurant? It's like that.

Don't try to rush your homeless patrons. Instead, take a few minutes to listen. Take a few minutes to explain. They will appreciate you, and appreciative people cause far fewer problems.

How to Prepare for Problems

Tool: The Training Wheels

On April 5, 1970, four California Highway Patrol officers were killed by two perpetrators in what became known as the Newhall Massacre. At the time, it was the deadliest incident in California Highway Patrol history. Consequently, California did a massive analysis of what happened, and many of those findings changed the way police forces around the world train and prepare their officers.

There is some disagreement as to the exact details, but the story goes something like this:

Two officers—Walt Frago and Roger Gore—pulled over a car just before midnight. The two people in the car opened fire on the officers, killing them both. Soon two other officers—George Alleyn and James Pence—arrived and engaged in a gun battle with the assailants. A former Marine who happened to be driving by—Gary Kness—stopped his car, picked up a gun, and tried to help the police. The two new officers were both killed and the former Marine ran out of ammo and hid. The bad guys escaped, but were captured three hours later (one killed himself during a siege and the other killed himself in prison in 2009).

During the "critical incident analysis" after the massacre, the investigators discovered problems that—with a little explanation—can help you run your library better:

- Some of the officers were using guns that they had not trained on. One officer accidentally ejected a live round during the battle and another held his shotgun the wrong way. In fact, the bad guy they captured later explained that he decided to shoot the officer when he realized he was holding his gun wrong. They had not practiced using their tools when the stakes were low. Consequently, they didn't know how to use them properly when the stakes were high.

- At least one of the officers put the spent shell casings from his revolver into his pocket. The theory is that when practicing on the firing range, he would put the shell casings into his pocket after shooting instead of dumping them on the ground and reloading.

On a firing range this saves you from having to crawl around on the ground to pick them up when you are done. In a live gun battle, though, taking the extra time to put them in your pocket can be the difference between life and death. What the officers practiced in low-stress situations is exactly what they did in high-stress situations, even things that were nonsensical to do when the stakes were high.

So, what can we learn from the Newhall Massacre? The first lesson is to learn from every incident, especially incidents that go poorly. The analysis in Newhall changed the way police around the world are trained. At Hesed House we have implemented a practice that is widely used by police, military, and fire person-nel—the After Action Review tool (see chapter 16 for how you can do it).

The second lesson is that you need to practice doing the right thing when the stakes are low. Then when the adrenaline starts pumping, you will do the right thing. Do the right thing during enough encounters with Level 1 problem pa-trons and you will likely do the right thing during a Level 2 encounter. Get good at handling Level 2 encounters and you probably won't freak out during a Level 3 encounter, and so on.

It is like how you learned to ride a bike. You probably didn't grab your par-ent's mountain bike and go down a steep hill your first time. Instead, you started with training wheels. Once you had mastered the basic technique of peddling and balance, your parents took off the training wheels.

How do you do this in the library? Take the tools in this book and practice them in low-level confrontations. Use the tools consistently *every single time* un-til it becomes as "easy as riding a bike." In the next chapter I am going to teach you how to stand and where to put your hands in order to de-escalate a situa-tion. Practice doing it during every conversation and you won't have to think about how to stand when someone is yelling at you. In chapter 7, I am going to teach you what to say and what not to say. If you catch yourself saying something wrong during a minor encounter, take note of your mistake and get better. That way when you have a truly problematic patron, you won't accidentally say some-thing that makes the situation worse.

You can do role-playing to practice doing and saying the right thing. I don't find it very effective, though, because it is never the same as a real situation. I rec-ommend instead to practice on people who are actually mildly annoyed or slightly angry. Practice it while actually doing it.

Similarly, I recommend you have key phrases that you always use in certain situations. So, for example, I have a catch phrase that I *always* use when some-one is shouting at me in the shelter. I calmly ask, "Would you mind turning the volume down a notch or two?" while turning an imaginary dial in the air. (*Note:*

Pretty soon I am going to have to get a new phrase because these pesky millennials have never turned an old volume nob, so they don't know what that means.) I am very consistent. If someone's volume is slightly elevated, I say that. If someone is shouting with spit flying everywhere, that is what I say. In fact, I suspect that if someone pointed a gun at me and shouted "Stick 'em up!" I would probably ask them to "turn down the volume a notch or two" out of sheer habit. That sounds funny, but it wouldn't be the worst thing I could do.

In the appendix to this book, I have a list of situations where it is helpful to have a standard phrase. You can use one of my suggestions or make up your own. It doesn't matter. What matters is that you figure out what works and stick to it. Don't try to be creative, thinking up something clever and different to say every time. Similarly, I recommend that you have a one- or two-sentence explanation for why each of your major rules exists. This is also in the appendix.

Conclusion

It all starts with your attitude. If you don't have the correct attitude when engaging homeless patrons, you will resort to punishment-driven enforcement and fire tools. After you have your head right, though, you are ready to learn the water tools for properly positioning your body for empathy-driven enforcement.

Notes

1. Louise Penny, *A Rule Against Murder* (New York: Minotaur Books, 2008).
2. Ohio State University Kirwan Institute for the Study of Race and Ethnicity, "Understanding Implicit Bias," http://kirwaninstitute.osu.edu/research/understanding-implicit-bias/.
3. Bob Herbert, "In America; A Sea Change on Crime," www.nytimes.com/1993/12/12/opinion/in-america-a-sea-change-on-crime.html.

Step 2: Your Body Tools

Yes, librarians use punctuation marks to make little emoticons,
smiley and frowny faces in their correspondence,
but if there were one for an ironic wink,
or a sarcastic lip curl, they'd wear it out.

—Marilyn Johnson[1]

Gary was one of the nicest residents at Hesed House . . . when he was sober. After a few drinks, though, he was a total ass.

On one particular night, Gary had imbibed more than a few drinks before arriving at the shelter and was in rare form. I tried to calm him down, but he was having none of it.

Gary screamed at me, spit flying everywhere, but mostly on my face and chest. He threatened to beat me up. He threatened to beat up my parents. He even threatened to beat up my deceased great-grandparents. I didn't mind the threats. Gary was—as they say in Texas—all hat and no cattle. All of my relatives—dead and alive—were safe.

What I minded was the audience. There were two volunteers a few feet away while Gary described his personal genocide against my ancestry. Middle-aged suburban men who came to the shelter with their church once a month to serve dinner. One of the men, a short stocky blond guy who worked in the information technology department of his company (or maybe it was human resources), stood at my side. His hands were balled into fists and every muscle in his body was tense, ready to protect me from my spittle-wielding assailant. I don't know how he didn't get a cramp. I'm sure he was sore the next day.

The other guy was a newer volunteer that I didn't know. He had seen a few more winters than the blond guy, and was tall and slender. He sat in a brown folding chair, his feet propped up comfortably on the table in front of him, watching the drunken spectacle with amusement.

Eventually—and against my best efforts—Gary crossed a line and I had to ask him to leave for the night. As I escorted Gary to the door, my blond

Figure 6.1: Head, BODY, words

volunteer-protector flanked my side like a portly Secret Service detail. The other volunteer never even took his feet off the table.

With Gary safely outside, the shelter quieted down and the two volunteers started talking. The blond guy asked the other volunteer (his feet still up on the table) how he had remained so calm in the face of such obvious peril. The other man smiled and said, "I'm an FBI agent and that guy was obviously full of s--t. He wouldn't hurt a fly."

• • •

Your Body Matters More Than You Realize

Remember from chapter 2 that homeless people pay way more attention to body language than you (because they have a smaller vocabulary). Thus, you need to be much more aware of your body language. (See figure 6.1.) You don't need to walk around paranoid and self-conscious, though. Instead, you should practice the tools in the following six categories (plus one "advanced" bonus tool):

1. How to approach a homeless patron
2. How to stand
3. Where to stand
4. Eye contact
5. Your face
6. Handshakes
7. Bonus advanced tool

Let's take a look at each of them...

How to Approach a Homeless Patron

Tool: The Walking Man

In 1987, Arnold Schwarzenegger starred in a movie about a dystopian America that had become a totalitarian police state ruled by a reality television host. It was set in the years 2017–2019 (I'm not making this up!). The movie was called *The Running Man*. The protagonist, Ben Richards—played by the Governator himself—spent a lot of time running around killing people. Don't do that. Ever. This is one hero I do not want you to emulate. *Don't run.*

Every conversation/confrontation starts with how you approach the patron. It is literally your first impression (and you know the saying about how many chances you get to make a good first impression). Whenever possible, approach a homeless patron calmly at a normal speed (even if it means you have to run the first 30 feet and then calmly walk the final 15). Running up on a homeless patron will automatically raise his anxiety level and make him defensive (or aggressive). Think about it: how do you feel when someone runs up to you?

How to Stand

Tool: The Fight and the Flight

When you are talking to a homeless patron (especially if the conversation is tense in any way) there are two equally bad ways to stand:

a. *Backing away in fear ("Flight")*—Do not back up. It sends the message that you can be physically dominated. If a patron thinks he can get what he wants by physically dominating you, he will be encouraged to do so.

b. *Moving towards the person in an aggressive manner ("Fight")*—If you lean in or over the person and invade his personal space, it sends the message that you are trying to physically dominate him. You can inadvertently trigger a "fight or flight" response in him. A "flight" response isn't the end of the world, but a "fight" response could make for a very bad day for you!

The key is to remove physical domination from the equation entirely. This is a library, not a boxing match: no one should be physically dominating anyone!

Okay, so if you shouldn't back up and you shouldn't move forward, what should you do? You should use a technique I call the Pool Shot.

Note: In a similar vein, if you are talking to someone who is sitting down (and you are standing up), do not physically lean over them. It sends a similar message of physical domination. Instead, squat down next to them so that you are at the same level as them.

Tool: The Pool Shot

There are two key aspects to how you should stand:

- Distance
- Body angle

Honestly, I'm not too worried that you will stand too close or too far away. Most people do it correctly without thinking about it. According to proxemics—the study of human use of space—"social space" begins at four feet, though that seems a bit far for me. (In the next tool, the Jerry Seinfeld, I'm going to teach you how to handle someone who invades your personal space.)

Far more important than your distance is the angle of your body. Just like in playing billiards, it is all about the angle. When I do live trainings, this tool is the one that excites people the most. It will change your work life (and possibly your sex life).

Here's what I want you to do:

> When you are talking to a homeless patron, turn your body 15 degrees so you are not facing exactly at him. Instead, your body will be pointing just to the outside of his shoulder. (See figures 6.2 and 6.3.)

Another way to think about this is to imagine how you stand when three people are talking. When three people are talking, no one is facing directly at each other. Everyone points towards the collective middle. I want you to stand that way when talking to only one person (as if there is an imaginary third person).

Facing your body at a slight angle reduces the emotional tension in the conversation. Squaring off at each other is a "confrontation," whereas a slight angle is a "conversation." Put down this book for a minute and go find someone to try this out with. It will change your world.

I was doing a training for security guards at a casino when one of the security guards got excited, saying, "My father taught me this technique." I was intrigued to find out how his father knew this tool. He continued, "He said if you are trying to pick up a woman at a bar, make sure you stand at a slight angle rather than facing her straight on. You'll be less intimidating and you're more likely to get her into bed." While I can't endorse this "fatherly" advice, the principles behind it are the same: turning your body slightly lowers the emotional tension and is viewed as less aggressive.

Figure 6.2: How not to stand: directly facing each other, with shoulders squared off

Figure 6.3: Instead, turn your body at a 15-degree angle in order to reduce the tension of the conversation

The key to this technique is to do it all the time in every conversation. Stand at an angle when at parties, when talking to coworkers, when talking to housed patrons, when talking to everyone. Eventually it will become the default way you stand and you won't have to think about it.

To see a video demonstration of how to stand properly, go to www.home lesslibrary.com/stand.

Tool: The Jerry Seinfeld

In the fifth season of the hit sitcom *Seinfeld*, Elaine (Julia Louis-Dreyfus) starts dating a guy named Aaron (Judge Reinhold). Aaron is a "close talker," someone who stands too close to people, invading their personal space. The episode is funny because we have all encountered a close talker who made us uncomfortable with their distance (or lack thereof). I have a few tips for handling close talkers:

a. Invite the person to "talk while you walk." Tell him that you want to talk to him, but that you need to restock some books (or get papers, or whatever) and then have him follow you. This allows you to control the distance between the two of you.

b. Try to position something (like a table) between the two of you, so that the natural barrier keeps the person at a distance. The key to this (and the hard part) is to casually slip behind the table without being obvious.

c. Invite them to talk to you sitting down (on opposite sides of a table).

d. If nothing else works, you can use a little alternative fact. Ask the person if you can take a step back because you forgot deodorant this morning (or forgot to brush your teeth, or whatever). This works because you aren't making it about them and because it is just weird enough to be disarming for most people. (*Note:* You are going to ask if *you* can step back, not ask the *patron* to step back.)

The Praying Ninja

You also need to be mindful of your hands. There are four things to avoid with your hands:

- *Arms crossed*—This says "I'm judging you."
- *Hands on hips*—This says "I don't approve of you."
- *Pointing at the person*—This says "I don't like you."
- *Hands balled up in fists*—This says "I'm going to punch you."

It is amazing how much talking your hands can do. Be very careful of what they are saying for you.

Instead, you want to send a message of calmness and casualness. The two easiest ways are to put your hands in your pockets or behind your back. Both send the message "I'm comfortable around you." Many experts recommend keeping your hands at your sides (instead of putting them in your pockets or behind your back) because the latter can make someone with paranoia nervous, but I have never personally experienced this. I, personally, almost always have my hands in my pockets when I'm talking to homeless guests at the shelter.

I say "almost" because there is one situation where you do not want your hands in your pockets or behind your back: if there is any chance you might get punched or shoved. You simply can't protect yourself or catch your fall when your hands are in your pockets or behind your back.

When I think there is any chance I might get punched, I switch to the Praying Ninja. With this technique, you put your palms together in front of your face (like you are praying) and "talk with your hands." You know how some people are really animated and are constantly moving their hands when they talk? You want to do that. The Praying Ninja is effective because it allows you to have your hands in front of your face to protect it (like a Ninja), but it doesn't look like you are trying to protect yourself.

I strongly recommend you go to www.homelesslibrary.com/prayingninja to see a video demonstration of the Praying Ninja because it is a *lot* easier for me to show you how to do it than it is to tell you. You will also better understand why I call it the Praying Ninja.

Where to Stand

Tool: The Less Public Library

Whenever possible, move a conflict between you and a homeless patron to somewhere "less public." I did not say to move it to somewhere private. It simply isn't safe to take an agitated individual (of any housing status) behind closed doors by yourself. You can take it somewhere "less public," though, by moving it from near a cluster of tables to twenty feet away. Similarly, behind a bookshelf works well (people will hear you call for help, but not hear you talking).

The goal here is to remove the audience. This accomplishes two things:

1. It allows the homeless patron to "save face." He doesn't have as much pressure to "tell you a thing or two."
2. It also removes the audience for you. You won't feel as much of a need to be a "tough guy" without a bunch of people watching.

Eye Contact

Tools Related to Eye Contact

Eye contact is incredibly important. Eye contact releases oxytocin, which creates bonding and relationship. It is also very important for giving respect. Unfortunately, human beings are making less and less eye contact, thanks to our smartphones. Good eye contact is essential, though, for empathy-driven enforcement.

The following are four tools (but you should only use the two water tools):

- The Floor of Disrespect (a fire tool)
- The Laser Beam (a fire tool)
- The Goldilocks (a water tool)
- The Pirate (an advanced water tool)

Fire Tool: The Floor of Disrespect (Don't Do This!)

Have ever seen a movie where a father was so disappointed in his son that he couldn't even look at him? Hopefully, that has never happened to you. In most Western cultures, avoiding eye contact is a sign of immense disrespect. If your goal is to disrespect someone, then staring at the floor while talking is a remarkably effective tool for accomplishing it.

It is equally disrespectful (and damaging) to stare at your phone, computer screen, or book while having a conversation. You wouldn't have a conversation with your grandmother while checking your e-mail. Why not? Because it is rude. Don't do it with homeless patrons either.

Fire Tool: The Laser Beam (Don't Do This!)

Have you ever seen an X-Men movie? I hope so, or this next analogy is going to fall a little flat. One of the mutant superheroes is called Cyclops, and his superpower is that he can shoot laser beams out of his eyes (according to Wikipedia, those laser beams are technically called "Optic Force Blasts," but that just sounds corny). These laser beams melt rocks and kill people and do all sorts of other really bad things.

You probably can't shoot actual laser beams out of your eyes, but you too have the ability to cause all sorts of damage with your eyes. You do this by glaring menacingly and relentlessly at someone (without blinking if you can manage it). People become very uncomfortable when glared at. If your goal is to make someone uncomfortable, then—by all means—glare away. I will warn you, though, that uncomfortable people tend to act in highly unpredictable ways (and libraries tend to function poorly with unpredictable people).

Water Tool: The Goldilocks (Do This Instead!)

Once upon a time, there was a little librarian named Goldilocks. She went for a walk in the stacks. Pretty soon she came upon a few patrons arguing. With the first patron Goldilocks stared too long and the patron exclaimed, "This eye contact is too much!" With the second patron, Goldilocks didn't look at him at all and he cried out, "This eye contact is too little!" For the third patron, Goldilocks made just the right amount of eye contact and the patron proclaimed, "This is just right! I will follow all of your rules!" Goldilocks got a raise, married Prince Charming, and lived happily ever after.

Here is what research has taught us about eye contact:

- *Too much*: If you stare for longer than 10 seconds, it is considered creepy and aggressive.

- *Too little*: If you make eye contact for less than 7 seconds, you are considered "untrustworthy, unknowledgeable, and nervous." You also inadvertently send the message that you are inferior to the other person.

- *Just right*: The ideal eye contact is about 7–10 seconds. In other words, you look at the person for 7–10 seconds, then look away for a few seconds, than look back again. The ideal "eye contact to non-eye contact ratio" for emotional connection and oxytocin release is 60–70 percent.[2]

Don't get out your stop watch or your calculator, though, to make sure you are at seven seconds and 60 percent. Now, that would be creepy. Instead, make eye contact for a while and then glance down at your feet for a few seconds. Then look back into the patron's eyes. Just do this over and over until the conversation is over.

To see examples of the eye contact tools, go to www.homelesslibrary.com/eyecontact.

Advanced Water Tool: The Pirate

Imagine that you are talking to a vicious, bloodthirsty, and murderous pirate. We'll call him Ned.[3]

Now, imagine that Pirate Ned wears an eye patch over his left eye. If you were talking to Ned, which of his eyes would you look at while he talked? His right eye, of course. If you stared at his patch he would probably make you walk the plank.

I want you to do that with your library patrons, too, when they are talking. Pick one eye and focus on it when the person is talking. Our natural instinct is to move our gaze back and forth between both eyes. This makes you look distracted,

Figure 6.4: Seeing a picture of a smiling child provides the same neurochemical pick-me-up as eating 220 pounds of chocolate

like you aren't fully paying attention. If, instead, you focus your attention on only one eye, the other person will feel like you are paying closer attention.

Your Face

Tool: The 22-Pound Chocolate Smile

I care enough about you, dear reader, to give you the same emotional high as eating 220 pounds of chocolate (but without any of the calories). Here goes:

Researchers at Hewlett-Packard discovered that looking at the smiling face of a child gives you the same emotional reward as eating 2,000 chocolate bars (~220 pounds).[4] A smile from a friend is only worth 200 bars of chocolate (~22 pounds), but that's still pretty good! (See figure 6.4.)

So, you can give your patrons an emotional high, too. You don't have to carry around a picture of a smiling baby (unless you want to). All you have to do is smile at them.

> *Disclaimer*: I am painfully aware of the fact that I run the risk of winning a "Captain Obvious" award for telling you that it is good to smile at people, but it is amazing how quickly we forget to smile at people, *especially homeless people*. So few people smile at homeless people that I am willing to risk being ridiculed for offering this basic advice.

Smiling is an all-around great tool: it makes you happier. It makes the other person happier, forcing him to smile[5] when his mirror neurons fire. In addition, when you smile at someone, researchers have found that the other person views you as more likable, more courteous, and even more competent.[6] And if that isn't enough, researchers discovered that people who smile live longer.[7]

A couple pieces of random smile advice:

- You don't need to smile through an entire conversation. Unless it is a happy, joyous topic, smiling incessantly is just creepy. Instead, focus on smiling at someone when they approach you (even if they aren't smiling).

- Practice smiling in the mirror. I used to be absolutely horrible at smiling. There are very few pictures of me from before 2005 where I am smiling. After seeing my sour mug on a picture (with a major donor holding a large check), I became determined to learn how to smile. I stood in front of the mirror (alone and with the door locked) and practiced smiling. Eventually I learned how to smile! Now, as Buddy said in the movie *Elf*: "I just like to smile, smiling's my favorite!"

Handshakes

Tool: The Secret Handshake

I am going to teach you a secret handshake that is remarkably effective with homeless patrons. (We aren't in a fraternity, so you don't get to invent your own secret handshake.) But you must do it *exactly* as I teach you. Are you ready to learn it? Good. Here goes. When a homeless patron approaches you, follow these exact steps in *precisely* this order:

Step 1: Make eye contact with the patron.

Step 2: Smile at the patron.

Step 3: Reach out your hand in the direction of the patron.

Step 4: Say "good morning" or "good afternoon."

Step 5: Lean in slightly.

Step 6: Shake the patron's hand.

I know what you are thinking: "But Ryan, that's not a secret handshake. That is exactly how I shake everyone's hand!" You are correct. And that is the secret. When you treat homeless people like you would any other person, they are insanely grateful. Homeless people appreciate being treated like "people," not "homeless people."

A handshake is enormously important for several reasons:

- It conveys an enormous amount of respect. When you refuse to touch people, you treat them like a biblical leper or an Indian untouchable.
- Shaking hands is remarkably effective at creating relationship because a single handshake releases as much oxytocin as three hours of face-to-face conversation.

Shake hands with your homeless patrons as often as you can. When I am walking through the shelter at Hesed House, I bet I sometimes shake 40 hands in a 20-minute span. In fact, I shake so many hands that when I'm done I promptly wash my hands. It isn't that I don't trust homeless hands; I would wash my hands after touching 40 surgeons' hands, too.

Here is what experts tell us are the ingredients for a perfect handshake:

- It should be "balanced." What this means is that both parties' hands should be vertical. If you twist your hand so that your hand is horizontal over their hand, it is a sign of dominance. If you twist your hand so that it is horizontal below their hand it is a sign of submission. Keep it equal.

- Your handshake should have the pressure of squeezing a peach. Imagine squeezing a peach. Too light and you'll drop the fruit. Too hard and you'll bruise it. If you can keep from giggling, imagine peaches while shaking hands.

- Shake men's and women's hands the same. Apparently, it used to be socially appropriate for a man to shake a woman's hand differently than another man, but the times they are a-changin'!

- Your hands should meet at the middle point between you and the other person. Do not pull the person's hand towards you. This is considered highly aggressive because it literally pulls the person off balance.

- Take your left hand out of your pocket. It is considered disrespectful to shake hands while keeping one's other hand in one's pocket.

- Three shakes and hold for two to three seconds.[8]

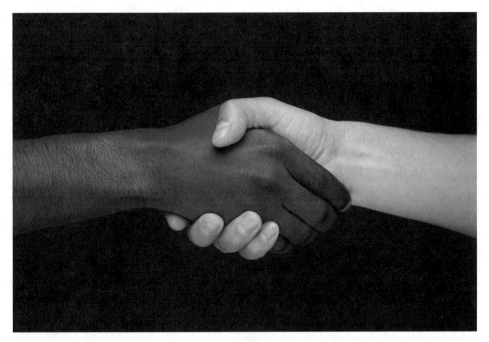

Figure 6.5: The correct way to shake hands: balanced so that both hands are perpendicular to the ground

Figure 6.6: The wrong way to shake hands: turning your hand "over" the other person's in a display of dominance

Do you think you are good at shaking hands? Good for you. Do you know who else thinks they are good at shaking hands? Every single person who is bad at shaking hands! Do yourself a favor and ask a few friends and colleagues if you can shake their hand and get feedback. Is it too hard? Too soft? Unbalanced? Too long? Too short? (See figures 6.5 and 6.6.)

Once you have mastered the Secret Handshake, you are ready to learn two advanced tools called the Bill Clinton and the Barack Obama.

Tool: The Bill Clinton

No one shakes hands better than William Jefferson Clinton. He is the master. Here's how you shake hands like Bill:

- Reach out with your right hand to shake the other person's right hand.
- After your right hands are touching, immediately bring your left hand around and also grab their right hand (forming a "hand sandwich").
- Shake hands.

Don't pull out the Bill Clinton (or the Barack Obama) for every handshake. Save it for when you are really excited to see someone. If you use it with someone else it can come across as a little too personal or intimate.

But when you want to convey warmth and affection, nothing beats the Bill Clinton . . . except maybe the Barack Obama. (See figure 6.7.)

Tool: The Barack Obama

Barack Hussein Obama is also pretty good at shaking hands (not quite as good as Bill Clinton, but that's just my opinion). Here's how you shake hands like Barack:

- Reach out with your right hand to shake the other person's right hand.
- After your right hands are touching, immediately bring your left hand around, and put it gently on the person's right bicep, elbow, or shoulder.
- Shake hands.

Tool: The Hot Stove

Shaking hands is the *only* time you should touch a homeless patron. In a confrontation with a homeless patron, don't ever touch him or her (or his or her belongings). There are two main reasons for this:

Figure 6.7: The man on the right is doing the Bill Clinton. The man on the left is doing the Barack Obama.

- It is illegal. You are not the police. You do not have the right to touch someone else against their will, except in self-defense. There is a name for touching someone who doesn't want to be touched. It is called battery (as in "assault and battery").
- It is a fire tool (punishment-driven enforcement) that escalates the situation substantially.

I am not just talking about punching or shoving. I am also talking about

- Leading someone to the door by their arm
- Putting your hand on someone's back to lead them towards the door
- Putting your hand on someone's shoulder to get their attention in a conflict
- Picking up someone's bag

Remember from chapter 2 that homelessness is inherently dangerous. Anyone who has been homeless for very long has been physically assaulted. People who have been physically attacked in the past are understandably skittish about having others touch them. It triggers a serious "fight or flight" response. Remember, if they have a "fight" response, you are going to have a very bad day!

A few years ago, one of our residents in the shelter was agitated (and intoxicated). He was trying to pick a fight with everyone who walked by. I approached him from behind and lightly touched the back of his arm to get his attention. Immediately he spun around on me, wild-eyed, his arm cocked back with a fist in a tight ball preparing to punch me. It happened so quickly, I didn't have time to respond. Time seemed to freeze at that moment and I vividly remember thinking, "Oh s--t. I'm about to get punched." In hindsight, I am ashamed that I couldn't think of something more clever, but this was all I could muster at the time.

As I braced myself for his inevitable fist, his whole demeanor abruptly changed. A wide grin spread across his face and he said, "Hey Ryan! How *you* doin'?" the way Joey Tribbiani says on the sitcom *Friends*. He lowered his fist and shook my hand, while I stood limply in disbelief. I asked him later—when he was sober—if he was actually going to punch me or if he was just faking. He replied with a smile, "Oh yeah. Totally. I really really wanted to punch you."

And that, my friends, is how I learned to *never* touch an agitated individual (homeless or otherwise).

Bonus Advanced Tool

Tool: The Echo

> *Disclaimer*: I almost didn't include this tool in the book because it is hard to do well.

> If this sounds too complicated or doesn't make sense, just skip it.

Postural echoing (not my term) is where you adopt a posture, stance, and gestures that are similar to those of the person you are talking to. If they stand casually, you do the same thing. If they stand tall with arms crossed, you do the same. Humans naturally do postural echoing when we are emotionally "in sync" with someone else. It can also be used to create connection, though, too. In a seminal research study, researchers had an assistant do postural echoing with half of the research subjects. In a post-study interview, the individuals who had been "echoed" liked the research assistant more than those who hadn't.[9] In fact, Match.com even teaches people how to use postural echoing as one of its "flirting tips"![10]

Here are my tips, though, if you choose to try postural echoing:

- This is most effective when a patron is standing casually. Adopting a less rigid stance will help you seem more approachable.
- Do not echo aggressive or hostile postures. This is just "following" a patron into bad behavior, not leading them into good behavior.

Question: How do I stand in order to convey authority?

Answer: That is a great question. The answer is simple: You don't. If you try to stand "authoritatively," you will most likely convey aggression. Instead, do the opposite: try not to convey weakness or fear. The easiest way to do this is by not backing down and by making appropriate eye contact.

Conclusion

Your body language is incredibly important. Homeless individuals and other individuals from a culture of poverty pay far more attention to body language than you do. Consequently, you need to learn to not "punish with your body language."

To close out this chapter, let's try an exercise. Take a look at figure 6.8 and try to pinpoint how many mistakes the people are making.

Figure 6.8: How many mistakes can you find in their body language (that display aggression or disapproval)?

I found four (perhaps you found more):

1. Leaning in aggressively
2. Squaring off straight on, rather than turning at an angle
3. Pointing fingers
4. Glaring at the other person intensely

Notes

1. Marilyn Johnson, *This Book Is Overdue!: How Librarians and Cybrarians Can Save Us All* (New York: HarperCollins, 2010).
2. Sue Shellenbarger, "Just Look Me in the Eye Already," https://www.wsj.com/articles/SB1000 14241278873248098045785112908222228174.
3. Wikipedia, "Edward Low," https://en.wikipedia.org/wiki/Edward_Low.
4. The Scotsman, "One Smile Can Make You Feel a Million Dollars," www.scotsman.com/news/one-smile-can-make-you-feel-a-million-dollars-1-738272.
5. Ulf Dimberg and Sven Söderkvist, "The Voluntary Facial Action Technique: A Method to Test the Facial Feedback Hypothesis," *Journal of Nonverbal Behavior* 35, no. 1 (2011): 17–33, available at https://link.springer.com/article/10.1007%2Fs10919-010-0098-6/.
6. Alicia A. Grandey et al., "Is 'Service with a Smile' Enough? Authenticity of Positive Displays during Service Encounters," *Organizational Behavior and Human Decision Processes* 96, no. 1 (2005): 38–55, available at www.sciencedirect.com/science/article/pii/S074959 7804000743.
7. Ernest L. Abel and Michael L. Kruger, "Smile Intensity in Photographs Predicts Longevity," *Psychological Science* 21, no. 4 (2010): 542–44, available at http://journals.sagepub.com/doi/abs/10.1177/0956797610363775.
8. Daily Mail, "Firm Squeeze and Three Shakes: Scientists Devise Formula for the Perfect Handshake," www.dailymail.co.uk/sciencetech/article-1294962/Scientists-perfect-handshake-formula-Firm-squeeze-shakes.html.
9. H. McGinley, R. LeFevre, and P. McGinley, "The Influence of a Communicator's Body Position on Opinion Change in Others," *Journal of Personality and Social Psychology* 31 (1975): 486–90.
10. Nausheen Qureshi, "Flirting Tips," http://datingtips.match.com/flirting-tips-body-language-13443241.html.

Step 3: Your Word Tools

7

Never argue with a librarian;
they know too much.

—CAROLE NELSON DOUGLAS[1]

I arrived at work with a little more pep in my step than usual; I love Halloween at a homeless shelter. The kids are all high on candy and the adults are extra-jovial. Looking at my calendar for the day, though, my heart sank. Oh, no! I forgot I had to meet with Jill—one of our more "famous" paranoid schizophrenic residents. Jill's tirades were the stuff of legend. I took a deep breath, girded my loins, and made my way towards the lobby, prepared for battle.

It wasn't until I saw the horror on Jill's face that I remembered that it was Halloween and I was dressed like Tinky Winky, the purple Teletubby. (See figure 7.1.) Before I could explain, she jumped up and screamed, "Who the f--k are you?!?" I smiled sheepishly and answered, "I'm Ryan, the executive director. You asked to meet with me?" It took five minutes to convince her that I was the executive director.

I left the door of the conference room open and sat in the chair closest to it, just in case. I asked Jill why she had asked to speak with me. Apparently, a few days earlier she had been kicked out of the shelter because she had screamed "F--k you!" at a staff member. After a few probing questions, Jill explained that she had been a little upset about one of our transgender residents (her exact words were "That she-male ain't

Figure 7.1: Author in a Teletubby costume / Me as Tinky Winky. Minnie Mouse is my daughter Hailey.

Figure 7.2: Head, body, WORDS

fooling nobody! I know she's got a d---k!"). Yes, the total bizarreness of talking to someone with paranoid schizophrenia about a transgender individual—while dressed as a Teletubby—was not lost on me.

When a female staff member had asked Jill to stop talking about the other resident, Jill turned on the staff member and screamed the obscenity that got her ejected. Jill did not deny that she had cussed at the staff member. It was unfair, though, she said. Only a few days earlier she had heard another resident say "Ah, you ain't s--t" to a staff member he really liked (he had said it with affection, not malice). Why had she been kicked out, but he hadn't?

I spent the next thirty-five minutes trying to explain the difference between screaming "F--k you!" at someone and affectionately saying, "You ain't s--t." Jill simply could not grasp the difference. Having this conversation was interesting at first, but it quickly grew frustrating.

Just as I was about to give up, Jill's eyes got big and she exclaimed, "I get it now! I get it! I know what I did wrong! I know what I have to do next time!"

I smiled, proud of my ability to get through to someone so troubled.

"I was wrong to scream 'f--k you.' I see that now," Jill said with deep earnestness. "Yeah, next time staff pisses me off, I'll scream 'You ain't s--t!'"

Not exactly the epiphany I was hoping for, but a step in the right direction, I suppose.

• • •

Magic Words

Okay, you have the right mindset. Your body language is oozing cooperativeness, rather than hostility. Now it is time to learn the magic words that will dramatically improve your library.

There are many tools that involve your words. They fall into four categories:

1. Basic tools that you should use 100 percent of the time
2. Things you should *never* do
3. Tools that will help you prevent future problems
4. Tools to use in a conflict with a patron

Let's take a look at each of them . . .

Basic Tools That You Should Use 100 Percent of the Time

Tool: The Limbo

Did you ever do the Limbo Dance as a kid? That's the dance/game where you lean back and try to dance under a pole without touching either the pole or the ground. The pole is then lowered an inch and everyone who didn't touch it in the last round goes again until only the winner remains. You want to do a version of that—with your voice—when talking to an angry homeless patron.

You want to "talk quieter" when speaking to an angry homeless patron. The reason is that a homeless patron will always be one decibel level above you. If an angry patron is at a decibel level 3 and you raise your voice to level 3, where will he go? Yup, level 4. If you then get louder and join him at level 4, where will he go? Of course, level 5! It is an arms race that you cannot win.

Instead of following a homeless patron into a shouting match, you want to lead him or her into a quieter conversation. It works like this: if an angry patron is at a decibel level 5 and you want him at a level 3, what is the loudest you can be? Yes, level 2. If you want him at a level 2, what is the loudest you can be? Correct, level 1. The trick is to accept that an angry homeless patron will always be louder than you, so you have to speak more quietly than you want him or her to speak.

I find it helpful to speak absurdly quietly when someone is shouting at me. If someone is shouting at me and I respond with a whisper, it can be very confusing to someone who expects me to shout back. More often than not, they whisper back without me having to ask them to talk more quietly.

If the Limbo Dance is not enough, it is very helpful to have a go-to phrase that you always say, so that you don't accidentally say "be quiet" (which usually elicits a louder response). As I explained in chapter 5, when someone is shouting at me, I *always* calmly ask, "Would you mind turning the volume down a notch or two?" while turning an imaginary dial in the air.

Tool: The Hypnotist

Take a minute and think about how a hypnotist talks to his or her subject. The hypnotist speaks very slowly, very calmly, and very smoothly without a lot of animation and excitability. The reason why hypnotists talk like this is because it is calming to the listener. You want to talk the same way for the exact same reason. Obviously, I don't want you to say to an agitated patron, "You are getting sleepy. When I snap my fingers, you will bark like a dog." I do, however, want you to take three things away from hypnotists:

1. *Speak slowly.* In fact, if you are slightly uncomfortable with how slowly you are speaking, you are probably getting close to the correct speed.
2. *Take pauses.* Force yourself to take pauses and not talk continuously. It will be more relaxing to you and to the patron. You can even take pauses in the middle of sentences.
3. *Breathe.* It is important that you breathe. Do you know what it is called when someone can't breathe? It is called asphyxiation and it is very bad. When you stop breathing, you are asphyxiating yourself. The lack of oxygen automatically makes you anxious. If you breathe, you will calm down and you will also unconsciously remind the other person to breathe (similar to how people often yawn when someone else yawns). If you have oxygen and the homeless patron has oxygen, everyone will be calmer.

Just as you want to avoid a "volume arms race," you want to avoid a "frantic-ness arms race." Lead them to calmness. When you can say, "If you do that again, I'll have to ask you to leave the library" with Zen-like calmness, then you know you are nearly a Jedi master of empathy-driven enforcement water tools.

Tool: The Oprah

The Oprah is probably one of the top five most important tools in de-escalating patrons. Since I live in Chicago, I have several friends who have worked for Oprah Winfrey. They all talk about how Oprah is an amazing listener. One producer told me, "When you talk to Oprah, she *really* listens in a way that no one has ever listened to you before. It is like you are the only person in the world and listening to you is the only thing she wants to be doing at that moment. It is truly amazing when Oprah listens to you."

So, I want you to be like Oprah and listen. Don't interrupt your homeless patrons. Don't talk over your homeless patrons. Homeless individuals don't like to be interrupted or talked over any more than you do. In fact, homeless individuals like it even less than you do because they are constantly interrupted.

When a homeless patron wants to explain to you why he broke a rule, give him a minute to plead his case. Listening to him does not mean you have to agree with him. It is miraculous how often just the mere act of listening calms the other person down. Just last week I had an angry resident complain to me that he was kicked out of the shelter for two weeks. I let him vent and complain for about ten minutes. I didn't say a word. When he was done talking, he took a deep breath, thanked me for my time, and left. He never even asked me to reduce his time out of the shelter. He just wanted someone to listen!

In fact, the mere act of listening can convert an enemy into a friend. So few people take the time to listen to homeless people that a simple courtesy like listening can turn a homeless patron into your biggest fan. It is a lot easier to solve problems when someone is your fan!

Tool: The Mirror

The Oprah is a good tool, but there is a more advanced version of it called the Mirror (also called "active listening" or "reflective listening"). With this technique you are going to reflect back at the patron—in your own words—what you believe his concerns are. For example:

- "*I understand that* you are frustrated that you cannot get a library card."
- "*I believe you that* it must be very difficult to sleep in the shelter."
- "*What I think you are saying is* that you need more time on the computer."

When you reflect back to a person, it accomplishes three things:

1. Reflective listening releases oxytocin in the speaker, which builds trust.
2. The person feels truly listened to. If you have children, have you ever gotten frustrated by them not listening and asked, "What did I just say?" Of course you have; every parent has! By reflecting back what the person is saying, you preemptively prove to him that you are listening.
3. It clears up misunderstandings. A couple weeks ago I was talking to a woman who was upset about being kicked out of the shelter. I said, "So, if I understand you, you do not feel that you should have been kicked out for what you did." She immediately shot back, "No,

I deserved to be kicked out. I just don't like the way the staff person talked to me while he was kicking me out." It was really helpful to know that, because until this point I hadn't understood the real reason for her being upset.

Tool: The Monica Lewinsky

On August 17, 1998, President Bill Clinton delivered the most important speech of his life. Speaking from the White House map room, Bill had cleared it of everything except a bowl of flowers and a reading lamp. The four-minute speech hinged on—and is most remembered for—two sentences: "Indeed, I did have a relationship with Ms. Lewinsky that was not appropriate. In fact, it was wrong."

Why did Clinton do this, after having been so insistent before in saying, "I want you to listen to me. I did not have sexual relations with that woman." We don't have to speculate. He told us in the same speech: "It is time to stop the pursuit of personal destruction . . ." Clinton sought—by admitting a mistake and apologizing—to be able to clear the air and move on.

We can all debate the sincerity of Clinton's comments, but there isn't any credible argument against their effectiveness. A few months after his admission of guilt, Clinton's approval ratings reached 73 percent, the highest point of his presidency. For some context, the highest Ronald Reagan ever got was 71 percent and Barack Obama only reached 69 percent.

You and I can learn a thing or two from Bill. If you make a mistake, admit it and apologize. Many people are afraid to admit mistakes because they think people will respect them less. They are disastrously wrong.

Do you know who is especially appreciative when others admit their mistakes and apologize? You got it, homeless people! Very few people who commit a wrong against a homeless person admit it and apologize (because they don't have to . . . there is nothing a homeless person can do to them). So, if you screw up, say so and then say you are sorry. This is true for all mistakes, not just "library mistakes" like accidentally reshelving a book that someone asked you to hold. For example, if you lose your temper and kick someone out prematurely—or say something you regret—simply apologize the next time you see him or her. You will convert a potential enemy into an ardent fan (and it is quite possible that you will become a better person in the process too).

Tool: The Wizard of Oz

Do you know what the single most common word is in the movie *The Wizard of Oz*?[2] I'll give you a hint:

We're off to see the Wizard

The wonderful Wizard of Oz

We hear he is a whiz of a wiz

If ever a wiz there was

If ever, oh ever a wiz there was

The Wizard of Oz is one *because*

Because, because, because, because, because

Because of the wonderful things he does

You can sing Judy Garland tunes to your patrons if you want (see the Weirdo section later in this chapter), but that isn't my point here. My point is that you should use the word "because." Offering a (short) explanation for why you want someone to do something is magical in gaining compliance. If you are asking a patron to do something (or to stop doing something), offer a brief explanation why.

Harvard professor Ellen Langer demonstrated this in a classic study[3] where research assistants asked if they could cut in line at the photocopy machine (this was the 1970s when photocopier machines were slow and jammed a lot, so it was a big deal). When the research assistant had a lot to copy, saying "because I'm in a rush" doubled the number of people who agreed to let him cut in line. What is more interesting is that when the research assistant only had to make a few copies, even a dumb reason—"because I have to make copies"—was as effective as a valid reason. Human beings are hard-wired to be more compliant when someone gives us a rationale for their request. For small requests, our brains don't even care if it is a good reason, as long as they make the effort.

Things You Should *Never* Do

Tool: The Vogon

The Vogons, in *The Hitchhiker's Guide to the Galaxy*, are a race of green humanoid aliens that run the Universe's bureaucracy. They have so completely mastered the use of bureaucratic jargon that their poetry is described as "the third worst poetry in the Universe."

Don't be a Vogon.

Each profession has its own language with its own words that don't mean anything to anyone else. Librarians are no different. Resist the urge to throw around a bunch of library jargon. This is especially true with homeless patrons. While not generally unintelligent, homeless people are extra-sensitive to being talked to like they are stupid. If you throw around a lot of technical terms, you risk your homeless patrons feeling like you are talking down to them.

Want to know how it feels? Read this sentence from the U.S. Labor Department's Employment and Training Administration:

> States must use the schedule to determine Federal military wages for UCX "first claims" ONLY when the Federal Claims Control Center (FCCC) responds to a request for information indicating that there is no Copy 5 of the Certificate of Release or Discharge from Active Duty (DD Form 214) for an individual under the social security number provided.

Do you have any idea what this means? Nope. Me neither. Do you feel smart when you read this? Nope. Me neither.

I'm sure you can come up with a better list of no-no words than I can, but this should get you started:

1. Periodicals
2. Serial
3. Reference
4. Interlibrary loan
5. E-journal
6. Index
7. Circulation

Also, get rid of all acronyms. I know that you value accuracy, but the ALA's website has a list of *hundreds* of library acronyms. My favorite is the LSSDDPMAG of the ASCLA (the Library Service to Developmentally Disabled Persons Membership Activity Group of the Association of Specialized and Cooperative Library Agencies). Stop it!

Don't feel bad, though. You're not alone. Hesed House frequently has to submit an AHAR from our HMIS to HUD through our CoC if we want to receive the next NOFA.

Tool: The Parent Trap

According to Ruby Payne (culture of poverty guru), there are three primary "voices" that we use when we talk to other people:

1. *Child voice*—Your "child voice" is basically how you whine. It is not relevant for our purposes today.
2. *Adult voice*—Your "adult voice" is how you talk to someone of equal status to you. You use it to *inform* and to *negotiate*.
3. *Parent voice*—This is how you talk to children and people that you believe are "beneath" you either in intelligence or status. It is very judgmental.

Here are some examples of each:

Parent Voice	Adult Voice
"You can't do that!"	"Sir, we have a rule against sleeping in the library."
"Why would you do that?"	"Sir, please do not look at lingerie ads on the library computers."
"What is the matter with you?"	"Sir, please do not stand on a pile of books in order to reach the top shelf. We have a stepladder."

Many middle-class individuals automatically switch to their parent voice when talking to homeless people (as well as immigrants, the elderly, and people with disabilities). Not surprisingly, homeless individuals find it insulting to be talked to like a child or like they are stupid. Don't do it.

Tool: The Six Unforgivable Curses

I have a confession. Please do not stop reading this book after I make this confession. Okay, here goes: I have never read any of the Harry Potter books. I know. That makes me a horrible person. I have, though, seen all of the movies, if that redeems me any.

In the Harry Potter movies (and I assume the books), there were "Three Unforgivable Curses" that were banned in the Wizard world (extra points if you can name them). Just as there were certain things that Harry Potter could never say, there are certain things you should never, ever say. Ever. These phrases are fire tools of the worst kind. They immediately make a person's blood boil over in rage and turn him into an evil troll who wants to eat your liver. Okay, maybe it's not that bad, but these phrases do piss people off, which is bad for you.

So here are the "six unforgivable curses" you should never say under penalty of a really bad day:

1. *"Calm down!"*—When my brother and I were kids, I would frequently tell my brother to "calm down." He always became enraged, which was the main reason I said it. Now that we are adults, it still has the same effect.
2. *"...or else!"*—When someone can't think of a punishment quickly enough, they sometimes say, "Don't do that or else!" It is a very weak and ambiguous threat. It escalates tension with the other person while making you look feeble at the same time.
3. *"Come here!"*—Who do you say that to? A dog. Who doesn't like being talked to like a dog? A human. Don't ever talk to a

person—homeless or otherwise—like they are a dog. It will not make them more disposed to do what you want.

4. *"You can't do that!"*—As we will discuss in the Multiple Choice Test section of this chapter, don't tell a person what he has to do or he may go out of his way to prove you wrong.

5. *"Why would you do that?"*—Who do you say this to? A child. Who doesn't like being talked to like a child? An adult. Don't ever talk to an adult—homeless or otherwise—like they are a child. It will not endear you to them.

6. *"What is the matter with you?"*—There is only one time when it is appropriate to ask this question: when your toddler is finger-painting on the dog with the brown paint he found in his diaper. Never talk to an adult—homeless or otherwise—like they are a feces-wielding baby Picasso. Seriously, though, this question is really unhelpful even when someone is doing something truly bizarre. Don't say it.

Tools That Will Help You Prevent Future Problems

Remember the Cup of Pennies tool from chapter 5? You have a cup of pennies and every time you do something positive for a patron, you add a penny to the cup; every time you do something negative (punishment-driven enforcement and fire tool) or have to enforce a rule, you remove five pennies from the cup. The following tools are specific ways to add pennies to your cup.

Tool: The Name Game

In dealing with homeless patrons, there are two names that are really important:

1. *Theirs*—According to Dale Carnegie, author of *How to Win Friends and Influence People* (30 million copies and counting), "A person's name is—to that person—the sweetest, most important sound in any language." Taking the time to learn someone's name conveys great respect and instantly endears you to them. This is true for every human being, but doubly true for homeless human beings (because no one else bothers to learn their names).

2. *Yours*—Encourage patrons—homeless and otherwise—to call you by your *first* name. Asking others to call you by your first name humanizes you and makes you more likable. It also puts you on the same level as the other person, which homeless people really appreciate (because most people act superior to them). Many people think they will be respected more if they insist on formality ("Call

me Mr. Dowd"), but this is almost never true. At Hesed House, I have everyone call me "Ryan" and often walk around in a T-shirt and flip-flops. I don't have any problem with respect or authority.

A few other tips about names:

- For problematic patrons, call them by their last name ("Mr. Jones" or "Ms. Smith") even while asking them to call you by your first name. Sometimes a little extra dose of respect is all it takes to assuage a battered self-esteem (which makes them more pleasant). For less problematic patrons, use their first name after you get to know them.

- Names are especially important when a patron is angry. I know that when someone is shouting, the last thing you want to do is give them your name, but it actually helps calm things down.

- I know that libraries have a culture of anonymity and confidentiality (and many patrons are leery of Big Brother Government tracking them). Two tips for this: (1) offer your name first before asking their name ("Good morning, I'm Ryan, what's your name?"), and (2) if you happen to be one of those freakish people who can actually remember names, you can avoid upsetting paranoid patrons by downplaying it: "Your name is Bob, right?"

Tool: The Knight and the Lady

Do you know what the most common name of homeless people is? It is "Hey You." Okay, that's not actually their name, but I bet that homeless individuals get called "Hey You" twenty times as often as they are called anything else. Do you know who likes being called "Hey You"? No one.

Try this instead: if you don't know a homeless patron's name, go out of your way to call them "sir" or "ma'am." This conveys great respect, and homeless individuals are rarely treated with such respect. It will make their day better, which will make your day better. Homeless individuals are *much* more respectful to people who are respectful to them.

Tool: The Walmart

In 1980 the Walmart store in Crowley, Louisiana, was experiencing significant shoplifting. They tried adding a greeter at the door (the now ubiquitous "Walmart Greeter"). This immediately had its intended effect and shoplifting went down. It also had a pleasant unintended consequence: the paying customers liked it. Walmart had accidentally stumbled on an ingenious tool. By merely greeting everyone upon their arrival, the good customers got the message, "Walmart is friendly," while the bad customers got the message, "Walmart is watching you."

I recommend that you do "the Walmart." When patrons come into the library, greet them. Make eye contact and say "good morning" or "good afternoon." If you are skeptical, try an experiment. Greet every single homeless patron with a smile for a day and see if you don't have significantly fewer problems with them.

Tool: The Weather-Person

Take the time to actually engage in small talk with homeless patrons. Talk about the weather. Talk about sports. Talk about their life (or yours). Talk about anything. Just talk!

I know that you are busy. I know that you have 50,000 looming deadlines. I also know that if you take a little time to show the simple kindness of a little conversation, you will be paid back tenfold with fewer problems (which will save you a lot of time later). Taking a minute or two to talk to someone conveys respect and converts you from a nameless, faceless authority figure into "Sally, the Friendly Librarian."

It can be very tempting to rush people into "getting to the point," but that is very short-sighted. Homeless individuals are constantly rushed along, so when someone shows a genuine interest in them, they are usually exceedingly grateful. And gratitude translates into fewer problems later.

Tool: The Dalai Lama

The roots of all goodness lie in the soil of APPRECIATION for goodness.

—DALAI LAMA

Do you know who likes being appreciated? Homeless people. Do you know who else likes being appreciated? Everyone else! Appreciation is a very effective empathy-driven enforcement tool for two reasons:

1. It is a great way to put pennies in your cup. Remember from chapter 3 that compliments are one of the four building blocks of relationship.
2. It reinforces behavior you want and creates psychological inertia in the right direction. Do you want someone to keep being helpful? Compliment them on it. Do you want someone to keep following the rules? Compliment them on it.

Most people are terrible at appreciation because they use it too infrequently. Honest appreciation of other people is free, and yet most people are very stingy. *The secret to appreciation: Be appreciative of the little things, too, not just when people go above and beyond*. Don't save it for the truly spectacular. Take a minute to appreciate every little thing that is good. If you are glad that something happened, say so:

- When someone is pleasant to you
- When someone helps you in a small way
- When someone does something well
- When someone speaks softly in the library
- When someone cleans up after themselves (or someone else)
- When someone disagrees with you respectfully
- When someone leaves at closing time without being reminded
- When someone follows any of the rules voluntarily

Tool: The Robin Williams

According to the "culture of poverty" theory, poor individuals value humor more than their middle-class neighbors. The reason is that poor individuals have less access to expensive entertainment, and so jokes between friends are more important. Personally, I just assume that everyone likes a good joke (which works for me in a homeless shelter).

There are two sides to this:

1. Don't be afraid to use humor yourself. In my experience, even a failed attempt at humor is appreciated. Learn one decent joke and then share it with everyone. You work in a library; there has to be a book of jokes lying around somewhere!

2. Appreciate the humor of your homeless patrons (even when it isn't very funny). In the shelter there is a man who tells me the same lawyer joke every week or so ("Did you hear about the time it was so cold that a lawyer had his hands in his own pockets?"). It was moderately funny the first time he told it to me, but it lost its charm about the fifth time. I laugh at it every time, though, and he loves me for it.

My wife made me promise not to do this, but I am going to ignore her and offer you three jokes to get you started:

1. There are two muffins in the oven. One muffin turns to the other muffin and says, "Boy, it's hot in here." The second muffin says, "Oh my God! A talking muffin!"
2. Why did Tigger stick his head in the toilet? He was looking for Pooh!
3. A guy in a library walks up to a librarian and says, "I'll have a cheeseburger and fries, please." The librarian responds, "Sir, you are

in a library." The guy says "Oh, I'm sorry," and whispers, "I'll have a cheeseburger and fries, please."

Yeah, my wife was probably right . . .

Tool: The Foot in the Door

Remember from chapter 3 that people who like us are more likely to comply voluntarily? And remember that people who have helped us like us more? It is this virtuous cycle: if you can get someone to do you a small favor, they will like you more and they are more likely to do you a big favor. You just need to get your foot in the door.

In one study, people were seven times more likely to comply with an obnoxious request (putting a huge ugly sign in their front yard) if earlier they had agreed to a small request (putting a tiny sign in their window).[4] The Foot in the Door tool works because it makes you more likable, creates psychological inertia, changes the self-perception of the patron ("I'm the type of person that is helpful"), and puts pennies in your cup because it shows you trust the person. That is a lot of psychological goodness packed into one tool.

Remember, start with a small favor:

- "Ma'am, would you mind recycling that bottle when you are done?"
- "Sir, would you mind helping me with this heavy box?"
- "John, would you please put that newspaper back when you are finished?"
- "Sally, would you mind helping me with your friend Susan? She seems to need a little help with the stairs today."
- "Jill, could you turn off computer no. 5 when you are over there?"

Tools to Use in a Conflict with a Patron

Tool: The "Do Ask, Don't Tell"

In 1994 the United States began the policy of "Don't Ask, Don't Tell," allowing closeted gay and bisexual individuals to serve in the military, as long as they were not open about their sexuality. This tool has absolutely nothing to do with that.

The "Do Ask, Don't Tell" Policy tool is that you want to—whenever possible—*ask* a homeless patron to comply with a request rather than *telling* him what to do. The difference between a question mark and a period (or exclamation point) at the end of your sentence is huge.

Consider this:

"Sit down!"

vs.

"Sir, would you mind sitting down?"

Which one would you rather have directed your way? Telling someone what to do is a fire tool (punishment-driven enforcement) that escalates tension. Asking someone to do something is a water tool (empathy-driven enforcement) that de-escalates tension.

It is odd, but a lot of people are afraid to ask someone to do something out of a fear that they might say "no." The misguided thinking is that if you ask someone to do something and they say "no," then all of a sudden you can't do anything. But asking someone to do something doesn't preclude you from telling them what to do later. Remember what I said about your two types of tools: always try the water tool first. If it doesn't work, you can always switch to a fire tool. By contrast, if you tell someone to do something and they refuse to comply, you can't then switch to a question without looking like an idiot.

Tool: The Multiple Choice Test

No one likes being told that they "must" do something. Homeless individuals are no different. Telling someone what they "must" do is a fire tool and escalates tension. In addition, when you tell someone that they must do something, you are lying.

Consider this: if I tell a patron that he must leave the library right now, I am lying. He does not, in fact, have to leave right now. If he wants to prove me wrong, he can say, "Oh yeah? Watch me," and sit down on the ground.

A person *always* has a choice. The choices might not all be good ones, but there are always choices. For example, in my example above, the patron can choose between (a) leaving now voluntarily, or (b) leaving later in handcuffs. Obviously option (a) is much better than option (b), but he does have a choice. If I escalate the conflict between us by telling him what he "must" do, he may choose option (b), just to prove me wrong and be difficult.

Instead of telling someone what to do, instead—whenever possible—lay out a person's options for them. It looks something like this:

> "Sir, I have asked you to leave. Please leave now. If you choose not to leave now, I will—unfortunately—have to call the police. They will probably arrest you and you will go to jail. You don't want that and I don't want that."

We tend not to think about a person's options because some of the options are so bad that we would never consider them as real options (e.g., going to jail, getting banned from our beloved library, etc.). Homeless people, though, are not like you and I in many ways that we have already discussed (e.g., short time horizon, habituated to punishment, etc.). For them, it might be worth going to jail just to make your life difficult because they feel you were rude. Water tools (like this tool) do not illicit as much entrenched stubbornness and therefore are more effective at getting compliance.

Tool: The Baby Steps

Whenever possible, you want to break up a request into a series of mini-requests. Once someone has started to comply, psychological inertia will begin to take over and they are more likely to keep going. The trick is to make the request small enough that it isn't a big deal to comply with it.

So, for example, if you are asking someone to leave the library, you can break it up into mini-steps. Instead of just immediately demanding that the person leave, you can say:

1. "Sir, can you please collect your belongings so we can talk over here?"
2. (After conversation near the door): "Unfortunately, I am going to have to ask you to leave the library for today."

Similarly, if someone is breaking several rules at once (food, taking over multiple tables, and taking their shoes off), pick them off one by one. Pick the easiest one first and work your way up to the harder ones.

Tool: The Bad Cop

Have you ever seen a movie where someone is being interrogated by the police? Often, one of the cops plays the "bad cop," bullying and threatening the suspect. After a while, the "good cop" steps in to protect the suspect from the bad cop and try to help. In gratitude and relief, the suspect confesses all his crimes to the good cop.

You can use a similar tool when enforcing the rules. The good news is that you get to be the "good cop." The best news is that you don't even need a "bad cop." In fact, it is better if you don't have a bad cop! You are going to shift the blame to some nameless, faceless authority figure who makes the rules. You aren't the enemy. You are merely a humble employee who is following orders. In fact, you are on his side, but "The Man" makes the rules and you both have to follow The Man's rules. You are not the bad guy. You are merely a messenger of bad news.

Here are some (weird) examples:

- "I would love to let you smoke from your three-foot-tall bong, *but I have to enforce the rules.*"
- "I would let you in with a penguin that you stole from the zoo, *but the bosses say* no pets."

- "I don't mind if you draw pictures of naked men on all the tables, *but the Board of Directors is really picky about* that for some reason."
- "I would let you walk around naked if I could, *but I think the bosses would fire me.*"
- "Hey, I don't care if you urinate on the Harry Potter books, *but the politicians have a* no urinating *policy.* Therefore, I have to ask you to stop."

The Bad Cop tool works best if you are ambiguous about who the bad cop is. My favorite culprit is "the bosses" because no one really knows who the bosses are (but they know that they suck). It is effective because almost every homeless person has had a job where they had to follow the rules of an unreasonable boss. They can relate to your plight of having to enforce rules that you didn't make.

A few final thoughts on the Bad Cop tool:

- If you are squeamish about "passing the buck," remember the Michael Jordan tool (page 81): your only goal is to get compliance with the rules. Your goal is not to convince every patron of the virtue of your rules. Who cares what they think about the rules (or "the bosses," for that matter), as long as they follow them?

- This tool works even if you are "The Man" (i.e., the boss). I am the executive director at Hesed House and when people don't like my decision, I just blame the Board of Directors or the federal government. If the board had any idea how many times I blamed them for things, I would probably get fired!

- Never shift the blame to someone who is in the room. Don't say, "Hey, I would love to let you pour Coca-Cola on Stephenie Meyer's debut novel, but Mrs. Jones, the director sitting over there at her desk—yeah, her, the one with a purple dress—she will kick you out." You will have just shifted the conflict from you to your boss (which will not get you on the fast track to a promotion!).

Tool: The Sad Librarian

In my experience, there are two—and only two—types of people in this world:

1. People who enjoy mistreating the vulnerable.
2. People who feel sad when vulnerable people suffer.

Researchers at the University of British Columbia and the University of Texas at El Paso recently discovered that a low-grade form of sadism—what they termed "everyday sadism"—is actually quite common. It turns out that a not-insignificant portion of human beings get some pleasure from inflicting pain or harm on others.[5]

In my opinion, these "everyday sadists" are drawn to homeless people like moths to a flame (or perhaps—more accurately—they are the flame, looking for homeless moths to burn). Everyday sadists seek out homeless individuals because homeless individuals lack the power to stop them. Think about it this way: if you mistreat me, I am going to call the police (who will believe me) and I might even sue you (I'm a lawyer . . . that's what we do). If you mistreat a homeless person, though, there is nothing he can do. The police are unlikely to take his side and he can't afford a lawyer. Remember my story from chapter 2 about the government employee who was rude to me when she thought I was applying for food stamps, but syrupy sweet when she realized I wasn't poor?

Because of the prevalence of everyday sadists—and their fondness for mistreating the poor—homeless individuals are very sensitive to anyone they think enjoys mistreating them. In fact, homeless individuals look for creative ways to retaliate against everyday sadists. Retaliation usually doesn't amount to much more than just being ornery, but it is still enough to give you a bad day. As you are enforcing rules in the library, you do not want patrons to accidentally think you are an everyday sadist. How do you do that?

As I said above, there are two types of people in this world: people who enjoy causing harm (everyday sadists) and people who are *saddened* when others suffer. The easiest way to prove you are not the first type of person is to show that you are the second type of person. Show homeless individuals that you are actually saddened by having to enforce rules against them. I call this the Sad Librarian tool. It works especially well when you are asking someone to leave the library for the day. Here is what the Sad Librarian looks like with some exaggerated examples:

- "Hey Josh, since you stabbed that guy in the arm, I'm going to have to ask you to leave for today. I'm really sorry. I know it's cold out there."
- "Sally, *please* stop making voodoo dolls of our director. I may have to ask you to leave, which I really don't want to do because you're my favorite."

The keys to this tool are not only the words you use, but also your facial expression and tone of voice.

Tool: The Alternative Fact

I'm a lawyer. I would never tell you to lie. Lying is bad. Don't do it!

It can be—however—helpful to suspend the exact details of reality for a few minutes. Here's how you use the Alternative Fact tool. When someone is breaking a rule, pretend that they didn't know the rule existed (even if they obviously did). There are two phrases that work particularly well:

1. *"You probably didn't know we have a rule against* campfires in the bathroom, but we do."
2. *"You probably didn't see the sign* explicitly banning rocket-propelled grenades within the library, but it is right over there."

The reality is that the patron knows he broke a rule. And you know he broke a rule. And he knows that you know. But everyone pretends that he didn't know so he can save face and you can avoid a protracted battle. Allow him to simply apologize as if his infraction was one of ignorance, not willfulness, and everyone can go back about their daily business. Remember, your goal is to get people to follow the rules, not shame a confession out of someone. If a little lie (I mean, alternative fact) gets the job done, then so be it!

Tool: The Shot Across the Bow

Has a patron ever denied breaking a rule, even though you knew with 100 percent certainty that he did break it? Perhaps you watched him sneak food out of his bag and chew it. When you confront him, he denies it, even though there is food in his beard. Maybe you saw her tear a page out of a periodical. When you ask her not to tear pages out, she says she didn't—even though the magazine in front of her clearly jumps from page 42 to 45.

When this happens to you, it can be infuriating. Not only is the patron breaking the rules, but he or she is lying about it, too! What do you do? I recommend that you use the Shot Across the Bow tool.

This tool gets its name from naval warfare. If one ship wants to provide a "warning shot" to another ship, it literally shoots its gun so that the shell lands a few hundred yards ahead of the other ship. This tells the other ship two things: (1) you are in range and I can hit you from here, and (2) I don't want to have to sink you, but I will, so please leave now.

So, how do you do this in a library? If someone breaks a minor rule and they deny having done so, say something like, "Okay. I could have been mistaken. As long as you weren't doing it—and you don't do it in the future—we don't have a problem. Have a good day." There are three parts to this phrase: the acceptance of their lie, the warning about the future, and the pleasant ending. Even though you are accepting their lie as truth, the reality is that they know they broke a rule and they know that you know it, too.

You accomplish three things with this tool:

- You put the person on notice that they were caught (even if they won't admit it);
- You explicitly warn them not to do it again;
- You avoid a lengthy argument that could get out of hand.

Remember the Michael Jordan tool from page 81. Your only goal is to get compliance with the rules. Your goal is not to prove to someone that you are right. If you can get compliance with the rules by accepting a little white lie, then so be it. Anything else is just your own pride.

Tool: The Appointment to Argue

When people hear about the Appointment to Argue tool, they are usually skeptical. I can tell you, though, that it is remarkably effective when someone is emotional and argumentative. To employ this tool, you simply tell an argumentative patron that you are happy to have a full discussion about the matter, but you are unable to do it right now. You then offer to make an appointment to discuss it and provide an alternative time. That time can be in twenty minutes, two hours, tomorrow, or next week (though the farther out you pick, the less likely it is to work). You can literally break out your calendar right there.

The purpose of this tool is to stop an argument when a person is highly emotional/irrational and delay it until he has calmed down. One of three things will happen if you use this tool successfully:

1. Occasionally, the person will decline the appointment, but he will allow you to disengage from the argument. Just offering to talk later is enough to calm many people down (because it shows that you are willing to listen to them).

2. The most likely outcome is that the person will never show up for the appointment. That's okay. Either the person came to his senses, or he realized it just wasn't worth the argument. I would guess that for every ten times I use this tool, only one person actually shows up for the appointment.

3. Sometimes, the person shows up for the appointment after he has had a little time to calm down and think the situation through. It also allows you to physically move the confrontation to somewhere less public where there isn't an audience. It is amazing how as little as twenty minutes can convert a "fight" into a "discussion."

This tool is particularly effective when you are kicking a patron out of the library and he wants to argue about the validity of the rule that started the confrontation.

A person who feels like this is his last opportunity to plead his case is much more likely to cause a scene. If—on the other hand—he knows that he can make his case to you tomorrow at 2:00 p.m., he is much more likely to leave quietly.

Tool: The John McCain

The way you have bipartisan negotiations, you sit down across the table…and you say, "OKAY, here's what I want, here's what you want. We'll adhere to your principles, but we'll make concessions."

—John McCain

Many of our modern politicians have forgotten the art of negotiating. Not John McCain! You should be like him!

Conceding a minor point goes a long way in getting what you want. It is true in politics. It is true in marriage. It is true in libraries. It is true everywhere. In fact, it is so true that psychologists have given it a fancy name: "graduated reciprocation in tension reduction." This definition gives us two interesting insights:

- "Reciprocation" = conceding a minor point, and this uses the principle of reciprocity. Basically, when you give a little bit, the other person feels psychologically indebted to give up something too.
- "Tension reduction" = minor concessions that reduce tension between parties. These concessions also create psychological inertia in the right direction.

Here are some examples:

1. "Okay, John, I'll waive your fine for the late book this time, but please promise me you'll get books in by their due date from now on."
2. "The rule is that you can only have one bag in the library, but I'll let you bring in two if you keep them stashed under a table where no one can trip over them."
3. "The rule is that you only get 30 minutes on the computer, but I think I can look the other way for an additional 10 minutes this time."

Remember the Michael Jordan tool from page 81. If you can achieve basic compliance by conceding on the rules in an insignificant way, that is a win. One final piece of advice: if you make a concession, make sure you (subtly) point it out. If the other person doesn't know that you have conceded something, it doesn't create any psychological debt.

Tool: The Counteroffer

The Counteroffer is a version of the John McCain tool. Here is how it works: if someone asks for something that you cannot do, reject their request, but them offer them something else in that direction. It is a form of concession that works on the same principle of reciprocity. If someone asks for 30 extra minutes on the computer, offer them 15. If someone asks if you can research for them the origin of the word "hooker," offer to show them how to use Google and Wikipedia.

I recommend combining this tool with the Sad Librarian (page 129) (and possibly the Bad Cop, page 128) from earlier in this chapter: "I'm sorry. I wish I could let you do your laundry in our restroom, but I would get in trouble. How about you brush your teeth really quick and call it a day?"

Tool: The Favor

This tool is especially useful with patrons that you know a little bit. It still works with strangers, but not quite as well. Here is how you do it: you phrase requests— even requests to follow the rules—as a favor to you.

Here are some examples:

1. "Hey Joe, *will you do me a favor? Will you* throw away your gum before my bosses see you with it? I don't want to get in trouble."
2. "Hey, your buddy is really drunk. *Can you guys do me a favor* and see if you can get him to leave before he does something he is going to regret?"
3. "*Can you do me a favor?* When you leave, *will you please* remember to clean up your area? A few people have left big messes and management is really riding us about that."
4. "Hey Bill, *will you do me a favor?* I heard that you and Gary have been giving Janet—the new librarian—a hard time. *Can you* cut her some slack at least until we've finished training her? And if you see Gary, ask him too. *Thanks!*"

The operative phrase here is "Can you do me a favor?" Human beings are hardwired for reciprocity. We want to do favors for people who are nice to us. If you have been respectful and kind to your homeless patrons, you can leverage that relationship with the Favor tool.

Tool: The Negative

When someone is complaining, it can be helpful to point out something small that you (or the library) could do better. It makes you more credible. (Researchers have found that letters of recommendation are more effective if they say something negative about the person.)[6] If you always defend everything and don't admit that anything could be better, people don't believe you. But if you can point out one negative thing, people are more likely to believe the positive things you say.

Examples of good uses of the Negative are:

- Our renewal periods could be a little longer.
- Our computers could be a little newer.
- We wish we had a few more extra staff so the lines moved faster.
- Our "Teen Vampires in Love Triangles with Werewolves" section could be more robust.

The trick is to find something that is (a) related to their complaint, (b) something you actually could do better if you had infinite resources, but (c) is not so large as to create a new argument.

Tool: The Explainerator

Have you ever had a patron question why a rule exists? Have you ever had a patron try to debate you about a rule, trying to find a loophole that will get him out of having to follow it?

It might look something like this:

Library Staff: Sir, would you mind finishing your meat loaf and gravy outside, please?

Patron: Why can't people eat in the library?

Library Staff: Because food can damage the books.

Patron: But I'll be extra careful.

Library Staff: Even if you're extra careful, you might accidentally get a little gravy on a book.

Patron: I promise I will be really really careful.

Library Staff: I believe you, but even when I'm really careful, I sometimes still spill food.

Patron: Yeah, but I brought a napkin so I can wipe up anything really quickly.

Library Staff: But even if you wipe the gravy up, it can leave a residue that causes damage.

Patron: I'm a gravy ninja. I'll wipe it up before it can cause any damage."
    ...and on and on and on...

Many homeless individuals have learned how to be master debaters in order to survive. You want to avoid getting into a debate about the merits of a rule (and exceptions). It sends the message that the rules are "up for debate." It will leave you frustrated and create unnecessary conflict. Don't do it.

The other extreme is "dictating" where you take a "because I told you" approach. It looks something like this:

Library Staff: Sir, would you mind finishing your cotton candy and extra large Slurpee outside, please?

Patron: Why can't people eat in the library?

Library Staff: If you don't take your food outside right now, you're going to be banned.

Patron: But all I did was ask a question!

Library Staff: That's it! You're banned for twenty years!

If a person asks a question about a rule and you are unwilling to give any explanation, it sends one of two messages: (1) there is no rational basis for the rule, or (2) there is a reason, but you are unwilling to share it. You either look like an idiot or a jerk. Either way you lose. That is "dictating." Don't do it.

Somewhere between "debating" and "dictating" is "explaining." Here is how you do it:

- Offer a one- or two-sentence explanation for the rule, *but no more.* A few sentences says "this is the reason for the rule" whereas a five-minute monologue says, "I don't actually believe in the rule, so I'm going to keep talking until you go away."
- Do not get defensive about the rule. If it is valid, have some confidence in it. (Of course, if you don't have any confidence in the rule, it should probably be changed.)
- If the person continues to challenge the rule after you have given your one- or two-sentence explanation, then pivot to a different tool. I personally recommend the Blame the Rules tool.

"Explaining" looks like this:

Library Staff: Sir, would you mind finishing your chocolate fondue outside, please?

Patron: Why can't people eat in the library?

Library Staff: Because food can damage the books. EXPLANATION

Patron: But I'll be extra careful.

Library Staff: Hey, believe me, I would love to let you eat in here, but I'll get in trouble if my boss sees you eating in here.

I strongly recommend that you have a one-sentence explanation ready for the rules that get broken the most. That way, you will have an answer and won't get flustered under stress. I have included an appendix at the end of this book with some sample explanations for different rules (feel free to come up with your own answers, though).

Tool: The Tractor Beam

In *Star Wars* (the very first one), the Death Star used its Tractor Beam to pull in the Millennium Falcon and keep it from leaving. You can be like the Death Star. Here's how:

You want to establish a good reputation for a patron. He will be drawn to it like a Tractor Beam, forcing him to live up to it. It uses the empathy principle of "consistency." The idea is that people who think of themselves as honest try not to lie; people who think of themselves as strong try not to appear weak, and so on. Remember in chapter 3 we talked about how Anwar Sadat (president of Egypt) would tell the leaders of other countries before negotiations that they were known to be cooperative and fair.

You too can establish a reputation for the other person to strive for:

- "John, *you are so helpful. You always* clean up your space."
- "Sally, *I appreciate that you* are always honest with me."
- "Robert, *you seem like the kind of person who would* alert staff to a problem rather than take matters into your own hands."

The basic idea is that you want the patron to think of himself in these glowing terms. He won't want to fall short of the reputation you have given him.

This tool works much better for patrons that you already know. It can still be done with strangers, but it is harder to be sincere (since you generally don't know what type of person they are).

Note: The person doesn't have to be universally consistent in living up to the value for you to point the value out. For example, most people think of themselves as generally honest, peaceful people. Appeal to that self-image by reinforcing it.

Tool: The Weirdo

This is one of my favorite tools. It is also very hard to do well.

Here is how it works. When you are trying to stop two people from arguing,

Question: What do I do when a patron continually talks over me and won't let me talk?

Answer: Great question! First, let me tell you what not to do. Don't try to talk over him or shout louder. All that will do is encourage him to be even louder and more aggressive. Instead, you should:

- Stand quietly in as calm a posture as you can, with your body at a 15-degree angle.
- Let the patron talk for a while without any interruption. Simply letting the person talk will take a lot of the gasoline out of the fire.
- When there is a break ask, "Would you like me to respond now?" Wait for him to say "yes."
- Then talk. When he interrupts you now, say calmly, "Hold on, you said it was my turn to talk."

you do something completely unexpected and off the wall (and weird). Doing something utterly unexpected distracts them and pulls their attention away from each other onto you. The humor lowers the tension. Often, this creates enough of a "gap" in the argument for you to separate the parties. You can tell a joke, but self-deprecating humor is the best because it is really hard to ignore. If they are too loud to hear you, you might have to do something physically odd to get their attention.

Here are some examples:

Situation	Example of the Weirdo Tool
A husband and wife are shouting at each other, ignoring all staff efforts to intervene.	You sit down cross-legged on the floor between them.
Two older gentlemen are agitated with one another, getting louder by the minute.	You say, "So I went on this blind date last week. It was horrible. I had a stain on my pants in the most awkward place."
Two groups of teenagers are starting to get loud with each other.	You ask, "Did you hear the one about the polar bear that walked into a bar with a talking duck under each arm?"

Obviously, there is a lot of context you have to factor in. That is why the Weirdo tool is so hard to do correctly. For example, you don't want to sit down between people who are violent or if there is a large audience of other patrons who won't understand what you are doing.

The trick here is to use weird and unexpected behavior to create a gap for you to intervene. Quickly move onto another tool once you have their attention (the point isn't to have a stand-up comedy act).

Conclusion

Your words matter. They have the ability to calm even the most enraged patron. Your words can also create problems where none existed. So, get your head right. Position your body correctly. Learn what to say (and what not to say). After you have these three basics down, you are ready for more advanced tools.

Notes

1. Carole Nelson Douglas, *Cat in a Red Hot Rage* (New York: Forge Books, 2008).
2. Actually, I have absolutely no empirical data for this, but it sounds plausible!
3. Ellen Langer, Arthur Blank, and Benzion Chanowitz, "The Mindlessness of Ostensibly Thoughtful Action: The Role of 'Placebic' Information in Interpersonal Interaction," *Journal of Personality and Social Psychology* 36, no. 6 (1978): 635–42.
4. Robert B. Cialdini, *Influence: Science and Practice*, 5th edition (Boston: Allyn and Bacon, 2008), 60.
5. Erin E. Buckels, Daniel N. Jones, and Delroy L. Paulhus, "Behavioral Confirmation of Everyday Sadism," *Psychological Science* 24, no. 11 (2013): 2201–09.
6. Cialdini, *Influence: Science and Practice*, 193.

Advanced Tools

8

Rule number one: Don't f--k with librarians.

—NEIL GAIMAN

It was a beautiful summer day, not a cloud in the sky, with a nice breeze that smelled of freshly cut grass. Someone told me two guys were arguing outside, which was the only excuse I needed to head out into the sun.

I found the argument quickly. One of the gentlemen—Andrew—was in his early twenties and had only recently been released from prison. He had obviously spent all of his time in prison lifting weights because he looked like a professional wrestler. The other gentleman—whose name I don't remember—looked like Drew Carey (before he lost weight), except much older. Drew just simply wouldn't stop antagonizing the much younger—and much stronger—Andrew, despite my pleadings.

Drew and Andrew took a step towards each other and I stepped in between them, putting a hand on each of their chests and pushing them apart. It was something I had done 100 times before (and have done 300 times since). Unlike any time before, though (or since), Andrew knocked my hand away and pointed right at my face. He said something. I don't remember what he said because that was the moment I realized that he was not pointing at me with his finger. He had a knife in his hand, and the blade was no more than eight inches from my face.

I had left my cell phone in the building and the odds of a police officer accidentally arriving at that moment were slim. I was totally, utterly, and completely on my own.

Except I wasn't.

Within seconds, the residents of Hesed House had formed a ring around us. There was Tony and Jake and Sam and Herbert and Bruce. There was Eight Ball and Juice and Skeletor and Blackie and Red and Miami and more. No human being on the face of the planet has ever been so excited to be surrounded by a mob of angry homeless men. They spoke to Andrew sternly. They told him that he needed to put the knife away. Andrew looked nervously from face to face. He could easily take on any one of these guys. He couldn't take on fifteen, though. A few seconds more and there were twenty guys. When the crowd had grown to twenty-five men, Andrew folded the blade back into the handle and put it in his pocket.

Ten of the residents stood by Andrew to make sure he didn't try to leave before the police arrived. The rest made a circle around me. Skeletor put his hand on my shoulder reassuringly and said, "Don't worry, Ryan. We've got your back."

• • •

Tool: The Nuclear Option

Calling the police is the biggest fire tool at your disposal. It should be viewed as the nuclear option, something you don't do unless you have exhausted every other option. I have some advice for when to call and when not to call.

> *Disclaimer*: Libraries have different policies about when to call the police. I have absolutely no idea what your library's policy is. If my advice conflicts with your library's policy, please follow your policy. I can't fire you, but your library can. Okay, now with that out of the way, onto the advice.

I believe that there are two—and only two—situations where you should call the police:

1. When you have asked a patron to leave the library and he has refused and you have completely and totally exhausted *everything* you can think of to get him to leave.
2. When the situation is dangerous or out of control.

You don't want to call the police unnecessarily for seven reasons:

- If you call the police too quickly, you won't learn how to handle difficult situations. If you call the police every time you have a minor problem, you simply won't have the skills if the police are ever slow in arriving for a major problem.

- The police take your calls more seriously (and respond faster) when you call them less frequently. Remember the boy who cried wolf? When Hesed House has a lot of new staffers who call 911 frequently, the police take a lot longer to show up.

- Bringing in the police escalates the tension and makes future interaction with the patron more difficult (because calling the police is a fire tool).

- It causes extra disruption in your library. Every once in a while when you call the police, sixteen officers are going to show up. Do you know the most common reason why sixteen officers show up for a call? It isn't an active shooter situation. The most common reason is that nothing interesting is happening in your town and they're all bored, so they swarm to a routine call to give themselves something to do. The problem with sixteen officers showing up for a routine call is that it sends a message to all of your other patrons that Armageddon is happening in the library. They feel much less safe when they think that a library needs sixteen officers to maintain control. If you don't call unnecessarily, you have less risk of sixteen officers showing up.

- It takes longer. A skilled staff member can almost always get an ornery patron to leave faster than it takes to wait for the police to arrive and deal with it.

- When other patrons see you handle a difficult situation well without the police, they feel safer. They think, "Wow, these library staff are really good at handling problems!"

- Some patrons have had very bad experiences with the police and they get very uneasy. Maybe they are undocumented. Maybe they have an unpaid parking ticket. Maybe they were roughed up a long time ago. Maybe they suffer from paranoia.

There is a corollary to the rule about when to call the police: you should only threaten to call the police when you are prepared to *immediately* follow through with your threat. Never threaten to call the police over something minor. For example, a patron raises his voice and you say, "Sir, if you don't lower your voice I will call the police." If the patron now says "What?!" loudly, you are in a pickle. You either have to ignore your threat (and lose credibility) or follow through on it (and call the police for something minor). Either way, you lose. Constantly threatening to call the police also makes you look like a dictator.

When I threaten to call the police it usually looks something like this (after a few minutes of begging and pleading with no mention of the police):

Ryan: John, will you *please* leave? Dude, if you don't go now I'm going to be forced to call the police, which I don't want to do. You'll get arrested, which I don't want. So, *please* leave.

Resident: I don't care. Call the police.

Ryan: Okey dokey. Your choice. [I exit stage left and call the police.]

Tool: The Mr. Bobby

You may find yourself in a situation where you want a coworker to call the police, but you don't want an irate patron to know that the police are being called. What do you do? Well, the secret—believe it or not—lies in nineteenth-century London. You see, in 1829 Sir Robert "Bobby" Peel created Scotland Yard. Ever since then, some people in England have called police "Bobbies."

But what does this have to do with you? I'm glad you asked. If you are in a tense standoff with an angry patron and need the police, turn to your coworker and say, "Would you mind getting Mr. Bobby for me?" Now your coworker knows to call the police, but the patron thinks that a manager is coming over.

Obviously, you don't have to use "Mr. Bobby" as a code word for the police. In fact, if anyone who works in your library is actually named Bobby, you should definitely come up with something different. It doesn't really matter what name you use as long as everyone knows what it means. There is nothing more awkward than asking a coworker to call "Mrs. Pinkerton" and having your coworker ask, "Who is Mrs. Pinkerton?"

Tool: The Sidekick

Sometimes a conflict with a patron gets bad enough that you don't want to handle it alone. You need backup! There is no shame in that. All the best superheroes have sidekicks. Batman has Robin. Han Solo has Chewbacca. Frodo has Samwise. Sherlock has Dr. Watson. You get the point.

There is a wrong way to do backup and there is a right way to do it. Almost everyone does it wrong, because it is the most natural way.

First, the wrong way: you see a patron getting loud and rude with one of your coworkers. He slams a book on a table and is waving his arms around wildly. Your coworker is visibly shaken by the patron's anger. You rush over to help, standing at her side in solidarity. You don't want her to feel alone. Your coworker is trying to talk, but the angry patron just shouts over her, not listening to a word she says. You try to interrupt him, so that he will give her a chance to talk. Pretty soon all three of you are talking at the same time, each trying to be heard over the others.

Yeah, don't do that. There are four reasons why this doesn't work:

1. Three people talking is much more chaotic than two. Chaos is the enemy of calm.
2. The person feels ganged up on. When people feel outnumbered they feel justified in being more hostile to defend themselves, even if they are the original aggressor.

3. There is no clear and consistent strategy because different people handle things differently. Who decides what to do next? Your co-worker? You? Do you take a vote?

4. The more aggressive/emotional staff member (who uses more fire tools) usually seizes control of the situation from the calmer staff member (who uses water tools).

There is a *much* better way. The two people each have different roles. One person is the superhero (primary person) and the other is the sidekick (back-up person). They do different things:

- *Superhero (primary person)*—This person does *all* of the talking and makes *all* of the decisions.

- *Sidekick (back-up person)*—This person does not talk; instead, he or she should:

  - Stand to the side of the staff member and patron, about five to eight feet away. You want to stand where both of them can see you. You want to stand far enough away that you are obviously observing the conversation, but are not a natural part of the conversation.

  - Handle any other patrons who might try to join the confrontation. Sometimes a patron's friends (or even another patron) will try to join the fray. You control the audience so your coworker can focus all of his or her attention on the problem patron.

  - Call the police if—and only if—directed to do so by the primary person. There are a few ways to do this. You can simply ask the person to call. You can make a little phone out of your hand with your thumb and pinky and hold it up to your mouth (the way someone signals "call me" across a crowded bar). You can also use the Mr. Bobby tool from page 144.

  - Intervene if it gets truly out of hand. This should be the absolute last thing you do, though.

It is like "tag team" wrestling in professional wrestling. Only one person is allowed to be in the ring at a time. And like tag team wrestling, you can switch out. If the situation is getting out of hand and the Superhero needs to switch roles with the Sidekick, you literally switch places. You physically switch places. The Sidekick becomes the Superhero and assumes control of the situation. The Superhero stands back and to the side and assumes the Sidekick roles (handle the crowd, call the police, etc.). Just make sure if you are now the Sidekick that you stand far enough away that the angry patron doesn't try to bring you back into the argument.

It may be obvious, but during high-stakes confrontations, the more seasoned staff member should be the Superhero and the newer staff member should be the Sidekick. This allows the newer staffer to learn by observing a more experienced colleague. What is not so obvious, though, is that in low-stakes confrontations the newer staffer should *always* be the Superhero and the experienced staffer should be the Sidekick. *This is the single greatest training tool at your disposal.* This allows the green staffer to get practice in a safe place where she can be bailed out if necessary. Also, after the confrontation is over, the experienced staffer can debrief with the newbie, allowing her to get feedback on what went well and what didn't.

A few other comments about how to provide backup to a coworker:

- If you are going into a situation where you think you might need backup, simply ask a coworker. For example, if two patrons are arguing, grab a coworker on your way over to stop the argument.

- If you aren't sure whether a coworker needs backup, simply ask him or her. You don't need to say, "Hey, do you need me to be your sidekick?" A simple "Do you want me to stick around?" will suffice. Better safe than sorry.

- Okay, ladies, you don't have to read this bullet point. This one is just for the gentlemen. Okay, guys, I know that you have watched a lot of movies where the Knight rides in to save the Damsel in Distress from the bad guy. Guess what? You aren't a knight and your female coworkers are definitely not damsels in distress. If a female coworker is in a heated conversation with a patron, resist the urge to rush up to her side and defend her. You should be her Sidekick, not take the confrontation away from her. Acting like your female coworkers can't handle their jobs is not chivalry. It is chauvinism. Don't do it.

To see the Sidekick done right and done wrong, go to www.homelesslibrary.com/sidekick.

Tool: The Ejector Seat

Even if you have done everything correctly, you will—occasionally—be forced to kick a patron out of the library. There is a right way to do it. This is the final test of whether you have mastered the water tools. If you can do this well, you have earned your black belt because it requires you to use all of your water tools simultaneously.

The trick to kicking someone out properly is to leave them with as much dignity as possible. I know what you are thinking: *Why do I care about someone's dignity while I am kicking them out? How do I even eject someone in a dignified way?* I can tell you with total sincerity that it is possible to kick someone out with compassion, and that doing so is in *your* best interest.

A few years ago, we had a gentleman who worked at Hesed House who had an absolute gift. When Justin kicked someone out of the shelter for misbehaving, the person almost always hugged him before leaving. It didn't matter why the person was being kicked out. It didn't matter if it was noon or midnight. It didn't matter if it was raining outside or five degrees below zero. People almost always hugged Justin when he asked them to leave. Justin was an absolute Zen master Jedi with a black belt in water tools.

I'm not that good. I don't usually get hugs from people I'm ejecting. I do, though, get a fair amount of handshakes. That is always my goal. If you can get someone to shake your hand (or hug you) before leaving, you know you have mastered your water tools.

Here's how to kick someone out of your library in a way that preserves their dignity (and possibly earns you a hug/handshake):

a. *Take a minute to listen.* It can be tempting to try to move the person out as fast as possible. Resist the urge. It is actually faster to allow a person to explain his actions for two minutes than it is to try to rush him out the door. Remember the first condition for legitimate authority in chapter 3: willingness to listen. People who feel heard feel respected. People who feel ignored feel frustrated. Frustrated people do more damage than respected people.

b. *Make it clear that you don't think negatively of the person.* I know this sounds weird, but it is important that you try to convey that you don't think the patron is a bad person. Often a person is frustrated with himself for screwing up and is afraid that he has ruined his relationship with you ("Now my favorite librarian hates me!"). You can allay this fear by saying something like, "Hey, I still like you John— you are a Stephen King fan, like me. But you broke a rule, so you have to go for today. We're still good, though! I'll see you next week." You want to give the person something to lose by not leaving peacefully ("I can leave quietly now or I can cause a scene and risk my favorite librarian hating me"). This is quirky advice, but it is really effective.

c. *Offer a fresh start.* Just as people can be afraid that their mistake ruined a relationship with you, they can also be afraid that they will forever be branded a troublemaker ("Now every time I come into the library they're going to be hard on me and kick me out because of one stupid decision"). You can allay this fear by saying things like, "You're out for three days, John, but when you come back on Thursday you'll have a clean slate and we can start over. See you Thursday!" Again, your goal is to give the person something to lose by not leaving peacefully ("I can leave quietly now or I can cause a scene and risk being branded a troublemaker").

d. *Be sad.* You want to prove to the person that you are not enjoying kicking him out. The easiest way to do this is to demonstrate that you are sad about having to kick him out (see the Sad Librarian tool on page 29).

e. *Use the Baby Steps* (page 128). Ask the person to talk to you near the door. Then ask the person to go get his belongings. Then ask the person to come outside with you. Then tell him that he must leave. Only then do you tell him that he cannot return for a month.

Conclusion

When problems escalate, it can be difficult to know when to call the police or kick a patron out or how to back up a fellow staffer properly. The good news is that by utilizing the police and your own staff properly, you can dramatically reduce problems in your library. This is good for you, your library, and homeless patrons.

Part III

Special Situations

Everyday Predicaments

9

When the going gets tough, the tough get a librarian.

—JOAN BAUER

I will never forget the first fight I broke up.

It was my first winter working in the shelter. Actually, it was my first month. Everyone had just finished dinner (baked spaghetti with a side dish of tater tots, with orange Tang to wash it down).

Suddenly I heard a deep voice yell out "I'm not going to take it anymore." I searched the sea of faces (most of them stuffed with homemade brownies). Before I could identify the source of the voice, another voice—even deeper than the last—cried out from behind me, "You want to step outside?!" I spun around, but couldn't identify where this person was either. Not knowing what else to do, I just stood there, waiting.

Eventually one of the men—in his late thirties and probably weighing 280 pounds—slowly rose, revealing his position. He stretched his back like Rocky before a bout, while muttering something about the other man's mother. The other man—younger than the first but twice as wide around the middle—set his fudge brownie down and stood up, hitching his pants up as he did. Now on their feet, they each started toward the other, slowly narrowing the twenty-five feet that separated them.

My brain understood the danger and rose to the challenge. Deep in my brain, my medulla released a flood of adrenaline into my bloodstream, like a dam breaking upriver from an unsuspecting hamlet. My pupils enlarged (a physical response that allows your body to see more acutely). My breathing and heart rate increased (as my body took in extra oxygen for my anticipated fight or flight). The paper cut on my left hand stopped hurting (adrenaline blocks pain receptors). My muscles tensed, ready to unleash the fury of every karate movie I had ever seen. I spread my legs slightly, assuming a boxer's stance.

Just then, my boss—a woman in her mid-fifties—came out of an office. She assessed the situation in an instant and snapped, "You two stop it. Sit down and eat your damn brownies!" Each man sat down obediently, grumbling, "I would have kicked your butt," and "Man, are you lucky she came when she did."

My boss looked at me with amusement, saying, "You, too. Eat a brownie before you hurt yourself. They're good tonight, just the right amount of nuts."

• • •

Predicament: Two Homeless Patrons Are Arguing

It is the middle of winter. The talking heads on TV say that a "polar vortex" is stuck over the region, creating a week of bitterly cold weather. Consequently, everyone is on edge. You normally look forward to the end of your shift (closing time at the library) because it means you can go home and watch cable television. Tonight, though, you are dreading it. In fifteen minutes, you will have to tell everyone that they have to leave for the night. You know that some of the patrons have nowhere warm to go, even in this weather. You hope they don't try to stage a sit-in. To distract yourself, you start thinking of things you might watch on Netflix tonight.

Suddenly you hear yelling from the other room. "You don't talk to her!" Another voice responds angrily, "I'll talk to anyone I want."

You rush into the other room and see three middle-aged individuals (two men and one woman) arguing. A young mother in the corner whisks her wide-eyed son out of the room as you approach.

"I've had enough!" one of the men shouts, beginning to take off his coat.

What do you do?

Empathy-Driven Enforcement Method

The first thing you need to know is that there are two types of homeless fights:

1. *A Peacocking Fight*—Peacocking is not a real fight. There is a lot of noise and posturing, but no actual violence involved. The vast majority (over 90 percent) of homeless "fights" are actually just Peacocking, where no one involved actually wants to get into a fight. The two telltale signs is that they are *loud* and they are *slow*.
2. *A Real Fight*—A Real Fight is totally different than Peacocking. In a Real Fight, the two parties' only aim is to hurt one another. A Real Fight is the exact opposite of Peacocking: it is *quiet* and *fast*.

You address these two different types of fights *very* differently:

Peacocking

Stopping a Peacocking Fight between two homeless patrons is much easier than you might think. The reason is that these "fights" do not involve any actual physical violence. There are two intersecting "truths" that explain this:

1. *Truth #1*: Homeless individuals want other people to think they are willing to fight. This keeps the person from being viewed as weak and being preyed upon. Remember from chapter 2 that it is really dangerous to be homeless, so many people want to look scary.
2. *Truth #2*: Most people—homeless or not—don't actually want to get into a fight. No one likes getting a broken nose or a night in jail.

So, you have two people arguing, and neither of them wants to fight, but both want everyone else to think that they are willing to fight. So, what do they do? Peacocking! There is a very uniform and predictable pattern: two individuals begin yelling at each other from relatively far apart (twenty or more feet). They continue to shout *loudly* at each other while walking relatively *slowly* towards one another. The noise they create gets staff attention. Their slow speed gives the staff time to get there and intervene. Then the staff member breaks up the "fight." Each side grumbles that "if staff hadn't gotten here first I would have beaten you up." Everyone saves face without having to actually fight.

This is how most homeless "fights" play out . . . mere Peacocking. So, how do you handle a Peacocking Fight? You intervene. The two would-be combatants *want* you to "break it up." They are purposely being loud and slow so that you will intervene. Send them each to a different corner if it wasn't that bad, and send them both out of the library if it was. The catch with a Peacocking Fight is that you *have* to intervene. If you don't break it up, eventually the two individuals get close enough to actually fight. They don't want to fight, but if you won't stop it, they don't have a choice.

One final note about breaking up a fight: if you do kick both people out of the library, make sure you send them away five minutes apart. Just ask one of them to wait five minutes while the other person leaves (most are happy to accommodate you because they don't want to fight). If you kick them out at the same time through the same door, all you have done is move the fight from the library to the library parking lot. Not a win!

A Real Fight

A Real Fight is nothing like a Peacocking Fight. Real Fights are dangerous. And they are—fortunately—rare among homeless individuals. Here's how you know you have a Real Fight on your hands: the first indication that there is a fight is that people are actually punching each other or grappling on the ground. There is no loud posturing. There is no slow walking towards one another. They just start punching without any warning. They don't warn staff with loud posturing because *they don't want you to break it up.* They want to hurt each other.

What do you do with a Real Fight? Stay the hell out of it! Don't try to break it up. Instead, call the cops, get the other patrons out of the room, and let them duke it out. If you try to intervene, there is a real chance you could get hurt. I can tell you that this just isn't worth it (and your library's workers' comp company agrees with me).

Additional Effective Tools for This Predicament
- The Hot Stove (page 108)
- The Appointment to Argue (page 132)
- The Training Wheels (page 91)
- The Nuclear Option (page 142)
- The Sidekick (page 144)
- The Ejector Seat (page 146)

Predicament: A Patron Is Going Through the Trash

You are sitting at your desk on a quiet Thursday afternoon. A meek, middle-aged, middle-class woman approaches your desk and sheepishly says, "Excuse me, but there is a man going through the garbage in the lobby." You thank her and quietly make your way over to the lobby. Sure enough, there is a man in dirty clothing and a long beard pulling objects out of the trash can and inspecting them one by one.

What do you do?

Empathy-Driven Enforcement Method
- Assume that the person is probably struggling with some sort of mental illness. This is not a 100 percent certainty, but in my experience it is probably best to assume it.

- Begin the conversation *very* calmly. And I don't mean "merely mellow." I mean "you-just-got-a-four-hour-massage-on-a-beach-while-smoking-marijuana" calm. Most individuals will feel at least some embarrassment at being questioned about going through the trash, and your calm demeanor will keep the situation from escalating. See the Marijuana Plant tool (page 89).

- Don't judge. If you were mentally ill and really hungry, you might be doing the same thing. See the Anti-Judge Judy tool (page 87).

- I recommend that you begin the conversation by saying something like, "Good morning, sir. Can I help you with something? I have to ask you not to go through the trash can." If the person immediately stops, simply thank him and consider the matter closed.

- It is possible that—because of mental illness—the person will try to tell you that it is okay to go through the trash because no one wants anything in there, anyway. Do not get pulled into a debate about the ownership rights of garbage. You cannot win. Use the Explainerator (page 135) followed by the Bad Cop (page 128).

Additional Effective Tools for This Predicament
- The Pool Shot (page 98)
- The Anti-Procrastinator (page 174)
- The Six Unforgiveable Curses (page 121)
- The Goldilocks (page 103)

Predicament: A Patron Is Making Sexual Comments

Your library is right down the street from the local community college. You get a lot of students, especially when their library is closed for holidays. It is late afternoon, closer to dinner than lunch.

A meek young female college student approaches. "Excuse me," she says timidly. She is embarrassed, hesitant to speak. "Some guy just asked me if he could see my boobs." At the final syllable, her face becomes visibly red. She motions towards a middle-aged gentleman sitting at a table and then she heads for the exit.

You take a deep breath and head over towards the man.

What do you do?

Empathy-Driven Enforcement Method

Unwanted sexual comments towards other patrons is one of the more difficult situations you face. It is not only an awkward conversation, but it is fraught with possibilities for it to get downright nasty. Here is my advice:

- This one needs to be addressed immediately (see the Anti-Procrastinator on page 174). It doesn't go away on its own. It always gets worse because the perpetrator is emboldened by your silence.

- Expect an argument. Individuals who are sexually aggressive are usually verbally aggressive in every way. This doesn't mean you are in danger, but it does mean that the person is likely to argue with you. Be prepared.

- Because an argument is more likely than not, always bring backup with you (see the Sidekick on page 144).

- Don't debate the merits of his words (see the Explainerator on page 135). The person will likely deny making any comment or deny that it was inappropriate ("It was a compliment"). Don't let him suck you into a debate. Instead, calmly and firmly make it clear that his comment was inappropriate and cannot happen again. The truth is that he does know that his comment was inappropriate; he just doesn't care.

Additional Effective Tools for This Predicament

- The Hypnotist (page 116)
- The Stick and the Stone (page 82)
- The Floor of Disrespect (page 102)

Predicament: A Patron Is Panhandling

You are working the circulation desk. It is an hour before closing time and you are mentally preparing dinner in anticipation of your shift ending. It was a good day, but your feet hurt a little bit. You make a mental note that it is time to get new shoes.

Your mental meanderings are interrupted by a well-dressed—but frazzled—man approaching with a little boy in tow. The toddler's diaper obviously needs to be changed, but you don't say anything. The man says, "Hey, some guy over in the DVDs is asking everyone for money. You all need to get this kind of stuff under control. I don't pay taxes so I can be harassed." You apologize meekly and thank him for alerting you. As he walks away, you notice that his son's shirt is on inside out.

You make your way over to the DVDs and, sure enough, there is a middle-aged man with corduroy pants (three sizes too large) who is quietly talking to a woman with an uncomfortable expression. She says, "I'm sorry, but I don't have anything on me," and the man shuffles away quickly. He is obviously panhandling inside the library.

What do you do?

Empathy-Driven Enforcement Method

Panhandling is difficult because most people are discrete about it. If you see it, though, or get complaints about it, here are my suggestions:

- Be *extra* calm when engaging someone who is panhandling. (See the Marijuana Plant on page 89.) Most people who have resorted to panhandling have had a pretty rough life and are very street-smart. They also don't usually fear confrontation. Panhandling causes so much confrontation that they have gotten over any qualms they may have had about it.

- If you actually witness the person panhandling, walk up *immediately* (see the Anti-Procrastinator in on page 174).

- If you don't actually witness it—but instead receive a complaint—I recommend that act like you did see it to avoid an argument. Simply say, "I noticed you asking people for money . . ." This alternative fact will save you a "he said / she said" argument.

- If the person denies panhandling, use the Shot Across the Bow (page 131). Simply say, "I may have been mistaken. As long as you don't ask anyone for money in the future, we'll be fine." It puts the person on notice that he was caught without causing an unnecessary argument. Remember, your goal is to stop the panhandling, not prove that you are right.

Additional Effective Tools for This Predicament
- The Cup of Pennies (page 83)
- The Walmart (page 123)
- The Secret Handshake (page 105)
- The Alternative Fact (page 130)

Conclusion

Most libraries face nearly identical problems from a segment of their homeless patrons. Learning how to keep your cool and address the problems with empathy-driven enforcement will make for a safer and more inclusive library.

Mental Illness

10

Do I have to talk to insane people?
You're a librarian now. I'm afraid it's mandatory.

—JASPER FFORDE[1]

Hesed House had just spent $25,000 on a new video camera surveillance system. A person sitting at the front desk could monitor every square inch of our property without moving. At the unveiling, we were as excited as little kids on Christmas morning. We switched between different cameras, and the monitor rotated between different angles outside of our building.

When we got to camera #9, we paused. Something wasn't right. One of our residents, Steven (who looked a lot like Shaggy from Scooby Doo), would take three steps forward, pause, and then back up three steps like someone hit "rewind." Then he would take the same three steps forward, pause, and again "rewind." We watched quizzically for a few minutes before unplugging the system and waiting for it to reboot. We found camera #9 again only to see Steven. Three steps forward. Pause. Three steps backwards. Over and over and over. Crud! $25,000 down the drain for a video camera system that is locked in a never-ending loop!

I said some unpleasant things about the company that had sold us the system. I vowed to make them replace every camera, every wire, everything. "Wait!" said Chris, our unofficial IT guy. "Look closer. Look behind Steven." I leaned in closer to the monitor. Front and center was Steven—trapped in perpetual motion—but behind him were other residents moving about normally. They were walking around, talking, laughing. And still, Steven continued to take three steps forward, pause, and then take three steps backwards.

We ran outside and around to where camera #9 was mounted. All the residents—except Steven—looked up at us, surprised by a dozen staff descending on them simultaneously. Steven took three steps forward, paused, and then took three steps backwards. Even in person it looked like someone was hitting the "reverse" button on an old VCR. While we had a new problem—what to do about Steven—at least we didn't have to replace the video camera system!

As an aside, a few months later a staff member somehow tracked down Steven's parents in California. Apparently, he had walked out of the family house one afternoon while his mother was at the store. Somehow, he made it to Chicago in spite of his semi-catatonic spurts. His parents flew out to Chicago to bring their son home, grateful that he was alive.

• • •

Mental Illness Basics

National estimates are that about 20–25 percent of homeless individuals struggle with mental illness (compared to 6 percent of the general population).[2] There are several things worth noting about homelessness and mental illness:

- Many people with mental illness also struggle with substance abuse. Don't try to add the statistics from this chapter with the statistics from the next chapter about substance abuse to get the rate of people who are mentally ill or addicted.

- Mental illness and homelessness have a symbiotic relationship. Mental illness can—obviously—cause homelessness. Homelessness can also cause mental illness, though. The enormous trauma one experiences being homeless is very damaging to the mind. I am always shocked by how "normal" people become after we get them rehoused.

- While the national statistic is that about a quarter of homeless individuals struggle with mental illness, it is not spread out uniformly among everyone who is homeless. Chronically homeless individuals—one year or longer—are *much* more likely to suffer from mental illness. It is not 100 percent, but it is pretty close. Most people without a severe mental health issue can eventually find their way out of homelessness.

Personality Disorders

This isn't a book about mental health, so I won't go into all the possible diagnoses (schizophrenia, bipolar disorder, severe depression or anxiety, etc.). There is one group of disorders that warrants a little more explanation, though: personality disorders.

There are lots of different types of personality disorders (e.g., antisocial, paranoid, narcissistic, borderline, schizoid, schizotypal, etc.), but the basic things you need to know are:

- Individuals with personality disorders are unable to act in the way that society expects of them. They do things that are "bizarre" by normal standards.

- Individuals with personality disorders are unable to learn from their mistakes. They repeat the same damaging behavior over and over, and are genuinely shocked every time by the poor outcome.

- Other people think they are jerks. When someone has a personality disorder, it is not obvious that they have a mental illness. They don't talk to themselves or stare catatonically. Their disorder is hidden under a layer of rudeness.

- There is no cure for personality disorders. They can be "managed," but only with professional help (and even then, not very well).

- While individuals with personality disorders can be found everywhere, there are two places where the incidence is particularly high: prisons and homeless shelters. Studies have found that as many as 71 percent of homeless individuals have a personality disorder.[3] Similarly, in prisons, the number is often put at 60–70 percent (with many inmates suffering in particular from antisocial personality disorder).[4]

I have two pieces of practical advice for library staff:

- When a patron—especially a homeless patron—is being a jerk, pause and consider that the person might actually have an undiagnosed mental health issue. This doesn't make their behavior acceptable, but it might help you keep your cool and respond appropriately. This is especially true when a patron keeps making the same mistake over and over, and is unable to learn from the consequences.

- Be on your guard for "staff splitting." Many people with personality disorders are very good at getting staff members to fight one another. They treat one staffer as a savior who needs to protect them from someone who is persecuting them. It is very easy to get sucked into this drama. Don't do it!

Tool: The Mental Illness Disrupter

In my experience, the symptoms of mental illness (talking to one's self, pacing, etc.) are worse after a person has gone a long time without talking to anyone else. It is as if the person has retreated into his own mind and been cut off from the "real" world. Consequently, an interesting thing often happens when you talk to a person who is talking to himself or pacing: it "snaps" him out of his mental world and brings him back to reality. The patron often stops talking to himself and pacing because he becomes aware again of the outside world.

This isn't a silver bullet that works every time—nothing is—but it works often enough that it should be one of your tools for working with mentally ill patrons. How do you do it? Simply walk up to a patron and start talking to him or her. Ask how their day is going. Ask if you can help find a book. Ask about their favorite book. Ask if they saw a recent sporting event (or movie). The operative word here is "ask." You don't want to just talk *at* them. You want to get them to genuinely engage with you. It is really hard to have a conversation with someone and be immersed in an alternative fantasy simultaneously.

Predicament: A Patron Is Talking to Herself

"How do you expect me to know which rabbit has the microchip?"

> Unsure of what that sentence even means, you shuffle in the direction of the speaker, expecting to find teenagers debating the latest sci-fi novel.

"The president ate it. And when the balloon popped, North Korea invaded Salt Lake City."

> You come around the corner of a bookshelf to find a woman by herself, gazing intently at her feet. She is obviously agitated, though she doesn't seem to notice you standing there, a mere three feet away.

"No! No! You're wrong. J. Edgar Hoover did not build the dam himself."

> You clear your throat loudly and take a step towards the woman. You notice that her left foot has two socks and her right foot has none.

"Fine! Fine! I said fine, so leave it alone! If she wants to put Kool-Aid in her computer, why do you care?"

What do you do?

Empathy-Driven Enforcement Method

Hearing a person talk to herself can be very unnerving, especially if she is having a full conversation. I have a few pointers for you:

- Unless the content of her monologue is violent, you are probably not in any danger. Most people who hear voices aren't any more dangerous than you or I.

- Approach the person *very* calmly, even if you aren't. (See the Marijuana Plant on page 89.) You want to be very "matter of fact," as if you are approaching someone who is talking to a friend.

- Wait for a break in the "conversation." If you interrupted someone who was having an actual conversation, she would find it rude. Remember, she doesn't know that she isn't having a real conversation.

- Do not draw attention to the fact that the person is talking to herself. Someone suffering from delusions is not going to suddenly get well because an armchair psychologist pointed out her mental illness.

- I recommend that you use this exact phrase: "Is everything okay, ma'am? Can I help you with a book or anything else?" These two questions put together are purposely ambiguous. It allows the person to ask for psychiatric help if she wants that. It also allows her to answer with a more "library-appropriate" question.

- Engage her in a few minutes of small talk. As we just discussed with the Mental Illness Disrupter, sometimes a little chitchat can help a person return to the real world.

Additional Effective Tools for This Predicament
- The Limbo (page 115)
- The Knight and the Lady (page 123)
- The Name Game (page 122)

Predicament: A Patron Is Delusional

You: Sir, I would be happy to reshelve those books for you. The Joel Osteen books don't belong in the cooking section.

Patron: I don't want the Russians to find them.

You: What?

Patron: The communist spies that have infiltrated our country hide their secret messages in Joel Osteen books. We have to keep them from communicating. That is why I am hiding them all over the library.

What do you do?

Empathy-Driven Enforcement Method

When someone shares their delusions with you, it is hard to know whether to laugh, correct them, play along, or run away. It is important to realize that being delusional does not equal being dangerous. Just become someone thinks he is the King of England today does not mean that he is going to think he is Jack the Ripper tomorrow. I actually knew a woman who thought she was the Queen of England and she was a very lovely woman (she made great tea). In fact, I know four different people who think the government has implanted chips into their brains to monitor their thoughts. None of these four have ever been violent in the years that I have known them. Their delusions simply don't hurt anyone (except themselves).

So, how do you handle delusions? First, let me tell you what *not* to do. There are two equally unhelpful approaches:

1. Trying to convince the person that he is delusional. Someone suffering from paranoid schizophrenia or some other serious mental illness is not going to suddenly get better because you correct him.
2. Playing along with the delusion as if it is true. While this is the path of least resistance, validating a delusion can be damaging. Just imagine the poor psychologist later when the patient explains, "But I know this is true. Go ask the librarian! She agreed with me!"

Instead, I want you to sidestep their delusions. The trick is to listen and be noncommittal. I personally like phrases like: "Even if that is true..." "I suppose that may be the case, but either way..." and—my favorite: "I'm not sure about that, but either way..." In this way, you aren't affirming their delusion, but you aren't directly contradicting it. This can allow you to avoid a direct confrontation about the truthfulness of the person's delusion.

My recommendation is that if a person's delusion isn't disruptive to the library, just ignore it. There are plenty of people who hold weird beliefs (and many have been elected to public office). If, on the other hand, a person's delusion is disruptive to the library (e.g., yelling, talking aggressively to strangers, staring, damaging books, etc.), you should focus on the disruptive behavior and not the underlying delusion. Sidestep the delusion using the phrases I suggested in the last paragraph and bring their attention back to the problematic behavior. A particularly effective tool is the Bad Cop (page 128).

Let's revisit the conversation above to see how my suggestions play out:

You: Sir, I would be happy to reshelve those books for you. The Joel Osteen books don't belong in the cooking section.

Patron: I don't want the Russians to find them.

You: What?

Patron: The communist spies that have infiltrated our country hide their secret messages in Joel Osteen books. We have to keep them from communicating. That is why I am hiding them all over the library.

You: Unfortunately, our Board of Directors insists that *all* books be put in the right section. If books are in the wrong place, I get in trouble.

Patron: What about the communist spies?

You: I'm happy to keep an eye out for any unusual activity around the Joel Osteen books, but I don't want to lose my job because all the books are in the wrong place.

Patron: Okay, but you will keep an eye out for Russians?

You: Thank you, sir. I will keep an eye on the Joel Osteen books.

Additional Effective Tools for This Predicament
- The John McCain (page 133)
- The Favor (page 134)
- The Your Momma (page 87)
- The Jerry Seinfeld (page 100)

Predicament: A Patron Is Fine One Day and Not the Next

You are working the circulation desk one afternoon when Tony approaches you, looking agitated. Tony has only been coming to the library for about a month, but he has arrived early most days for the last four weeks. He appears to be in his mid-sixties, but you suspect Tony is much younger than he looks. With his long white beard and camouflage jacket, Tony fits every stereotype of homelessness, except one.

Tony loves William Faulkner, whom he affectionately calls "Billy F." Inspired by Tony—and unable to keep up with his Faulkner trivia—you have already re-read *The Sound and the Fury* and are now onto *A Fable*. You aren't sure if it is okay to have a "favorite homeless person," but—with a gun to your head—you would admit that Tony is your favorite. He is smart and charming and educated.

You: Good morning, Tony. Did you know that *A Fable* is a precursor to Heller's *Catch-22*?

Tony: I don't give a %#$%@ about *A Fable*. What I care about are parents who can't control their kids. If they are going to let them run wild, they shouldn't have them.

You: What?

Tony: Those boys being disrespectful over by the magazines. They're monsters. Don't they know this is a library?

You: They look like they're just sitting around reading, to me.

Tony: No! They keep giggling. And talking. They won't stop. I can't take it anymore. I'm going to go teach them some manners!

You: Whoa, Tony! Hold on! Come back and talk to me! Tony!

What do you do?

Empathy-Driven Enforcement Method

Individuals struggling with mental illness have good days and bad days. You know who else has good days and bad days? You, me, and every other human being. Anyone who has been married for more than a weekend has experienced this fact intimately. Individuals with mental illness can have a wider swing between "good" and "bad" than their healthier counterparts, though. The triggers for a bad day can be obvious—hunger, exhaustion, intoxication—or a complete mystery. There are some things you can do when working with patrons whose mental illness makes them unpredictable.

On their "good days":

- Build a relationship. Put pennies in the cup (see the Cup of Pennies on page 83). When someone is in a good mood and being rational, use that day to build up some goodwill. Think about it like making deposits into the relationship bank. You will need to cash them out later on a bad day. It is easy to ignore patrons on their good days because they aren't causing problems. This is a mistake. Seize the opportunity you are being given.

On their "bad days":

- Have the staff member with the best relationship talk to them. If Patron Bob likes Librarian Nancy, then Librarian Nancy should talk to him on his bad days. Don't make things harder than they already are; leverage whoever has a relationship with the patron.

- Be calm. Remember, you want to lead a patron into the behavior you expect, not follow him into chaos. Your calm and caring demeanor may be exactly what your patron needs to break out of the anxiety that set him off.

- Confront problems early before they escalate. It is tempting to ignore a few infractions because "he's such a good patron normally." You want to get to the problem patron early. Your calming presence can prevent the situation from escalating.

- Consider asking the person to "take a day off." This isn't exactly kicking the person out. Rather you are trying to talk him into leaving voluntarily. If a person has a history of escalating problems on his bad days, it can be an act of mercy to get him to leave. This prevents him from doing something that could get him kicked out for much longer than a day. Even actually kicking him out is sometimes in his best interest.

Additional Effective Tools for This Predicament

- The Cup of Pennies (page 83)
- The Nashville Minute (page 90)
- The 22-Pound Chocolate Smile (page 104)
- The Weather-Person (page 124)
- The Robin Williams (page 125)
- The Tractor Beam (page 137)

Predicament: A Patron Is Pacing

Henry normally paces back and forth in front of the circulation desk. For some reason unknown to you, today he is favoring the reference desk. You and a coworker, Susan, do rock-paper-scissors to see who is going to go talk to Henry. You lose. As you walk toward the reference desk, you mutter to yourself, "Always pick rock."

What do you do?

Empathy-Driven Enforcement Method

Pacing is often accompanied by other problematic behavior (delusions, talking to one's self, etc.). There is advice for those situations elsewhere in this book. The advice in this section assumes that the person is not doing anything other than pacing. Here is my advice:

- Offer to help the person find a book. This is effective because it can help him break free from his own world (see the Mental Illness Disrupter on page 162) and because it subtly sends the message that pacing is discouraged.
- If there is somewhere else in the library where walking around would not be disruptive, consider suggesting that the person can go there. (See the Counteroffer on page 134).
- If the individual's behavior is genuinely disruptive and there is nowhere else for him to walk, ask him to have a seat (politely, of course). Use all the water tools you have learned throughout this book to keep the situation from escalating.
- If the person makes an effort to stop, but starts again, I would be inclined to offer several warnings before escalating to something stronger (like asking him to leave). Unlike staring (covered in the next section of this chapter), pacing by itself almost never escalates into more problematic behavior.

Additional Effective Tools for This Predicament

- The Your Momma (page 87)
- The Billy Bias (page 88)
- The Oprah (page 116)
- The Parent Trap (page 120)
- The "Do Ask, Don't Tell" (page 126)
- The Baby Steps (page 128)

Predicament: A Patron Is Staring

"Excuse me," whispers a middle-aged woman in expensive yoga pants. "Some guy won't stop staring at me." She motions with her head over her shoulder. Sure enough, a male patron is staring at her in a way that makes the hair on the back of your neck stand on end.

What do you do?

Empathy-Driven Enforcement Method

A patron who is staring at another patron is actually pretty serious. By the way, I don't mean casually glancing at others or puzzling at someone who is making a scene. I am talking about an intent fixation that creeps people out.

This is serious because it has a higher likelihood of escalating. Here is a process for handling a mentally ill patron who is staring at another patron (but not talking to her):

Step 1: Make sure the patron is actually staring at the person and not just staring into space. Many times I have thought that a person was fixated on another person only to discover that he or she was just "zoned out." There are a few ways to tell the difference: (a) if the person moves, does the patron's gaze follow? and (b) if you walk in between them, does the person try to peer around you?

Step 2: Go over and talk to the person staring and talk to him about anything (a book, the weather, etc.). See the Mental Illness Disrupter on page 162. In my experience, if the person is absolutely fixated on someone else, this usually doesn't work at stopping the behavior. It is effective, though, for determining how serious the situation is. If the person is unable to hold a basic conversation because he is so intently staring at the other person, you have a real problem.

Step 3: Pleasantly (but firmly) confront the patron by asking why he is staring. I recommend saying, "I have noticed you staring" instead of "The person over there said you are staring" to take attention away from the other person.

Step 4: If the patron continues to stare after you have asked him to stop, I recommend that you ask him to leave. I suggest this for two reasons: (a) if one warning is insufficient, it is unlikely that two or more interventions will be any more effective, and (b) this is one of the few mentally ill behaviors that—in my experience—has a higher likelihood of escalating into a much bigger problem.

Additional Effective Tools for This Predicament

- The Anti-Procrastinator (page 174)
- The Sidekick (page 144)
- The After Action Review (page 215)
- *La Bibliotecaria* (page 85)
- The Fight and the Flight (page 97)

Conclusion

Working with individuals struggling with mental illness can be very difficult (especially if you are early in your career). Fortunately, Hollywood is wrong about most mentally ill individuals being dangerous. Stay extra calm and use your water tools and you'll do great!

Notes

1. Jasper Fforde, *The Woman Who Died a Lot* (London: Hodder & Stoughton, 2012).
2. National Coalition for the Homeless, "Mental Illness and Homelessness," www.national homeless.org/factsheets/Mental_Illness.pdf.
3. E. L. Bassuk, L. Rubin, and A. S. Lauriat, "Characteristics of Sheltered Homeless Families," *American Journal of Public Health* 76, no. 9 (1986): 1097–1101.
4. United Kingdom Ministry of Justice, National Offender Management Service, "Working with Personality Disordered Offenders: A Practitioners Guide," https://www.justice.gov.uk/downloads/offenders/mentally-disordered-offenders/working-with-personality-disordered-offenders.pdf.

Substance Abuse

11

Of course it's all right for librarians to smell of drink.

—BARBARA PYM

Melvin was one of the sweetest old men I have ever met. He looked like Albert Einstein. Except Melvin was shorter...and black. All the volunteers at the shelter loved him because he was so charming. Melvin's signature move was to look deep into a woman's eyes and ask her if she would marry him. For most people that would be creepy, but somehow Melvin made it sweet and endearing. When he proposed to my wife she was flattered, until she found out that he had also proposed to my mother (her mother-in-law!). Melvin never met a woman he didn't want to marry. That was just his thing.

Skip was a nasty old drunk. When Skip entered the shelter, he immediately started picking fights with every man within earshot. More often than not, Skip left the shelter in handcuffs or with a bloody lip (or both). His signature move was to lean in close, point his finger at your chest, and attack your character. Skip never met a man he didn't want to insult. That was just his thing.

In a modern-day Dr. Jekyll and Mr. Hyde tale, if Melvin had even one sip of alcohol he transformed into Skip. It was like watching Bruce Banner turn into the Hulk. Except that Skip always got his ass kicked.

The staff at Hesed House learned how to spot Skip from across the room. If Skip walked into the shelter, the staff had explicit instructions to escort him right back outside again. It wasn't just that Skip caused problems for the shelter (though he certainly did). It was that Skip caused problems for Melvin, and we all loved Melvin. We learned that if we let Skip stay in the shelter he would do something that would get Melvin kicked out. It was more humane to ask Skip to leave for the night than to let him stay and do something that would result in a longer punishment (or broken nose).

Melvin passed away a few years ago. There was no obituary, but if there had been, the list of fiancées he left behind would have been impressive.

Substance Abuse Basics

National estimates are that about 38 percent of homeless individuals struggle with alcohol abuse and 26 percent struggle with other drugs[1] (versus general population rates of 6.6 percent for alcohol and 9 percent for drugs).[2] Many people struggle with both, so you can't add them up to get a "total addiction rate." There is a lot of overlap.

There are three things worth noting here. The first is that substance abuse and homelessness have a symbiotic relationship. Substance abuse can—obviously—lead to homelessness. But homelessness can also lead to substance abuse as individuals try to temporarily escape their reality. Many people don't develop a substance use disorder until after they are already homeless.

The second point here is that while about one-third of homeless individuals struggle with addiction, it is not spread evenly among the three types of homeless individuals described in chapter 1. A much higher percentage of chronically homeless individuals struggle with drugs or alcohol.

The third thing to note about substance abuse is that there is a strong correlation between substance use and mental illness. Mental illness often leads to drugs and alcohol as individuals try (ineffectively) to "self-medicate" their way back to normalcy. This is called "dual diagnosis," "co-occurring disorders," or MISA (mental illness substance abuse).

Substance Abuse Hijacks the Brain

It is important to understand that substance abuse hijacks the brain. It literally changes the brain. It changes both the chemical makeup and the neurological pathways of the brain.

Basically, drugs and alcohol trick the brain into thinking that they are essential for survival (like food, water, and oxygen). If you were deprived of food, water, or oxygen, how frantic would you get? What would you be willing to do to get it? It's like that for an addict. An addict's brain is telling him that he will die without his next fix. Remember this when you judge someone who is struggling to get clean.

Detoxing

A person who habitually uses drugs or alcohol can't just stop "cold turkey" without serious side effects. When a person stops drinking or using drugs, he goes into the "detoxification" process, or "detox" for short.

Detox from alcohol is particularly difficult. When a chronic alcoholic does not have alcohol, he can experience insomnia, sweating, heart palpitations, rapid heart rate, irregular heartbeat, high blood pressure, fever, confusion, hyperventilation, vomiting, headache, hallucinations anxiety, and delirium tremens (a form of seizure typically called "the DTs").

Does all this sound nasty? It is.

In fact, detoxing from alcohol can kill you. So, when a chronic alcoholic is acting like he could die if he doesn't get a drink, that might actually be true!

Heroin withdrawal—on the other hand—is unlikely to kill you. That said, anyone detoxing from heroin wishes they were dead. A few years ago I watched a man go through heroin withdrawal. He writhed around on a concrete floor, scratching at his body in a futile attempt to get the imaginary bugs off. It took the paramedics a while to get there, so I had a front-row seat to his nightmare. I don't recall ever seeing anyone in my life who looked so miserable.

There is a great quote in the movie *28 Days* with Sandra Bullock. Steve Buscemi's character—an addictions counselor—says:

> I would tell myself, "Tonight, I will not get wasted." And then something would happen. Or nothing would happen. And, uh, I'd get that feeling. I think you all know what that feeling is. When your skin is screaming and your hands are shaking. Uh, and your stomach feels like it wants to jump through your throat. And you know, that *if anyone had a clue how wrong it felt to be sober, they wouldn't dream of asking you to stay that way.* They would say, "Oh, geeze, I didn't know. Here. It's okay for you. Do that mound of cocaine. Have a drink. Have 20 drinks." Whatever you need to do to feel like a normal human being, you do it. And boy, I did it. I drank and I snorted, and I drank and I snorted, and drank and I snorted, and I did this day after day after day after night after night. And I didn't care about the consequences, because I knew they couldn't be half as bad as not using.

When I see someone desperate for their next fix or their next drink, I try to remember that they feel worse right now than I have ever felt in my entire life. I try to imagine it as similar to the flu combined with a hangover and chemotherapy. It doesn't make drugs and alcohol okay, but it does help me stop judging and try to understand.

Tolerance and Reverse Tolerance

You probably already know that as someone drinks more heavily, they develop a tolerance to alcohol. It takes more and more alcohol to get drunk.

But you probably didn't know that after a while it reverses itself. Towards the end stages of alcoholism, many people develop what is called "reverse tolerance." At this point, their liver is so damaged that it cannot metabolize the alcohol as quickly as it once did. Consequently, the individual gets drunk quicker off less alcohol and stays drunk longer. When you see a chronic alcoholic who is stumbling around drunk, it is natural to think that he or she has drunk a gallon of alcohol. That may not be true.

Wet Brain

Actually, he or she may not even be drunk. He or she might have "wet brain," which is often confused with alcoholism itself.

Wet brain (which is technically called Wernicke-Korsakoff syndrome) is an odd form of malnutrition. Chronic alcoholism leaches vitamin B1 out of the body. This vitamin B1 deficiency has very specific effects on the body and brain:

1. Confusion
2. Loss of muscle coordination
3. Speech problems
4. Loss of memory
5. Inability to make sense while talking
6. Difficulty forming new memories

If you met someone who was exhibiting these characteristics, what would you think of them? You would think they were drunk!

What is interesting about wet brain is that it doesn't reverse itself if a person stops drinking. It is quite sad, actually, to talk to someone who is exhibiting many of the telltale signs of being drunk, but you know they have been sober for a year. In fact, with someone who is still drinking, it is difficult to know whether they are stumbling around because of the alcohol that is in their body or the vitamin B1 that isn't.

Tool: The Anti-Procrastinator

In my experience, if you ignore a small problem, it will become a big problem more often than not. Do not ignore a small problem in the hope that it will go away. It is easier to solve a small problem now than a big problem later.

This is especially true in two situations:

1. When two individuals are arguing. Mild disagreements quickly escalate into big arguments and eventually fights. Cut off all conflict between homeless patrons quickly.
2. Intoxicated individuals. It is tempting to think "Well, he's not harming anyone," but individuals who are obviously intoxicated rarely get better soon. Because of liver damage, chronic alcoholics stay drunk much longer than individuals with healthy livers. If a person

appears to be getting more intoxicated with time, he or she is likely drinking in the library. Don't wait. Deal with it as soon as you become aware of the problem.

Tool: The Jane's Addiction

This tool is a mental trick to help you not judge a person who is struggling with addiction. Here's how it works: when you are talking to someone with an addiction, imagine that you are talking to their addiction. You aren't talking to Jane. You are talking to Jane's addiction.

Jane is a wonderful human being who played with dolls as a child and dreamed of being a ballerina when she grew up. But Jane's addiction has taken over Jane's life and crushed all of her aspirations. Jane idolized her father and was in love once with a man who didn't understand her. Jane's addiction doesn't care about anyone else. Jane is a good person. Jane's addiction is a liar and a thief. Jane is made in the image of God. Jane's addiction is a demon that has taken over her body for its own purposes.

I find that thinking about a person trapped in a body that has been taken over by a personified addiction helps me to empathize. I can have compassion for someone—even someone who has made bad choices—when I recognize that chemicals now control every aspect of that person's life and personality. I once talked to a woman a few months after she got clean from heroin. She sobbed as she recounted how she had sold her body to fuel the addiction. "That wasn't me. I didn't do those things," she said. "I mean, yes, obviously it was me. But it wasn't *really* me. I don't know if that makes any sense."

This tool is also effective outside of the workplace if you have a friend or relative who struggles with addiction. Know that your friend loves you and is a good person. Your friend's addiction—on the other hand—is a parasite that will take and take until it kills its host. Try to separate your feelings for your friend from your feelings about your friend's addiction. This will lower your resentment. Your job is to love your friend and help him or her to exorcise the demon that has taken over. Good luck!

Predicament: A Patron Is Drunk

You smell him before you see him. At first, you think it is rubbing alcohol, but with a second whiff, you get flashbacks to college and cheap vodka. You find Henry in a corner chair, muttering to himself. He is too drunk today to even bother hiding the bottle, which rests comfortably between his legs.

As you approach, Henry flashes a big grin on his face and says with great fanfare, "Wanna hear a joke about a penguin?"

What do you do?

Empathy-Driven Enforcement Method

Dealing with an intoxicated person is one of those scenarios where your skills matter a lot. Handle it well and no one will even know there was a problem. Handle it poorly and you will make the situation much worse.

There is—unfortunately—no silver bullet for dealing with a drunken individual. Instead, stick to your basic water tools:

- Deal with it quickly (see the Anti-Procrastinator earlier on page 174). It is very tempting to ignore someone who is only "slightly" intoxicated because of the potential for a major confrontation. In my experience, this often (usually) leads to a worse situation, albeit a slightly delayed one.

- Stay calm (see the Marijuana Plant on page 89). Intoxicated people can be real jerks. Don't lose your temper. It almost always makes the situation worse. Hide your frustration and speak to the person very calmly, with an almost disinterested (but firm) voice. Intoxicated individuals are extra-emotional, and your own emotion only feeds theirs.

- Don't get sucked into a debate (see the Explainerator on page 135). For some reason, drunk people love to argue. If you allow yourself to be drawn into a debate, the situation will only escalate. Tell them that you are more than happy to make an appointment another day to discuss their concerns (see the Appointment to Argue on page 132).

Additional Effective Tools for This Predicament

- The Jane's Addiction (page 175)
- The Anti-Judge Judy (page 87)
- The Michael Jordan (page 81)
- The Nuclear Option (page 142)
- The Less Public Library (page 101)
- The Wizard of Oz (page 118)
- The Multiple Choice Test (page 127)

Predicament: A Patron Has a Seizure

Your quiet library is suddenly chaotic. People are running around and yelling. Children are crying. You don't know whether to head towards the epicenter of the chaos or move away from it. Your better judgment loses the internal battle and you run towards the source of the noise.

In the quiet study section a man is on the ground convulsing violently. His arms, legs, and head jerk around erratically, and though his eyes are open, only the whites are visible. The other patrons—panic-stricken faces—look at you. You freeze, until a little girl in a red polka-dot dress tugs on your sleeve, pleading "Help him, please!"

What do you do?

Empathy-Driven Enforcement Method

The first few times you see a seizure it is scary. If you work with homeless individuals, though, they are inevitable. Here's what you do:

1. Stay calm. Most seizures last only 60–90 seconds, though it will feel like much longer.
2. Look around for dangers. If the person is not in a dangerous place, do not move them. Move furniture away from them.
3. Ask someone else to call 911. Say, "Call 911 and tell them we need an ambulance because a man is having a seizure." During a crisis situation, people need to be given *very* specific directions.
4. Do not leave the person unattended. That is why you need to ask someone else to call 911.
5. Do *not* hold a person down. Thrashing around is unlikely to hurt the person. You, on the other hand, can dislocate their shoulder or break a rib.
6. If the person is on the ground, cushion their head with something soft.
7. Do *not* put your finger or anything else in their mouth while they are seizing. That is a really good way to lose a finger.
8. Kneel next to the person until the seizure ends (and until the paramedics arrive).
9. After the seizure stops, place the person in the recovery position (on their side; see figure 11.1) while they wait for the paramedics to arrive. Also, check if anything is blocking their breathing like food or false teeth.

• • •

Figure 11.1: After the seizure stops, place the person in the recovery position: on her side with one knee extended forward

Epilepsy Society (www.epilepsysociety.org.uk)

1. Do not give food or drink to the person even if they ask for it.
2. Make note of the following so you can report it to the paramedics: how long the seizure lasted, how the person was acting before the seizure, and how the person acted immediately after the seizure.

Additional Effective Tools for This Predicament

- The Marijuana Plant (page 89)
- The After Action Review (page 215)
- The Scrimmage Game (page 217)
- The Anti-Metaphor (page 218)

Conclusion

Intoxicated individuals can be particularly frustrating. If you can leave your judgment at the door (it isn't helpful) and instead focus on the goal (compliance with the rules), you can solve a lot of problems by sticking to empathy-driven enforcement.

Notes

1. National Coalition for the Homeless, "Substance Abuse and Homelessness," www.national homeless.org/factsheets/addiction.html.
2. National Institute on Drug Abuse, "Nationwide Trends," https://www.drugabuse.gov/publications/drugfacts/nationwide-trends.

Hygiene

12

Librarians wield unfathomable power.

—ERICA OLSEN

July 6, 2011

Dear Diary,

Krissie and the kids are out of town so I slept at the shelter last night. The residents kept asking me if my wife had kicked me out. They couldn't understand why I would choose to sleep here. They didn't believe me when I said that I wanted to understand what they go through.

Last night was pretty uneventful. Woke up pretty early, though. My bladder served as an alarm clock (albeit one that goes off at 3:38 a.m.). It worked out well, though, because I smelled funky. Hesed House doesn't have enough showers for everyone, so only the early bird doesn't smell like a worm.

There are four individual shower stalls for the men—each with a relatively new curtain, I was happy to see. Residents had warned me that some have good water pressure and some don't. Three showers were already occupied, so I took the empty one. Obviously, the other men knew which one was the bad shower. The water literally just ran down the wall and I had to use my hand to splash it on myself. It was relatively warm, at least. In half an hour the hot water tank would be exhausted and everyone else would be taking cold showers (if they could even get one at all).

I immediately became conscious of the fact that—even before 4:00 a.m.— this shower had already been used by a dozen men this morning. I'm not normally skittish about such things, but I tried not to look at the different varieties of hair clogging up the drain between my bare feet. *Note to self:* Next time bring a pair of cheap flip-flops.

One of my three shower buddies was playing music on his cell phone. It was a manly song with a good beat and completely unintelligible words. A few people sang along, and I tapped my foot with the music.

When the first song was over, the next song on his playlist was the theme music from *The Lion King* ("Can You Feel the Love Tonight" by Elton John). The men stopped singing and the room was eerily quiet except for the trickle of water from four showers. Tension hung in the air of the tiny room as thick as the steam. I waited anxiously through the first verse to see if the other men would protest the Disney intrusion.

Quite unexpectedly, a single voice came in during the chorus, *"And can you feel the love tonight . . ."* I have heard that everyone's voice sounds prettier in the shower. This man was the exception. Then another gentleman—this one with an accent—joined in, *"It's enough for this wide-eyed wanderer that we got this far . . ."* At first sheepishly and then more confidently, the rest of us picked up the remainder of the chorus, *"It's enough to make Kings and Vagabonds believe the very best . . ."* I can't explain it, but at that moment it didn't feel weird to be singing a Disney anthem with three other naked men.

I finished my shower before Elton John and the Homeless Shelter Shower Band were done singing. I was only slightly cleaner than before, but it would have to do. I quickly got dressed and headed up to the dining room for breakfast. I was in my office and working by 5:00 a.m. Oh, it's going to be a long day . . .
All my love,

Ryan

• • •

Hygiene Basics

If you want to fully understand the homeless experience (and why homeless hygiene is sometimes less than stellar), there are four facts you need to know:

1. Homeless shelter showers are bad;
2. Laundry facilities are bad, too;
3. So are bathrooms;
4. And homelessness doesn't smell very good.

Homeless Shelter Showers Are Bad

I can tell you—from personal experience—that homeless shower options suck. Forgive my language, but there is no more accurate way to describe it.

If you ever become homeless, let me describe your "choices" (starting out with the best and working our way to the worst):

- If you stay in a large shelter, it will have showers. There will be a very long line to get in. Since you have to be out the door by 7:00 a.m., you will not get a shower unless you wake up early. All the hot water will be gone unless you get up really early. The shower will be filthy from overuse and will—paradoxically—smell of bleach in an unsuccessful bid to keep it clean. And this is the pinnacle of homeless hygiene. It only goes downhill from here ...

- If you stay in a small shelter—or one that rotates between churches—it may not even have showers. You will wait in a long line to clean up in a single church sink. You will brush your teeth and splash water on your armpits. It could be worse, though ...

- If you are unlucky enough to be sleeping outside, you will not have any shower anywhere in the world that you can use. You will clean up as best as you can in a public restroom, hoping that the McDonald's manager or librarian doesn't walk in. If they chase you away before you're done, you will have to find a public fountain to bathe in (unless it is winter).

These are the options available for someone who wants to take a shower. Many homeless individuals are reluctant to take a shower because of mental illness. Some people have delusions that make removing their clothes psychologically painful. They will go out of their way to avoid showering. We had one gentleman at Hesed House who would only wear clothing that was made in the United States and was a specific shade of blue. He wouldn't take his clothes off and shower until we could prove we had a whole new outfit that was his domestic blue. Even with Amazon, that is a really hard thing to pull off.

Now let us add another layer of shower complications: prior sexual abuse. In my experience, a greater portion of the homeless population was sexually abused as a child than the general population. To be clear, homeless shelter showers are not dangerous places (they are too crowded for anything to happen). For someone who was victimized before, though, even the thought of getting vulnerably naked can be terrifying. Oh, and at the risk of being too graphic, any individual who has spent time in prison may be understandably shaken by the thought of a group shower room.

At Hesed House, we often have to bend the rules for some people. We shut the bathroom down temporarily and allow a person to use the shower room alone, with the bathroom door locked. It is the only way to get them to shower. With hundreds of residents every day, though, this isn't something we have the capacity to do for many people or very frequently. Honestly, we only do this when one of two things happens: (1) other residents are threatening a person because they can't take the stench anymore, or (2) our local library calls us and begs for our help with a patron whose odor is driving away other patrons.

Homeless Laundry Facilities Are Bad

Let's talk about laundry options. As you can probably guess by now, they're no better than shower options.

First, let's get one thing out of the way: yes, laundromats exist, but they are also really expensive (relatively speaking).

Just like people who sleep on the streets don't have access to showers, they also don't have access to laundry facilities. You can do your best to wash your clothing in a public sink. This assumes, though, that you have a second set of clothing to change into while you are washing the first set. It also assumes that you can wash and dry your clothing before being kicked out of the bathroom.

At Hesed House we have sixteen washing machines and sixteen dryers. They run all day and much of the night. In fact, they are used so much that the commercial-grade washers we purchase are rated for five years of use, but burn out in one. Even with all those washers running continuously, it isn't nearly enough.

Individuals have to sign up to use the washing machines. They are allowed one load per day because all the slots fill up almost immediately when the shelter opens. Every single night, people walk right past the food and bed sign-up in order to try to get a precious washing machine slot.

Relatively speaking, the residents at Hesed House are really lucky. Many shelters—especially those run out of a different church every night—don't have any washing machines. Worse still, the biggest inner-city shelters make everyone disrobe every night and put on a hospital gown. Then all of their clothing goes into a room that heats up to 130 degrees. The room effectively kills any lice or bedbugs, but I can only imagine how clothing smells when it comes out in the morning.

Homeless Bathrooms Are Bad

My wife will not use a public restroom unless she has absolutely no other choice. She won't use a gas station bathroom under any circumstances. She would have a very hard time being homeless.

Obviously, there is a theme here. Homeless individuals lack access to adequate bathrooms. In fact, using a bathroom is a very unpleasant experience if you are homeless. Homeless shelter bathrooms are crowded. They get used constantly and consequently are really difficult to keep clean.

Have you ever used the bathroom at the end of a baseball game or concert? Did you have to wait in line? Were you sitting in a stall and could see the feet of the people in the stall to your left and right? Could you differentiate between the potpourri of different sounds coming from various directions? Was the scent a little sickening? Did you feel rushed because of the line of impatient people banging on the stall door? If you can relate to this, then you have a little bit of an idea of what it is like to use a homeless shelter bathroom. Except, imagine that this was your experience *every single time* you had to go.

And that crowded, smelly, loud, dirty bathroom is as good as it gets (almost… but I'll explain that in a minute). It actually gets worse when you leave the shelter. Most communities do not have public restrooms or port-a-potties. Consequently, when you are out in the community, you will have to "hold it" a lot. If you get desperate and try to sneak in unnoticed to a fast-food restaurant, you will likely be chased out. You might try to find a patch of woods or a hidden alcove to relieve yourself. Go quickly, though, because if the police find you and there are children anywhere near, you might end up on the sex offender registry. Probably better to just hold it. Again.

But now I want you to imagine that you arrive at your public library. You walk into the well-lit bathroom. It is blissfully empty, with a silence that calms your soul. You take a deep breath, inhaling the smell of "Cool Vanilla Sugar" air freshener (unless it is winter, then it is "Evergreen Pine Cone and Cinnamon"). The sink sparkles. The stalls even have those flimsy translucent paper sheets for the toilet seat that keep your delicate cheeks from touching a surface sullied by the cheeks of others.

Would you not savor that bathroom experience as a gift from God and take a little longer than normal?

Homelessness Does Not Smell Very Good

One final comment about homeless hygiene warrants mentioning: homelessness does not smell very good.

I don't mean that homeless people smell bad (though that is sometimes true). I mean that homeless people are constantly subjected to unpleasant odors. Whether it is sleeping in a crowded room next to someone else who hasn't bathed, or a shelter bathroom that is overused and under-cleaned. And that doesn't even include digging through dumpsters looking for cans to recycle. Homeless people are exposed to a lot of bad smells.

Consequently, they become desensitized to odor. I completely understand this. Having spent most of my life working in homeless shelters, my own sense of smell is irrevocably different. When I give tours of Hesed House, people will frequently comment on odors that I simply can't smell anymore.

What does this mean for you? Well, you know that guy sitting quietly in the corner of your library who has an unpleasant odor? He may honestly have absolutely no idea that he (or his bag) smells.

Tool: The Amigo

It can be really helpful for you to have a relationship with your local homeless shelter. The first thing to do is figure out how many shelters there are in your community. Some communities have multiple shelters; some only have one. If there is only one, life is simpler for you.

Call the shelter's executive director and ask for a meeting. Tell him or her that you have many mutual patrons and would like to discuss how you can work together. There are a myriad of ways that a shelter can help you:

- It can suggest how to deal with difficult patrons. Our local library was once struggling with a particular homeless gentleman. After we suggested that he likely had undiagnosed autism, they treated him differently (with great success).

- It can give warnings about dangerous people or problems that are brewing. Shelter staff are much more in tune with what is happening in the homeless community.

- It can help get someone to bathe.

- Joint behavior agreements. I personally hate these, but some shelters have joint behavior agreements with the public library. If an individual is kicked out of the library during the day, he is also kicked out of the shelter that night.

- Joint staffing. If you want to hire a social worker for your library, don't. Instead, subcontract with the local shelter (or other social service agency) to provide a social worker on-site. See page 234 for more details.

- Joint trainings. This book originated as a training I did as a favor for the local library.

There are actually a lot more ways that you can work with your local shelter, but this should get you started.

Tool: The Matthew 20:16

So the last shall be first, and the first last

—JESUS (MATTHEW 20:16 KJV)

You should make your *non*-homeless patrons go first in every situation (except one). Let me explain:

As we discussed in chapter 2, homeless individuals are very sensitive to being singled out (because they *are* always singled out!). If one of your homeless patrons thinks you are enforcing a rule against him that you don't enforce against your wealthier patrons, he will go out of his way to make sure you have a bad day.

I have a tip that helps: if you have to enforce a rule against two people—one who is homeless and one who is not—enforce it against the non-homeless person first. This allows the homeless patron to see that you are being fair with the rule and not just picking on him. You will encounter a *lot* less resistance.

This is particularly true for rules like:

- Too many bags—How many college students have just as many bags as homeless patrons?
- Noise—Teenagers are much louder than homeless people.
- Smell—That guy who just went for a jog smells bad too.

There is one exception—a rule that you should always enforce against a homeless patron before you enforce it against his non-homeless counterpart. If your library doesn't allow sleeping and two patrons are sleeping, wake up the homeless patron first. This way he will actually be awake to see you wake up the other patron!

Predicament: A Patron Smells

It is a rainy spring morning, the kind of day that makes you want to curl up on the couch with a good book. Instead, you are working. The library is pretty quiet, though, so you decide to reshelve some books. You grab a pile and head out. On your way to the stacks, you pass one of your regular homeless patrons, Larry.

Larry is a nice enough fellow. It is obvious that he got caught out in the rain today. Little puffs of steam escape from his clothing as he shifts in the chair. And then it hits you like a shovel in the face. A master sommelier would describe the aromatics as "pungent yet complex, a mixture of spoiled Chinese takeout and fermented armpit, with the slightest hint of unwashed anus." You retch a little, but manage to keep your Honey Nut Cheerios in your stomach.

What do you do?

Empathy-Driven Enforcement Method

We are pretty lenient about body odor at Hesed House, but there are times when someone smells so bad that we simply cannot ignore it. If we don't intervene, the other residents will, but with far less tact (fewer words, more fists). I have had to talk to many people about their hygiene. These conversations are about as pleasant as spraying yourself with pepper spray. I can't make it more comfortable for you, but I have some pointers to make the conversation more effective.

The first thing to recognize is that there are two possible conversations you can have with the person. They are very different and you need to know which one you are intending to have. The "Odor Suggestion" is when you suggest that a person *should* bathe. It is a helpful reminder to someone who may not be aware of the offense they are causing. The "Odor Eviction" is when you tell a person that he or she *must* leave now and may not return until after a shower. It is a non-negotiable order.

Here are a few tips, whether you are making *either an Odor Suggestion or an Odor Eviction*:

- Don't act uncomfortable. Your discomfort will only make the other person more uncomfortable (uncomfortable people are unpredictable people). Just be very "matter of fact" about it, like you are telling someone when their books are due.
- Whenever possible, do not talk to someone about their odor in front of others. Embarrassed people are unpredictable people.
- Be respectful. See the Knight and the Lady on page 123 and the Big Bird on page 90.

Obviously, an Odor Eviction is much more difficult than an Odor Suggestion. Here are some additional tips for doing it well:

- Be *very* clear about what you are asking the person to do. Do not hint. Do not be ambiguous. Do not use metaphors. Do not assume the person knows what you are asking him to do unless you clearly spell it out. Do not tell a person to leave until he "doesn't smell" (he probably doesn't think he smells now). I recommend that you specifically ask the person not to return until after he takes a shower and washes his clothes (never forget the clothes; they are often the real problem). If the problem is halitosis, be specific about brushing teeth.

- Be pleasant, but be firm. Someone who has really bad body odor most likely has a *very* strong aversion to bathing (probably because of mental illness). If you agree to allowing the person to stay for today if he bathes tomorrow, you are likely to be having the same conversation again tomorrow.

- If you know which shelter the person stays at, call the shelter and ask for help. They may be able to coax the person into bathing (or make special accommodations). See the Amigo on page 184.

- Be consistent about body odors of all types. If a non-homeless woman has an overpowering amount of perfume, she should be treated the same. If a businessman decides to use the library after hitting the gym, he should be treated the same. Homeless individuals are very observant about which rules only apply to them. Disparate treatment creates resentment and resentment creates problems (for you). See the Matthew 20:16 earlier on page 184.

- Avoid the "most sensitive nose" rule. Do not allow an odor autocrat to set the standard. Some people—patrons or staff—feel entitled to an odorless environment, which is just unrealistic. There is a certain amount of odor that we can expect whenever we go out in public. Other people use odor as an excuse to vent their prejudices. Don't let someone's hypersensitivity or bias rule the day if the smell really isn't that bad.

- That said, I personally don't think you need an objective standard for odor. I heard of one library that had a rule that any odor that could be smelled from six feet away was against the rules. I can imagine them getting out a tape measure in order to see if the rule was being violated. This is just going to cause a scene. Instead, if the odor is truly unacceptable, just be pleasant and respectful, but firm.

Additional Effective Tools for This Predicament
- The Anti-Judge Judy (page 87)
- The Time Machine (page 88)
- The Michael Jordan (page 81)
- The Vogon (page 119)
- The Jerry Seinfeld (page 100)
- The Counteroffer (page 134)
- The Multiple Choice Test (page 127)

Predicament: A Patron Is Bathing in the Bathroom

You are sitting in the break room eating your lunch (ham sandwich and Cheetos) while casually flipping through a *People* magazine that was on the table when you arrived. Mr. Jones—a library trustee who sold his company last year and now has a lot of opinions about how libraries should be run—sits down next to you. "So, there is a guy shaving in the bathroom. How should we handle this?"

Your eyes start to roll back in their sockets, but you manage to stop them before they do a full circle. "I got it," you mumble through a mouthful of Cheetos. You set down your sandwich and head over to the bathroom, knocking before you enter. Mr. Jones was wrong. The guy isn't shaving, at least not anymore. He's splashing water into his armpits. When you approach, he smiles cheerfully and says, "Good morning!"

What do you do?

Empathy-Driven Enforcement Method

This scene may or may not be a regular occurrence at your library. If your community has inadequate shelter capacity—or poorly run shelters—this will be more common. There are a few things to remember when addressing it:

- If you are disgusted by someone bathing where you wash your hands, make sure you hide it. Your revulsion is not helpful. See the Anti-Judge Judy on page 87.
- This situation is a particularly good candidate for the Bad Cop (page 128). It can be awkward, and blaming the rules removes some of the emotion involved.
- If you have the luxury of designing a new library (or remodeling an existing one), place the bathrooms near public areas rather than hiding them in a back corner.
- You can hire "bathroom attendants." The Philadelphia Public Library hires formerly homeless individuals to police the bathrooms for inappropriate conduct.

Additional Effective Tools for This Predicament
- The Billy Bias (page 88)
- The Big Bird (page 90)
- The Pool Shot (page 98)
- The Laser Beam (page 102)
- The Sad Librarian (page 129)
- The Shot Across the Bow (page 131)
- The Canary (page 218)

Conclusion

When I am doing live trainings, I ask the trainees what the most common problems are that they face with homeless patrons. The first answer is usually about hygiene. While not the biggest problem (in terms of disruption), it is a particularly awkward conversation to have. The trick to holding conversations around hygiene is to keep focused on the goal (and remember your water tools)!

Sleeping

13

No dueling. No summoning of imps or other manifestations of elements
potentially damaging to the records, including but not limited to:
elementals, imps, sprites, ifrits, goblins, vile maidens, elohim, and major, minor and
inferior spawn. No praying. No cursing, except by staff. The library is closed on public
holidays. Donations welcome.

—Demonia Library, Justina Robson[1]

Even in a deep sleep, my subconscious knew that something was wrong. I was cuddling up beside my wife, but it just didn't feel right. *She* didn't feel right. Too large. Too hairy.

I opened my eyes and was completely disoriented in a large darkish room. Where is my bed? Where is my bedroom? Where is my wife? Who is this person I am cuddling up beside?

Suddenly, the lumpy pad (and ache in my back) reminded me that I was at Hesed House. I had decided to sleep in the shelter for a week while my wife and children were in Atlanta visiting the in-laws. I do this periodically to get a better understanding of what it is like to be homeless in our shelter.

Okay, that answers the questions about my bed, bedroom, and wife…but who the hell am I cuddling up to?

The pads in our emergency shelter are six feet long, three feet wide, and only two inches apart. It is *very* easy to roll over onto your neighbor's mat. The large man—sleeping in a checkered flannel shirt and pants—made a noise and rolled over slightly. My arm was around him and my chest was pressed up against his back.

If you ever find yourself spooning with a strange man in a homeless shelter, the trick is to roll back onto your own mat quickly, but carefully, so as to not wake him. Anything else can lead to a very awkward conversation and possibly a black eye.

I was able to get away successfully, but I was lucky. Already awake, I decided to use the restroom. I didn't bother to put my shoes on, a decision I soon regretted. It is hard for most men to hit the tiny toilet in the middle of the night. By the width of the puddle, I calculated that I was probably the 40th person to use the bathroom that night (and at least a few guys had gone twice).

I found my way back to my pad but was now wide awake. I reached into the sweatshirt I was using as a pillow and pulled out my cell phone (it was unlikely that anyone would steal from the executive director while he was sleeping, but I wasn't taking any chances). It was 4:10 a.m. The lights would be turned on in less than two hours.

So I just lay there, staring up at the ceiling. I couldn't get comfortable. The mat was thin and lumpy. My sweatshirt-turned-pillow was thinner and lumpier. A chorus of men snored, but not in harmony and not in sync. I did my best to count how many men were snoring. I couldn't keep track after about 20, so I just guessed that about a third of the 88 men in the room were snoring. My large hairy neighbor (and former cuddle buddy) was one of them.

The residents had told me to choose my mat carefully. There is a hierarchy of locations. Any spot in front of a fan is premier because it is cooler and it keeps the smells from accumulating. The second-tier mats are along the walls because then you aren't surrounded by men on all four sides.

I had not been fortunate enough to get a fan or a wall. I had two sets of bare feet near my head. I could turn around to put my head on the other side of the mat, but that would just get me two different sets of bare feet. At least we had had spaghetti last night and not burritos.

I just lay there for nearly two hours, staring at the ceiling, trying to identify all the strange noises and smells. I had absolutely no idea how I was going to be able to work today. I hadn't been able to fall asleep until well after midnight, and what little sleep I got was choppy.

My last thought—before the lights went on and a staff member announced that we all needed to get up—was "at least I already have a job. I can't imagine having to go to a job interview this tired."

• • •

Homelessness Is Exhausting

There is no other way to say this: being homeless is absolutely exhausting. Imagine this:

- Last night you slept under a bridge on a piece of cardboard over gravel. A nearby dog barked all night, making you think that someone was coming to mug or rape you. The night before you slept in a crowded shelter with ninety other people in the room who kept snoring and farting.

- You walked ten miles today in bad shoes. You walked ten miles yesterday, and the day before, and the day before that . . .

- Every time you sit down on a bench or in a park, the police come by and move you along.

- You're hungry a lot. Your only meal today was out of a dumpster behind a taco joint. Yesterday you ate in the shelter, but they ran out of dinner early and you had to settle for a peanut butter and jelly sandwich.

- You are stressed out of your mind all day and all night, every day and every night. You don't know when—or if—you will ever work again or how you will get back into an apartment.

How tired would you be? Yeah, you would be really damn tired. At Hesed House, we do "poverty simulators" a few times a year. We take a group of ten college students and give them a 24-hour homelessness experience. The #1 epiphany from the students at the end is always, "I am so much more tired than I ever imagined!" In fact, they are so tired that I have learned that I have to build a "nap time" into the schedule. I tried not having a nap time and people would get migraines or throw up. The last group I put through a poverty simulator had planned—without me knowing it—to all go to a bar together when they were done. At the end, every single one of them immediately went home to sleep.

These are healthy 23-year-olds who can't even make it for 24 hours as homeless people without taking a nap. The students all say the same thing:

- I don't think I could go to work this tired and not get fired.
- I definitely couldn't go to a job interview like this.
- I finally understand why homeless people are always falling asleep in parks and libraries.

Homelessness Is Boring

Homelessness is really boring. I don't mean "gee-the-battery-is-dead-on-my-iPad-so-now-I-have-to-see-what-is-on-TV" bored. I mean "life-is-an-endless-series-of-identically-bland-days-and-my-brain-is-atrophying" bored. It is unlikely that you have ever in your entire life experienced the kind of boredom that homeless individuals experience most days. I have tried wandering around the city by myself without money for the day to see what it is like, and by noon I am going crazy out of sheer boredom. I can go a lot longer without food than I can go without mental stimulation.

Imagine:

- You have been cut off from your friends and family. No one that you know will take your phone calls or meet with you. They have made it clear that they want nothing to do with you. Ever.
- You have been unemployed for a long time. In fact, you are unemployable, and you know it. You know that you will never work again. Ever.
- You don't own a TV or a computer or a smartphone. You can't watch Netflix and you can't choose the channel on the TV at the shelter (and it mostly plays cartoons for the kids).
- You don't have money to go to the movies or theater or zoo or anywhere else.
- There is nowhere you need to be today. Or tomorrow. Or next week. Or ever.
- You have no reason to believe that any of this will ever change. As far as you know, this will be the exact condition of your life until you die.

How bored would you be? Yup, you'd be pretty darn bored!

What would you do? Well, given your profession, I have to assume that you would go to the library and read a book. And you know what? That is exactly what many homeless individuals do too!

If you were bored and also really tired, what would you do? Yup, you'd sneak a little nap!

Predicament: A Patron Is Snoring

You have been looking forward to leading the book discussion group all week. The selected tome, by Alisa Surkis, is called *The Big Book of Lesbian Horse Stories*. (Yes, that is an actual book, but according to one Amazon reviewer, it is only average-sized.) You are halfway through a lively discussion of the fifth short story ("Snake Eyes for Silky") when the elderly woman who was speaking is interrupted by the sound of loud snoring. She tries to compose herself and begin again, but the snoring only grows louder. You tell her to continue and politely excuse yourself to go deal with the source of the noise.

You find the culprit quickly. Harold—a regular patron and one hell of a nice guy—is sprawled out on a comfy armchair, his head tipped back rakishly and his mouth wide open. You have always felt bad for Harold. He tells the most vivid stories of when he was a star quarterback back in high school, before he started drinking and before "that damn draft." You sheepishly whisper, "Harold, wake up." No response. Nothing. A little louder the second time, "Harold, buddy, you gotta get up." He actually snores louder, and you can feel the disapproving looks of the book club searing the back of your head.

You kneel down next to Harold and gently touch his arm. Still nothing. You give his arm a little shake. Suddenly, and without warning, Harold jerks upright, his arms thrashing about wildly. You try to back away but his elbow catches you in the nose. You hear a distinct crunching noise like a june bug under a little boy's heel.

"Oh my God, I'm so sorry! Are you okay?" Harold is standing over you, trying to help you to your feet. You touch your nose and waves of pain make the edge of your vision fuzzy and black. You have a broken nose.

And it is your fault.

What should you have done instead?

Empathy-Driven Enforcement Method

Waking up a homeless patron is not like waking up a non-homeless patron. Homeless individuals are frequently the victims of violence. Many have PTSD from being woken up by a mugger (and by war, if they are a veteran). Waking an individual with PTSD is a delicate affair. Do it wrong and you will get a broken nose.

Let me teach you how to do it the right way:

- If at all humanly possible, try not to wake a homeless patron by touching him. Try to wake up a homeless patron with your voice from a safe distance of a few feet.

- Some people recommend waking up patrons by "accidentally" dropping a book on a nearby table or kicking their chair. While this is a safe way to wake someone, I don't recommend it because it is tacky and rude. It certainly won't endear you to your homeless patrons.

- If you are completely unable to wake up a homeless patron with your voice alone, be mindful of where you are standing when you touch him. The two best places for you are either directly behind the person (it is hard to hit someone directly behind you) or—if they are sleeping at a table—from across the table (where it is also hard to reach someone). Never ever, *ever* crouch or kneel beside a homeless patron to wake him up. This is the fastest way to get a trip to the emergency room. The patron will feel really sorry, but you will still have a broken nose.

Additional Effective Tools for This Predicament

- The Hot Stove (page 108)
- The Minimalist (page 212)
- The Red and the Blue (page 213)
- The Canary (page 218)
- The Counteroffer (page 134)

Conclusion

I firmly believe that everyone should do a poverty simulator and "walk a mile" in a homeless person's shoes. If we all did that, we might appreciate how bloody exhausting it is to be homeless. This insight might not change your library's rules about sleeping (or snoring), but it will help you to have a little more compassion for someone who nodded off. Like everything else, the solution is in employing all of your empathy-driven tools with consistency.

Note

1. Justina Robson, *Selling Out* (New York: Pyr, 2007).

Possessions

The perfect Librarian is calm, cool, collected, intelligent, multilingual, a crack shot, a martial artist, an Olympic-level runner (at both the sprint and marathon), a good swimmer, an expert thief, and a genius con artist. They can steal a dozen books from a top-security strongbox in the morning, discuss literature all afternoon, have dinner with the cream of society in the evening, and then stay up until midnight dancing, before stealing some more interesting tomes at three A.M. That's what a perfect Librarian would do. In practice, most Librarians would rather spend their time reading a good book.

—Genevieve Cogman[1]

Chicago's weather is beautiful for two weeks in the spring and two weeks in the fall (and miserable the rest of the year). This particular day was one of the fourteen beautiful days in spring. I drove into work early—7:30 a.m.—with the windows open. The wind would have blown through my long dark hair, but I'm bald so the wind just bounced off my shaved noggin.

As I pulled into the parking lot, I saw her sitting on top of a picnic table. Curly blond hair, skinny jeans, a T-shirt purchased at some boy band concert. I guessed that she was between sixteen and twenty years old. She looked upset. I got out of my car and walked over to the picnic table. From ten feet away it was clear that she was not merely distraught. She was hysterical.

She tried to stifle the tears, but when she saw my staff name tag, she began to sob uncontrollably. I did my best to reassure her, but when someone is having the worst day of her life, the author of Ecclesiastes says it best: "all words are feeble." After a few minutes, she was able to talk again, in between fits of hyperventilation. She was in high school. A senior. She was pregnant. Her parents found out. Last night. That morning her father had given her thirty minutes and told her to pack her bags.

Then the bastard personally drove his own daughter to the second-largest homeless shelter in the state and left her sobbing in the parking lot. She had watched as her father drove away, certain he would come back. But he didn't.

Another staff member—a female with excellent maternal instincts—joined us. She put her arm around the girl and said, "Honey, let's get you some breakfast. Are you hungry? I'm sure we can whip you up some eggs and toast. And milk. Do you like milk?" The girl looked down at her bags—two extra large grey garbage bags stuffed to overflowing—and asked, "What about my stuff?" The staff member comforted her, "Now you don't worry about that, dear. Ryan here will take care of your bags. He'll keep them safe. Won't you, Ryan?" They disappeared into Hesed House.

I picked up the garbage bags and they immediately tore, spilling their contents all over the ground. Staring at this girl's stuff, I suddenly felt the full gravity of the moment, a moment that would likely define her life (for good or ill). Here was her childhood, scattered about on a homeless shelter's parking lot: six teddy bears, a chemistry book, a lime-green tennis racket, a few bras that wouldn't fit her in a few months, sunglasses with leopard print frames, and a pink diary with the heart clasp dangling precariously from when it had been pried off with a knife or screwdriver.

• • •

Possession Basics

Remember from chapter 2:

- Homeless individuals value their possessions more than you.
- Homeless individuals look at space differently than you.

Homeless individuals view their possessions differently than you. Remember in chapter 2, when I had you imagine what it would be like to get evicted? You would have to pick one bag to take with you. You would have to go through all of your personal belongings to decide what to keep. Everything that didn't fit in the bag would get thrown out. You would care more about that bag than any other bag you have ever owned.

A few things you should know about homelessness and possessions:

- People have to make those tough choices about what to take with them after eviction every day. Every person who becomes homeless has to make tough choices about what to keep. Anything that makes the cut is absolutely precious.

- If an individual is lucky enough to be at a large "fixed site" shelter, they will get a little bit of storage space. At Hesed House, individuals get a locker that is about ten inches wide, ten inches deep, and three feet tall. That is about the size of a carry-on suitcase.

- Many shelters don't have any storage at all (for example, shelters that rotate between different churches every night). Homeless individuals from these shelters must carry all of their physical belongings with them everywhere they go.

- Homeless individuals who sleep on the street must—obviously—carry everything everywhere.

Homeless individuals also view space differently than you in two important ways:

1. Homeless individuals view every room as a multipurpose room. When growing up in a crowded house, every room is used for everything. The same is true in large homeless shelters. Don't be surprised if they don't share your need for each room to have a different function.

2. Homeless individuals don't have anywhere to go to "just be." After a tough day, there is nowhere they can go to be alone. The police—or others—can ask them to leave from anywhere they might go to just sit.

Predicament: A Patron Brings in a Lot of Bags

You are carrying a huge box across the library. It isn't heavy, but it is awkward, and very large—completely blocking your vision. You shuffle quickly, eager to dispose of this box and move on to more interesting work. Your foot snags on something and before you realize what has happened you are sprawled out on the floor. The box has tumbled off ahead and you can already feel a bruise forming on your knee.

"Oh my gosh! I am so so sorry! Are you okay? Here, let me help you up." It is Joan, one of your quieter homeless patrons. In fact, you realize that you have never actually heard her speak before. Joan helps you to your feet and you look back to see what tripped you. It is one of Joan's many black Hefty bags. The guilty bag is now sporting a sizeable gash and crushed aluminum cans have spilled out on the floor. Seeing where you are looking, Joan rushes over to the bag and sheepishly shoves the cans back through the tear into the bag.

What do you do?

Empathy-Driven Enforcement Method

When I do live trainings at libraries, I always ask what problems they face with homeless patrons. The most common answer I get is "Too many bags." This appears to be a universal condition of libraries with homeless patrons.

I offer these tips and suggestions for dealing with it:

- When you are formulating your policy—or enforcing it—try to remember that that bag may contain the entirety of that person's possessions. He likely has absolutely nowhere else that he can put the bag where it will not be stolen.

- Try to distinguish between actual possessions and garbage. Many homeless people collect cans to recycle for money. Others have a hoarding problem and literally collect trash. In my opinion, there is a difference between trying to make accommodations for a suitcase of clothing and making accommodations for a bag of garbage. I would personally be more likely to make an exception for a duffel bag than a shopping bag full of tattered old magazines.

- Consider a policy that bags must be "out of the way," instead of banning them entirely. Is a duffel bag placed under a table really a problem?

- Consider lockers. Some newly renovated libraries are adding banks of lockers for patrons—and not just homeless ones—to place their belongings in.

- Consider a parking lot. I heard that some libraries have installed "parking lots" for shopping carts and other large baggage.

- I recommend against agreeing to store a bag behind the counter or desk. If it is garbage, it isn't worth the hassle, and if it is prized possessions, that is a great responsibility. If someone steals a bag while you are supposed to be watching it, you are going to feel horrible (and the patron is going to be justifiably angry). If I had a separate room with a locked door, I might be more inclined to be helpful, but it still wouldn't be my first choice.

- Be consistent. Many a homeless person has complained to me that college students routinely bring in larger—and more—bags without any consequences. If it isn't a problem for college students, then it isn't really a problem.

- Expect stiffer resistance to rules about bags than other rules. Rules about how many bags you may bring into a public place feel like they are targeted at homeless people.

- Obviously, when enforcing bag rules, be sure to use all of the water tools that you learned throughout this book.

Additional Effective Tools for This Predicament

- The Minimalist (page 212)
- The Mirror (page 117)
- The Sad Librarian (page 129)
- The Counteroffer (page 134)
- The Less Public Library (page 101)
- The Wizard of Oz (page 118)

Predicament: A Patron Is Monopolizing an Area

It is the perfect storm: Saturday morning during spring break and it is raining. You know that soon the library will be overflowing with young families looking for a cheap outing. You and your coworkers hurry around to get a few last tasks done before the rush. Soon you will spend hours hunting velveteen rabbits, sourcing green eggs, and searching for the secret garden.

And that's when you see Dale, a harmless curmudgeon. On this particular day, Dale has pushed three tables together. His belongings and a few dozen magazines are scattered out across the tables and all of the accompanying chairs. Dale has single-handedly consumed the space for twenty human beings. Judging by the arrangement of the magazines and other items, it is clear that Dale is not working on some grand project; he is merely marking his territory. Public urination—while more effective—is frowned upon, so Dale uses magazines.

On another day, you might have overlooked Dale's spatial greediness, but your library is Asia circa the thirteenth century: wave after wave of tiny Mongol invaders will be overwhelming your defenses soon. You need that space!

What do you do?

Empathy-Driven Enforcement Method

Homeless patrons sometimes monopolize space. Remember, homeless individuals have exactly zero square feet in the entire universe that is truly theirs. The temptation to commandeer a little public space is strong. I'll be honest, if I was homeless, I would probably do the same thing. Sometimes, this just isn't going to work for your library, though. Here's what you do:

- Have a little empathy (see the Anti-Judge Judy on page 87). Be cognizant of the patron's lack of space elsewhere. This doesn't mean that you have to ignore the infraction, but try to have a little compassion.

- This situation is a prime candidate for the Alternative Fact (page 130). Approach the patron as if he simply doesn't know he has done anything wrong, even if you are certain he does. You'll encounter less resistance than if you treat him like a bad guy.

- Offer a compromise (see the John McCain on page 133). What is the maximum space allotment that is acceptable? Can you spare two tables? Can you spare three chairs? Sometimes a negotiated settlement reached peacefully is better than a war that is won.

- Don't debate. Have your one- or two-sentence explanation ready as to why he can't use so much space (see the Explainerator on page 135).

- This is a prime candidate for the Bad Cop (page 128). Simply state that while you don't mind him using so much space, the "powers that be" would be very angry with you for allowing it. Remember, your goal is compliance with the rules, not universal agreement with their merit.

Additional Effective Tools for This Predicament
- The Michael Jordan (page 81)
- The Multiple Choice Test (page 127)
- The Goldilocks (page 103)
- The Limbo (page 115)
- The Hypnotist (page 116)
- The Mirror (page 117)

Conclusion

It is hard for those of us who have never been homeless to understand how homeless individuals look at possessions and space. Their world is so completely different from ours. Try to understand where they are coming from and stick to your water tools and everything will go better for you and your homeless patrons.

Note
1. Genevieve Cogman, *The Masked City* (New York: Ace, an imprint of the Penguin Publishing Group, 2016).

Children

Librarians save lives:
by handing the right book, at the right time, to a kid in need.
—Judy Blume

He was surprised when staff emerged from the shelter kitchen with a birthday cake—or at least he was polite enough to pretend to be. It is hard to keep a secret in a homeless shelter. Jonathon smiled broadly as we sang the traditional birthday song to him, humored by our inability to pick one key in which to sing. He said that ice cream cake was his favorite, and we said that we knew. The chocolate-vanilla swirl cake was frosted with huge sticky gobs of orange frosting.

Jonathon deliberately and slowly counted the candles, very concerned that the cake have exactly sixteen (though I doubt he had seen the Molly Ringwald movie). His mother, Cindy, told him to make a wish. An uncomfortable look crept onto his young face as he bit his lip. It was totally quiet in the room for a few moments while Jonathon thought. You could actually hear the faint crackling of the sixteen candles.

I have no idea what Jonathon was thinking or what he wished for, but he grinned suddenly and let out a little chuckle before blowing out the candles—all sixteen in one breath. Everyone standing around the cake in the shelter dining room cheered, and Jonathon raised his hands in mock triumph—as if he had just beaten Apollo Creed (though I doubt he has seen a *Rocky* movie, either).

A Hesed House staff member cut the ice cream cake, giving Jonathon and his mom the first pieces. I watched Cindy's face carefully. It reflected a mixture of emotions: the milestone birthday of her only son—*but* celebrated in a homeless shelter; pride in *who* he was becoming—*but* sorrow at *where* he was; gratitude that he had a birthday cake—*but* disappointment that *she* couldn't afford to buy it for him. She smiled, genuinely, but fought back tears.

Noticing her pain, Jonathon gave his mom a hug, and a single tear slipped past her defenses. Cindy wiped it away quickly, telling herself that she made it disappear before Jonathon noticed.

Jonathon is one of the greatest kids I have ever met (straight-A student, respectful, funny, etc.). And I'm sure that the girls in school think he's "uber" cute. I would adopt him in a heartbeat, but that isn't our job . . .

• • •

Homeless Children Basics

Just as homeless adults are different from you in specific ways (view of respect, orientation to time, etc.), homeless children are not like your children. They have had *very* different experiences than your children.

Two Types of Homeless Children

The federal government uses two different definitions of homelessness:

1. The Department of Housing and Urban Development considers homelessness to be living in a shelter, on the streets, or in a place not fit for human habitation (e.g., an abandoned building).
2. The Department of Education also includes families who are "doubled up," living in someone else's home temporarily. Many families "couch surf," moving between friends' and family members' homes as they exhaust their welcome.

There are *way* more children who are "doubled up" than children living in shelters or on the streets. Most families can find someone to stay with. In fact, during the Great Recession, the number of children in shelters stayed relatively constant, while the number of doubled-up children skyrocketed.

This is important to know. Living in a shelter or on the streets has unique challenges, but they tend to be pretty obvious. It is less obvious to see the chaos in a child's life who is technically housed, but has been switching between homes every few weeks (or days). Similarly, many families who are doubled up will not self-identify as homeless. When you think about the needs of homeless patrons, don't forget the couch surfers.

Shelter Children Are Younger Than Other Children

Children in homeless shelters are younger than other children. I don't mean that they are "psychologically younger." I mean they are "chronologically younger." They actually are younger than other kids. I know; this doesn't make any sense.

To understand why, let's do a little thought exercise:

1. Imagine that you are a single parent with a sixteen-year-old child. You get evicted. Your son's friend says he can stay at their house, but you will have to go to a homeless shelter. Would you take your child to a shelter or let him stay with a friend?
2. Imagine that you are a single parent with a three-year-old child. You get evicted. Would you try to find someone who is willing to take your toddler, or would he come with you no matter where you are living?

Most families will find somewhere for their older children to live other than a shelter. Most families will keep younger children with them. Thus, shelters are full of babies, toddlers, and elementary school students. Junior high tends to be 50/50. Very few high school students live in homeless shelters.

I have no evidence for this, but I also suspect that parents with young children are more likely to become homeless than parents of older children. Most homeless families are headed by single mothers. If you have young children, it is harder to keep a job than if you have older children.

Keep this in mind when contemplating collaborating with homeless shelters. Harry Potter is good, but Dr. Seuss is better.

Homeless Children Have Experienced a Lot of Trauma

Several years ago, we built a special children's playroom in Hesed House. One of the walls has a mural that was designed to be calming for homeless children (a house, a momma bird feeding her babies, and a pretty tree). The mural was created by an art therapist who enlisted the help of the children to fill in the colors. The children loved it, but more importantly, it taught us a very important lesson about homeless children.

According to many art therapists, drawing trees is especially significant. When a child adds a knot (or broken limb, etc.) to a tree, it signifies a traumatic event in the child's life. Where on the tree the knot is placed signifies when it happened (e.g., if a six-year-old places a knot halfway up a tree, then something happened when she was three).

When our art therapist asked the children to help paint the tree in our mural, 100 percent of the children tried to add a knot on the tree. She saw an opportunity, carefully documenting where each child wanted to place the knot, so she could follow up with traditional therapy.

Every homeless child has experienced some obvious traumas:

- Poverty (e.g., skipped meals)
- Distracted and stressed-out parents
- Eviction

Homeless children are also *much* more likely to have experienced other traumas than housed children:

- Sexual abuse
- Violence
- Drugs

Traumatized children need much more help than non-traumatized children. Traumatized children also tend to have more behavior problems than other children. Anyone who wants to work with homeless children has to accept that some of the children will be difficult to handle. This isn't a reason not to serve homeless children, but it is a reason to be prepared (and to keep the ratio of children to adults low).

Homeless Children Are Academically Behind

At Hesed House, we just had a student who got a perfect score on the ACT. This is not normal. Unfortunately, homeless children

- Are sick twice as often
- Are twice as likely to repeat a grade
- Have twice the rate of learning disabilities
- Have three times the rate of emotional and behavioral problems
- Are two and a half times as likely to experience anxiety, depression, or withdrawal

Of course, getting a poor education creates a trap of intergenerational poverty, where homeless children don't learn the skills they need to thrive and they eventually become homeless adults. Their children then inherit the same disadvantages, and on and on. Some of the individuals who were homeless children when I started my career are now homeless parents. The cycle continues....

Oh, if only there was a profession of people who had access to knowledge and could help homeless children to catch up to their peers!

Homeless Children Are Clingy

Homeless children are often very physically affectionate with strangers. There are two reasons for this:

- Homeless children often do not receive sufficient attention from their stressed-out and distracted parents.
- Homeless children get very comfortable with strangers because shelters constantly rotate volunteers through.

Being able to show some attention to a child is always a good thing. Just be careful to protect yourself, though. *Never be alone with a homeless child.* Remember, homeless children are much more likely to have been sexually abused. If they get confused about which adult abused them, your life could be ruined. This is not a reason to avoid homeless children. But it is a reason to be careful, and to follow all protocols.

Homeless Children Have Special Education Rights

Once upon a time, three little children became homeless. The shelter was in a different school district than where the children had lived. The big bad school district sued the children to kick them out. The judge said that the children had to transfer schools. The three little children cried.

This angered the heroic people who ran the homeless shelter. The shelter mobilized their 5,000 volunteers to call legislators. Eventually, their state passed a homeless education "Bill of Rights" that was largely written by the homeless shelter staff. Soon other states became jealous, wanting their own homeless education laws. After several trips to Washington, DC, the homeless shelter—along with advocates around the country—was able to get a national law for homeless children. And everyone lived happily ever after . . .

This fairy tale is true. The homeless shelter was Hesed House (where I work!). Illinois passed the first homeless education rights bill in 1995. In 2002, the No Child Left Behind Act incorporated the Illinois law almost word for word.

The law has a lot of very important provisions:

- Homeless students can remain in their "school of origin" or transfer to the school where the shelter is.
- Homeless students receive transportation to whichever school they choose.
- Homeless students have a right to be enrolled immediately. All the paperwork (e.g., medical records, school records, etc.) can be sorted out after the child is in school.
- Each school has to name a "homeless liaison" to ensure that homeless students are identified and assisted.

For an exceptional explanation of homeless education rights written by a brilliant (and handsome!) young law student, see "No Other Choice: Litigating & Settling Homeless Education Rights Cases" in 23 NORTHERN ILLINOIS UNIVERSITY LAW REVIEW 257 (2003) by Ryan Dowd.

Homeless Children Have a Hard Time Doing Homework

Homeless shelters are crowded and loud. It is really hard to do homework in a shelter. Students often can't

- Be alone
- Go somewhere quiet
- Spread their papers out
- Use a computer whenever they need one
- Store large projects like a poster board

Libraries are essential for homeless students trying to do homework.

Homeless "Youth" (Age 18–24)

The government is putting a lot of effort into assisting homeless individuals who are between the ages of 18 and 24. The reason is that new research suggests that individuals who "come of age" during a recession are more likely to struggle with homelessness for their entire lives. The Great Recession may have created a cohort of homeless individuals. Right now, there are a lot of homeless 22-year-olds. In ten years, there will be a lot of homeless 32-year-olds. In 20 years, there will be a lot of homeless 42-year-olds, and so on ...

Homeless individuals who are old enough to be adults—but barely—are particularly challenging. Because they lack the impulse control of older individuals, they can be difficult. They are young enough, though, that a little extra assistance now can change the trajectory of their entire lives.

LGBT Homeless Youth

Consider this:

- 7 percent of the general youth population identify as LGBT.
- 40 percent of homeless youth identify as LGBT.

The all-too-common story is that a teenager comes out to his parents and is kicked out of the house. Be sensitive to this phenomenon when talking to children and youth living on the streets. These individuals have less resources than others and face additional stigmas. They are also especially susceptible to predators.

Tool: The Scholarship Hunter

Do you want to change the trajectory of a person's life? Help a homeless student apply for scholarships. The bad news is that homeless students have a hard time going to college; it is hard to prioritize higher education when your family doesn't even have a roof. The good news is that it is easier for homeless children to get scholarships than other similarly situated individuals. Some scholarships prioritize homeless students or give them special attention. Even for those that don't, everybody loves the idea of helping a homeless student overcome his or her circumstances and go to college.

College is one of the most effective ways for breaking the cycle of intergenerational poverty.

Predicament: You Want to Do a Program for Homeless Children

"Excuse me." You look down to see Sonya, one of the regular children in the library. As usual, she is clean, but her clothing is threadbare and a few sizes too small. She wears her poverty with as much dignity as she can. "Yes, Sonya," you say with a big smile.

"Do you have any books about how to build a papier-mâché volcano?" You spend a few minutes looking with Sonya, ultimately finding a craft book with detailed instructions. Eyes bright with excitement, Sonya scans the instructions. When she gets near the end, her body slumps and she sighs deeply, closing the book. As she begins to walk away, you ask Sonya what is the matter.

"I can't do it," she confides, "it has to dry overnight and the shelter won't have space for that."

(This has been adapted from the children's book: *Where Can I Build My Volcano?* by Pat Van Doren.)[1]

What do you do?

Empathy-Driven Enforcement Method

If you want to provide specific programs for homeless children, here are some tips for all programs (regardless of topic or type):

- Reach out to your local homeless shelter. Most shelters would be thrilled to work with you to serve their children. They will usually bend over backwards to facilitate your work. They will also know what is likely to be successful. See the Amigo on page 184.

- Focus on the parents. They are the key to children's programming. It is not enough to sell the children. You have to sell the parents. They are stressed and overwhelmed. Their attention is understandably elsewhere. Thus, a program at the local library may not be a priority unless someone has talked to the parent. This point cannot be stressed enough.

- Don't bother with planning and advertising weeks in advance. The advertising you do in the last 24–48 hours right before the event is most important.

- Schedule "self-contained" programs. Homelessness is chaotic, thus long-term planning and follow-through are difficult. One-time programs and programs that can be started and stopped midstream will be more successful than programs that require regular attendance. Make each session self-contained (someone doesn't need to have been to the prior session and doesn't need to come to the next one).

All children love arts and craft projects. Homeless children theoretically love them even more! The "culture of poverty" theory states that individuals raised in poverty have a more kinesthetic (touch-based) relationship with the world than their wealthier peers. Also, while wealthy children have ample access to expensive art supplies, these are a special treat (and luxury) for poorer students. A few pieces of extra advice for craft projects:

- As stated above, be careful that the project is self-contained. Do not choose a project that requires multiple sessions (e.g., pottery that must be fired and painted on different days). Focus instead on projects that can be started and completed in a single sitting.
- Be cognizant of space. Homeless students generally do not have a lot of storage space for their artwork. Thus, painting or scrapbooking is better than pottery or shadow boxes.

For a growing list of examples from libraries around the country, go to www.homelesslibrary.com/inspiration.

Additional Effective Tools for This Predicament
- The Scholarship Hunter (page 206)
- The Robin Williams (page 125)
- The Dalai Lama (page 124)

In Conclusion

Homeless children pose a lot of unique problems. They also present unique opportunities. The opportunity to fundamentally alter the trajectory of another's life is much greater when dealing with children. If you encounter homeless children in your library, take a little bit of extra time to get to know them. Who knows, you just might change their world!

Note

1. Pat Van Doren, *Where Can I Build My Volcano?* (P. V. Doren, 1999).

Part IV

Beyond Problem-Solving

Advice for Managers and Leaders

16

The most important asset of any library goes home at night—the library staff.
—Timothy Healy

3:00 a.m. The darkest part of night. The first big thunderstorm of summer.

It was a night she would try to forget. She would fail.

Rain poured off her straw-colored hair as she struggled to carry her three children by herself—a newborn and twin toddlers in car seats. She shuffled slowly along an urban bicycle trail. Her days-old C-section incision was infected. Events of the last few days had cast her into a nightmare.

Every flash of lightning must have thrown ghastly shadows. Every clap of thunder probably made her shudder. Every gust of wind almost certainly felt like even the elements were conspiring against her.

Can you imagine what this would feel like? I can't. I have tried. My imagination is unable—or unwilling—to conjure up such raw terror. My breathing gets tight when I even try.

Somehow, the police found her. Perhaps someone driving by the bike trail saw her, but was too afraid to pull over in the middle of the night. The police officer, overwhelmed by what he was witnessing, drove the woman and her three babies to Hesed House.

I wasn't there. I wish I had been. Only occasionally—even at a homeless shelter—do you have an opportunity to take care of someone who is in exactly the worst minute of the worst hour of the worst day of his or her life. That moment is what the fifth-century Celtic Christians called "a thin place," where the distance between heaven and earth is narrower. There is no better way to describe it.

However, I wasn't there. I was a few miles away, in my bed, sleeping soundly.

That night—like every other night—there was only one staff person on duty. He was responsible for 200–250 souls scattered over a 45,000-square-foot building with a lot of rooms and hallways. It is likely that he would never have a five-minute period in his life when he had a greater opportunity to impact another person's life.

Hesed House—an organization built on a 3,000-year-old philosophy and theology of radical hospitality and unconditional love—was counting on this single staff person to be the literal hands of God in that moment. Was he the right person for this sacred duty? Did he have the depth of empathy necessary for a task of such magnitude? Did he know what to do? Had we trained him adequately?

He immediately got the woman a warm meal even though the kitchen was closed. He prevented a dozen women on their way to work from taking a shower so she could bathe in peace. He left the building completely unattended while he rummaged through a trailer in the parking lot looking for dry clothes that would fit her. He put her in an empty dorm room in our transitional wing, a direct violation of federal grant guidelines.

Before the sun had crested over the horizon the next morning, this staff member had broken at least a dozen organizational rules. I have never been more proud.

• • •

Being a Manager Is Hard

Working with difficult homeless individuals is hard. Managing people who work with difficult homeless individuals is harder. There are two equally challenging problems:

1. Staff who are terrified of conflict and avoid all confrontation by not enforcing any rules.
2. Staff who think they are Rambo, turning every mild conflict into World War III.

It is *much* easier to help a timid staff member become assertive than it is to help an aggressive staff member be polite. I am not sure why this is, but hot-headed staff usually cannot rein it in for very long. They can get better for a little while, but eventually emotions take over and they lose their cool. Timid staff, on the other hand, only grow more confident as they get experience.

There are some tools that can make you more effective.

Tool: The Minimalist

Less is more when it comes to rules.

We tend to think that we need to make an explicit rule prohibiting every possible undesirable behavior that could possibly happen. And every time someone does something bad, we can add one more rule to the laundry list of prohibitions. This is highly ineffective.

The problem is that every time we add a new rule, it dilutes the other rules already in place. If you have four basic rules, it is easy for everyone (patrons, staff, management) to learn them and remember them. Everyone will take them seriously as "The Law." If—on the other hand—you have 106 rules that govern every specific behavior imaginable, your patrons will have trouble remembering them and your staff will have trouble enforcing them (which makes you look arbitrary).

How many rules can you remember from the Bible? Probably not too many. Even ten rules is too many, apparently. More Americans can name all the ingredients of a Big Mac than all ten commandments.[1] But if you get it down to one, most people can remember it. Consider how easy it is to remember the Golden Rule ("Do unto others as you would have them do unto you").

At Hesed House we have four rules posted on a big yellow metal sign outside of the shelter entrance:

1. No drugs or alcohol.
2. No weapons.
3. No fighting.
4. If you leave for the night, you may not return until tomorrow.

Every staff member—and most of the residents—can recite them from memory. There is no ambiguity.

Consider what some of your fellow libraries are doing:

- The Central Library in Dallas used to post a lengthy list of rules. When they instead focused on only five, they found that compliance went up substantially.
- The Helen Plum Memorial Library in Lombard, Illinois, took it even further. They got rid of all their rules and replaced them with a single rule: no one is allowed to interfere with someone else's use of the library. As long as a patron isn't bothering anyone else, they can do whatever they want.

Tool: The Red and the Blue

There are two types of rules:

1. Rules that should never be broken under any circumstances (Red Rules)
2. Rules that keep things running smoothly, but should be broken when common sense dictates (Blue Rules)

Some people view the red/blue rules concept as ludicrous. To them, a rule is a rule; if it is going to be ignored, it shouldn't be a rule. The problem with this thinking is that it is impossible to develop guidelines and rules for every possible scenario. It is much more effective to make a few hard-and-fast rules (red) and then a bunch of guidelines (blue rules) that work in most, but not all, situations.

For example, Hesed House has a rule that residents are not allowed to arrive later than 10:00 p.m. It is a blue rule. If someone shows up at 10:30 p.m. during a blizzard, I expect the staff to ignore the rule. If they don't, someone could literally die. We have another rule that violence is not permitted. If one resident punches another resident, staff does not have the authority to send the aggressor off to bed with a firm scolding. This is a red rule.

The problem for managers is that it is obvious *to us* which rules are red and which are blue. It is not obvious to the front-line staff (especially the new ones). Take the time to make sure that your staff know the difference. You can call the rules whatever you want that makes sense in your setting (though "red/blue rules" is common terminology in health care, business, and government).

Tool: The Anti-Witch Hunt

In February 1692, Betty Parris (age 9) and Abigail Williams (age 11) began to convulse on the ground. They described feeling poked by imaginary pins. Soon, other young people in the village complained of the same thing. The culprit was soon identified: Sarah Good, a mentally ill homeless woman, and her fellow witches. On July 29, 1692, Sarah was executed. Before the panic had subsided, twenty-five people were dead.

I don't think it is coincidental that the Salem Witch Trials began with a homeless woman. The most vulnerable among us are often scapegoated during periods of mass hysteria. The same thing happens today, whether it is immigrants, minorities, or—as is often the case—homeless individuals.

Guard against panic in your library. It is contagious. After something bad happens in your community (or in the news), people become unreasonably fearful. Suddenly they are terrified of something that has the same statistical likelihood as being eaten by a shark. Using that analogy, if I read about a shark attack, I am a little more careful swimming in the ocean, but I don't prevent my children from taking baths.

Our irrational fears can sound so reasonable in the moment. A registered sex offender just got a library card, so now all of our children will be kidnapped. A patron was overheard having a conversation with himself, so now Norman Bates is on the loose. A Wiccan group from the local college applied to use a conference room, and now we are afraid that our pets will disappear for ritual sacrifices. A mosque opens in a nearby town and we all Google the word "jihad." A coworker is mugged leaving a nearby restaurant, and we devise new ways to exclude homeless patrons (especially if they are African American).

By the way, homeless shelters are not—unfortunately—immune to mass hysteria about homeless persons. Consequently, I have dealt with my fair share of hysterical outbreaks.

Here is how you deal with mass hysteria and witch-hunts that seize hold of your staff:

- Confront it directly. Call a meeting to discuss everyone's concerns. This prevents people from accusing you of "not taking their safety seriously." Make sure that you schedule it at a time when the calm and rational members of your staff can be present. Contact them in advance to ensure that they will be there. The worst thing you can do is call a meeting and then discover that everyone in the room is paranoid. That just exacerbates it.

- Stay very calm. Demonstrate through your demeanor that you are not afraid. If you get frustrated and angry with your colleagues, it is easier for them to dismiss you.

- Lead by example. Find a tangible way to demonstrate that you are not afraid. Work the circulation desk for a while. Make a point of approaching your homeless patrons when your staff are watching. Hesed House had a tuberculosis outbreak, and the staff became panicky, accusing me of not taking the danger seriously enough because I was safe in my office. That night I moved into the shelter for a few days, eating, showering, and sleeping alongside residents. My actions showed better than my words that I believed we were doing everything in our power to contain the outbreak.

Tool: The After Action Review

After a battle or other significant event, the military conducts what it calls an "After Action Review" (AAR) to debrief the incident. Most police forces, fire departments, and hospitals also have some form of this in order to learn from mistakes and successes.

You, too, should do an analysis with your staff after something significant happens. If it is done well, it has the added benefit of allowing staff to talk through a stressful—or traumatic—event, which can be therapeutic.

It is absolutely essential, though, that the After Action Review be about learning lessons, not assigning blame. If staff feel like you are on a witch-hunt, they will omit key details and they will leave even more traumatized than before.

There are six steps to an effective After Action Review:

Step 1: The leader (i.e., you) accepts *all* of the blame for anything that went wrong. This clears the air and allows people to speak openly without fear of punishment. It is also true. Anything that went wrong is your fault, even if you weren't there when it happened. These are staff that you hired (or at least retained) and that you trained (or not) following policies that you created (or at least didn't eliminate). If you have been in your job more than three months, *everything* that goes wrong is your fault. This is just the burden of leadership. Own it. If you are not going to explicitly accept all blame, don't bother doing an After Action Review.

Step 2: Explain the purpose of the AAR. Tell the staff that you want to learn from what worked well and from what didn't. Explain that you will search for mistakes, but only because you learn more from mistakes than successes. Acknowledge that there are *always* mistakes, even when the outcome was a raging success. The Normandy Invasion on D-Day during World War II was an unqualified success *and* the Allied forces still learned valuable lessons from how poorly they inserted the paratroopers.

Step 3: Get clear on the facts. It is helpful to review the sequence of events. Not everyone will know all the details. Some people will have heard rumors and innuendo. I recommend just walking through it chronologically. Always start the historical review 30–60 minutes before the actual confrontation. Most of the mistakes are made early. When law enforcement review police shootings, the officer—while justified in the final moments—often made a mistake earlier that could have prevented him from having been put in a position of needing to shoot. I find the same thing to be true at Hesed House: a staffer was justified in kicking a hostile resident out, but when we "rewound the tape" we discovered that the resident wasn't hostile until the staff member was rude first.

Step 4: Review what went well. Always start with the good.

Step 5: Review what could have been done better. You go first: tell a story about a time when you handled a similar situation poorly. Explain something you could have done to help staff be more prepared for this incident. Your admission of guilt gives everyone else permission to do likewise.

Step 6: Close up. Review the lessons learned. Thank everyone for their honesty and their service to the community. Remind them that they serve on the front line of democracy, a sacred duty that can be challenging. Say thank you again.

Here are some questions to get you started:

- Where was there ambiguity about our policy?
- Where was there uncertainty about the staff's authority?
- Where did we have inadequate communication?
- Where did we not follow protocol (for better or worse)?
- How could this incident have been avoided?
- What did we do to de-escalate the situation?
- What did we do to escalate the situation?

In probing for lessons, I recommend always using the pronoun "we," even if the incident only involved one staff member. Alternatively, you can use the pronoun "I," and phrase everything in terms of how you could have done better (e.g., "How could I have ensured that staff communicated adequately?"). Never use the pronoun "you" when looking for mistakes if you want honesty.

Tool: The Scrimmage Game

In sports, a scrimmage game is where the team divides into two halves who play each other. You can do something similar through role-playing. Have your staff pair off and practice the techniques in this book. It isn't as good as practicing during the real thing, but it has its place. Role-playing is not very effective when practicing for very high-stress encounters (because you can't re-create the emotions). Role-playing is very effective, though, when practicing how someone should *physically* handle a situation. Two tools, in particular, lend themselves well to role-playing:

- *The Pool Shot* (page 98)—Have staff practice standing properly with their hands in the right positions. Muscle memory will make it more likely that they will actually use this tool if they have practiced it.
- *The Sidekick* (page 144)—Providing backup properly is more complicated because it involves coordinating the actions of two different staff members. Every other tool in this book can be done by yourself, but providing backup always involves someone else. Thus, it is especially important that everyone is on the same page with how to do it properly. It doesn't matter if I know how to provide backup correctly if you are the one backing me up.

Tool: The Anti-Metaphor

One night I was training a new staff member. I only made one mistake, but that mistake almost killed a man. It was bitterly cold outside, so we were trying really hard not to kick anyone out, lest they freeze to death. The new staff member and I were informed that one of our residents was being ornery in another room. I made the flippant comment "Okay, let's go yell at Mr. DiFranco." On the way over there, I explained that the new staff member would take the primary role and I would back him up (see the Sidekick on page 144).

When we reached Mr. DiFranco, the new staff member immediately began to yell at him. I didn't see it coming. This staff member was a pretty mellow guy, but he yelled at Mr. DiFranco like a professional wrestler taunting his opponent. Mr. DiFranco went from a level 2 jerk to a level 4 wild man in about three seconds. Realizing that soon we would have to send Mr. DiFranco away in subzero temperatures I said, "I've got this," and relegated the new staff member to the back-up role. I spoke calmly and quietly and within a few minutes, Mr. DiFranco was calm. Ten minutes later, he was in bed.

After the incident was over, the new staff member looked at me with bewilderment and said, "I don't understand. You told me to yell at Mr. DiFranco." I tried to explain that I hadn't actually meant to "yell" at him. I had screwed up. I had spoken imprecisely to a staff member who was not yet steeped in our culture and way of doing things. A longtime employee would have known that I hadn't actually meant "yell," but this new guy didn't.

With new staff, always speak precisely. Say *exactly* what you mean. Don't speak metaphorically. Don't exaggerate. Don't assume that he or she knows what to do.

Tool: The Canary

Miners used to take a canary underground with them. Canaries are more susceptible to gases than humans, so if the canary died, the miners knew it was time to get out of the mine. Homeless patrons are your canary. They die before your other patrons. While this is literally true, it is also metaphorically true for two reasons: (1) homeless individuals do not have the power to fight back through "normal" channels (the police don't take them seriously, etc.), and (2) many homeless individuals elicit an emotional response from us more quickly than other patrons.

A staff member who mistreats homeless patrons will also mistreat the elderly, children, and other staff members. Conversely, a staff member who goes above and beyond to help a homeless patron is more likely to serve all of your patrons zealously.

You want to know someone's true character? Watch how he or she treats homeless people.

Tool: The Trick Question

Some people are just naturally wired for calmness and respect. Other people get a power trip from exerting control over the weak. It is really hard to tell the difference during an interview. It isn't a male or female thing. It isn't a rich or poor thing. It has nothing to do with education. For years I have sought the trait that makes someone a bad fit for working in a homeless shelter. I haven't found it. The closest I got is the concept of everyday sadists (see the Sad Librarian on page 129). A psychologist named Aisling O'Meara at the University College, Cork, has even developed a test for this trait called the "Short Sadistic Impulse Scale" (SSIS). This test is, unfortunately, completely worthless in a job interview. It includes questions like "Do you have fantasies that involve hurting people?" (even Jack the Ripper would know how to answer this one properly).

After consulting experts who teach corporations how to do effective interviewing, I have concluded that there are only two tools for weeding out someone who is a bad fit: the trick question and the behavioral interview question.

The trick question involves asking a job candidate a series of questions that have no obvious correct answer outside of your workplace. As alluded to above, if I ask whether you "fantasize about hurting people," you will answer "no" even if you are a total sociopath. If—on the other hand—I ask you "which is worse, a rude person or a slob," there is no obvious correct answer. Through a series of such questions I can start to get a sense of your personality. It is hard for me to give you exact questions because it is culturally specific. The type of person you want to weed out of a library might not be exactly the type of person I want to prevent from getting hired at a homeless shelter.

You can also ask someone how they would handle a specific difficult situation. While this can tell you a little bit about a person's personality, people always handle hypothetical situations better than real ones. This brings us to the second tool, the behavioral interview question.

Tool: The Behavioral Interview Question

Behavioral interviewing techniques involve asking people questions about how they have handled certain situations in the past. Here are my favorite examples:

- Tell me about a time when you got really frustrated with a patron (or coworker).
- Tell me about a time when you lost your temper at work.
- Tell me about a difficult conversation you had with a patron.

The reason why these questions are effective is because they track actual (not hypothetical) behavior and most people haven't prepared for them. It is amazing the things people will admit because these questions force them to lower their facade for a minute while they recount a story. Actually, behavioral interview questions are generally effective for ferreting out all sorts of traits (not just everyday sadism). For example:

- Tell me about a time when your boss asked you to do something unreasonable. (What does he consider to be unreasonable?)
- Tell me about a time you handled a situation poorly at work. (Can she admit mistakes?)
- Tell me about a time when a team project ended poorly. (Can he work on a team?)
- Tell me about a time when you had to pull out all the stops to get a project done on time. (How is her work ethic?)

Tool: The Andy Taylor

Have you ever watched the *Andy Griffith Show*? The main character is Sheriff Andy Taylor (don't let the show's title confuse you). Sheriff Taylor is a great officer who doesn't just run around arresting people. He is a true problem-solver, always working with people to make the community better.

Your library needs a Sheriff Andy Taylor. Put another way, your library needs a liaison within the police department. It isn't enough to just call 911 when you have an issue. You also want an officer or two who looks out for you.

Your first choice should always be the community oriented policing (C.O.P.) officer assigned to your area. C.O.P. officers are trained to build relationships and proactively solve problems through community engagement. Your local C.O.P. officer wants to know you. The type of people who are chosen to go into these units are usually very friendly and enjoy working collaboratively.

If your jurisdiction does not have a C.O.P. unit, then you'll have to move to Plan B. Call the police commander who is responsible for your area and explicitly ask if there is a good person who can be your contact within the police department. The commander will know which of his or her officers would be a good fit and will usually assign someone accordingly. Also, the officer will feel more pressure to serve you well if he or she has been assigned by a boss. This is a much better tactic than trying to simply befriend a random officer.

One final tip about getting a police liaison: unfortunately (for you), the best police officers get promoted quickly. If you find a good officer and he or she gets promoted, ask for an introduction from that person to someone else who can be your main contact. You are more likely to get introduced to an equally good officer.

Tool: The Lawyer Repellent Spray

It is important for libraries to protect everyone's access to them. Sometimes when you fail, lawyers and courts intervene.

Kreimer v. Morristown (1991)

Richard Kreimer, a 42-year-old homeless man, was a problem patron for the Morristown (New Jersey) library. He was kicked out repeatedly for staring at patrons, following patrons around, speaking loudly/belligerently, and smelling very bad. He sued.

The library lost the case at the trial court, with the judge saying, "If we wish to shield our eyes and noses from the homeless, we should revoke their condition, not their library cards." The appellate court overturned the trial court, ruling in favor of the library—but not before the library's insurance company had settled for $80,000.

Armstrong v. District of Columbia Public Library (2001)

Richard Armstrong tried to enter the Martin Luther King Memorial Library in Washington, DC, one February afternoon. A security guard stopped him, saying that he needed to "clean up" before he could come in. Ultimately, the court held that the library's policy against "objectionable appearance" was unconstitutional because it was too vague.

This book is not a legal treatise, so I won't go in depth into the liability from homeless patrons. I will share this, though, from Mary Minow, a lawyer-librarian (how cool is that?), who offers the acronym FEND for keeping the lawyers away:

- *First Amendment* = Libraries must protect the right of free speech.
- *Equal Enforcement* = Policies must be applied consistently.
- *Notice* = All policies should be clearly posted or distributed.
- *Due Process* = A well-defined appeals process must be available to patrons who challenge policies.

Predicament: A Patron Brings a Pet into the Library

It is a pleasant Saturday morning in late spring. Sunlight streams into the windows on the east side of the library, where people have naturally clustered. Families and college students are strolling around the library amiably with books under their arms. This is the kind of day that makes your heart glad that you became a librarian.

Your bliss is interrupted by a strange noise. It doesn't sound like a book and it doesn't sound like a person. It doesn't sound like it belongs in a library. Maybe one of the children has turned the volume up on a computer. You follow the source of the noise and discover a woman with a large cat that smells of urine. As you approach the woman, she immediately shouts, "My Chester is a service animal. I have rights! If you say anything I can sue you!"

Your great day is officially over.

What do you do?

Empathy-Driven Enforcement Method

Before I tell you what to do, I need to give you a disclaimer: While I am a lawyer, I don't offer this section as legal advice. Your state might have more restrictive laws than the federal government, or federal rules could have changed. If you don't live in the United States, I have absolutely no idea what your laws are. With this disclaimer firmly in place, let me tell you what the Department of Justice says.

• • •

In 2010 the U.S. Justice Department issued long-overdue guidance on service animals. Here are the basics:

- The only two animals that qualify as service animals are dogs and miniature horses. This isn't a typo or a joke. Apparently miniature horses are excellent at providing support for people who are unsteady when they walk. This means that cats, ferrets, iguanas, hamsters, and goldfish can never be service animals (not even if they are wearing one of those cute little vests that says otherwise).
- The only time an "emotional support" animal qualifies is if it is for PTSD. But if your dog, Puddles, helps calm your social anxiety, that doesn't count.
- Service dogs must either be on a leash or under control. If a leash or harness would impede the dog from doing its job, the owner can control it with verbal commands.
- There are two—*and only two*—questions that you may ask of the owner:
    - "Is the dog required because of a disability?"
    - "What work or task has the dog been trained to perform?"
- You may *not*
    - Ask about the person's disability
    - Require documentation, certification, or identification
    - Ask the dog to demonstrate its skill

What if the dog (or horse) is a problem? Well, there are guidelines for that, too:

- You may *not* exclude the dog because someone is afraid of dogs.
- You may *not* exclude the dog because someone has allergies.
- You *may* exclude the dog if it is not under control.
- You *may* exclude the dog if it is not house-broken.
- If you exclude the dog, you must allow the owner to stay or return without the dog.

You can get the full text of the Justice Department guidelines at www.ada.gov/service_animals_2010.htm.

Additional Effective Tools for This Predicament

- The Homeless Golden Rule (page 86)
- The Fight and the Flight (page 97)
- The Parent Trap (page 120)
- The Lawyer Repellant Spray (page 221)

Predicament: A Non-Homeless Patron Is Complaining

"This is ridiculous," a man blurts out as he shuffles towards you. "I pay taxes and I can't even use the library. It is completely overrun with the homeless. You need to get them out of here. If you can't fix this, I'm calling the mayor!" It wasn't a question, but he stares at you, waiting for an answer anyway.

What do you do?

Empathy-Driven Enforcement Method

Working at a large shelter for most of my career, I have heard a *lot* of complaints about homeless individuals from non-homeless individuals. Sometimes the complaints are totally valid, and sometimes they are utterly ridiculous. I once had a guy at a "neighborhood meeting" shout at me for fifteen minutes. The essence of his complaint was that it was unfair that he had to "see those people." Some individuals feel that they are entitled to never witness the effects of poverty. I don't have a lot of sympathy for them.

My advice for dealing with ornery non-homeless individuals is as follows:

- Listen without agreeing or disagreeing. I usually just quietly listen until they get bored and move on. It is easier than fighting and usually more effective. Most people eventually realize (without being told) that they are being ridiculous. When you challenge them, though, they dig into their position even stronger. It might make you feel good to "defend" homeless people, but it doesn't actually change the person's mind. See the Michael Jordan (page 81).

- Here are a few phrases that work well: "We take the needs of *all* of our patrons seriously, regardless of their socioeconomic status." "Thank you for your concern. We have the situation under control," or "We are keeping an eye on the situation."

Similarly, many individuals feel that homeless individuals are not entitled to the same level of confidentiality as everyone else. They will ask prying and inappropriate questions about homeless individuals that they would never ask about someone else. My advice:

- Maintain as much confidentiality for homeless patrons as you would for non-homeless patrons. If a pregnant woman or elderly patron had a "bladder accident," you wouldn't share that news with a stranger who asked. Provide the same level of respect and dignity to your homeless patrons in the same situation.
- If a person is prying for details, hint that there is "more to the story" than is obvious (even if there isn't) and then stop the conversation.
- My favorite phrase: "It would really not be appropriate for me to talk about other patrons."

Additional Effective Tools for This Predicament
- The Pool Shot (page 98)
- The Stick and the Stone (page 82)
- The Goldilocks (page 103)
- The Bill Clinton (page 108)
- The Oprah (page 116)
- The Wizard of Oz (page 118)

Conclusion

It is hard to be a manager or leader on a good day. On a bad day—when the staff are freaking out and the community is making threats—leadership seems downright impossible. To steal a line from the poem "If" by Rudyard Kipling: "If you can keep your head when all about you / Are losing theirs and blaming it on you," then you just might be able to have a huge impact on the community. This world desperately needs your leadership. Teach your staff empathy. Teach your staff empathy-driven enforcement. Help the community to have a greater appreciation for the most vulnerable members. Thank you for shouldering the burden of leadership!

Note

1. Reuters, "Americans Know Big Macs Better Than Ten Commandments," www.reuters.com/article/us-bible-commandments-idUSN1223894020071012.

How Best to Help
Homeless Patrons

17

"So you're a librarian."
His eyes shifted back and forth.
"I prefer loremaster."

—BRANDON MULL[1]

From Jennifer Slone, public services coordinator at the Garnet A. Wilson Public Library of Pike County (Ohio):

> There is a homeless shelter right across the highway from my library. During the day, the shelter residents are made to leave the shelter to go out in search of work, homes, etc. Every day, they come to the library to do just that.
>
> A little over a year ago, a resident came in who was a victim of domestic abuse. She was meek and afraid to ask for anything, and I sensed this. One day, when she was wandering around the library, I asked her if she was looking for anything in particular. She confided in me that she didn't know where to start. She suffered from extremely low self-confidence, under the weight of everything else on her plate.
>
> So that's where we started. I helped her obtain books on self-confidence, attachment disorders, and domestic abuse. Once she had those for a while, she came back asking for help developing a résumé. She wasn't quite ready to pursue a job on her own just yet, but she expressed that it was kind of like a carrot. If she saw the résumé, the possibility of finding a job and creating a life on her own became more real.
>
> A few weeks later, after cycling through many self-help books and with our guidance searching for the kinds of jobs available in our area, she asked for help applying for jobs online. That proved somewhat fruitless, but after a bit more encouragement, I talked her into walking in to

some of the local businesses and inquiring about job opportunities. In a sleepy town like ours, word-of-mouth and direct human contact are often preferred.

Soon after that day, I realized that this lady had no longer been coming into the library. I hadn't seen her for a few days, then a couple weeks, then over a month. I wondered what happened to her, and hoped that she had found some sort of resolution/improvement in her situation.

And then, one morning, I opened our local newspaper, and there she was, in a photo of our local Walmart handing over a donation to a community organization. She was a Walmart employee, she had a huge smile on her face, full of confidence, and she was paying it forward. I knew then that I was in the right place, and that public librarianship was one of the most rewarding things I could have done with MY life. And I help countless people like that every day!

• • •

This Chapter Is a Little Different

Most of this book is about how to handle problems with difficult homeless patrons. This chapter is about how to help them. Before I tell you how to be most helpful, I need to share with you a few general pointers...

Don't Expect a Miracle

I don't say this to be cynical, but do not expect a miracle. You aren't going to change the trajectory of every homeless patron's life. This isn't because libraries aren't powerful. It is because homelessness is a *very* complicated and deep problem that requires a lot of assistance.

Know your limits. Your job is not to solve their problems. Like any other patron, your job is to help them find resources to solve their own problems. Celebrate the small victories and take the (frequent) defeats in stride.

New staff at Hesed House frequently invest a massive amount of emotional energy into "saving" a resident. More often than not the significant attention is enough for the person to get better for a few days or a week. Usually, though, the homeless individual backslides and the staff member is left bewildered and angry. Many staff members have quit after growing frustrated because "they don't want help." They fail to recognize the complexity and depth of the problem, thinking that they can step in and solve a long-standing problem with a little tender loving care.

If you want to help homeless patrons for decades, you need to protect yourself from the deep disappointment that comes from unrealistic expectations.

Don't Be Surprised by a Miracle

Don't expect a miracle, but don't be surprised by one either. I have learned to never ever *ever* write off anyone (ever!). Just when I think that someone is completely beyond all hope, something happens and the person finds sobriety, then a job, then a home. The human spirit is a mysterious and miraculous thing. While you cannot expect a miracle every time you help a homeless individual, if you help enough, you will eventually see one!

The Effect of September 11 on Homelessness

Imagine that someone stole every form of identification you have. They took your driver's license, social security card, birth certificate, and passport. You drive down to the local Department of Motor Vehicles to get a new driver's license. They ask to see your Social Security card. No big deal. You drive over to the local Social Security office. They ask to see your driver's license.

Uh-oh! Where the heck do you start?

It didn't used to be this hard. Everything changed on September 11, 2001. New security protocols have made it *much* harder to get an ID if you don't already have one. Many homeless people have lost all forms of identification in an eviction or subsequent theft. Case managers in homeless shelters spend an enormous amount of time getting the necessary documents in order to prove a person's identity. It isn't easy, even when it is your job to help people get an ID.

Please remember this the next time you tell someone to "just come back with an ID."

How to Help

Okay, now that we have these introductory concepts in place, let me tell you how you can best help homeless patrons. I get this question a lot in live trainings and my advice is always the same. There are eight things you can do to help:

1. *Respect, Dignity, Humanity*

   Actually, if I was making a list of things library staff could do to help homeless patrons, it would have 1,008 things on it and the first one through 1,000 would be to "treat homeless patrons with respect, dignity, and humanity." I'm not being trite. It really is the most important thing you can do for homeless patrons, *by a wide margin.*

Homeless individuals are treated so infrequently with respect, dignity, and humanity that they absolutely crave it. Remember what that crazy little nun from Calcutta said: "Being unwanted, unloved, uncared for, forgotten by everybody, I think that is a much greater hunger, a much greater poverty than the person who has nothing to eat." This isn't just a pretty meme to post on your Facebook page. It is also true! It is really easy to get free food in the United States. It is relatively easy to get free shelter. Obtaining dignity and your humanity, though, are much harder when you have no money.

Furthermore, when you say "Good morning, Joe" to a regular homeless patron, you may be helping him get a job and a home, even if you don't realize it. It is almost impossible for a person to get a job if he has no self-worth left. When you treat a homeless patron like he is worthy of your respect, you help him to feel worthy of respect. And that shows through in an interview.

Many a homeless person has found the courage to reach for a better life because of the simplest kindness bestowed by a stranger. Remember this when you are tempted to roll your eyes in frustration. A smile really can change the world.

2. *Be a Library*

The second most important thing you can do for homeless patrons is to simply "be a library." Help them get library cards. Help them find a book. Help them use the computers. Help them research jobs or benefits. Help them with online databases.

According to the "culture of poverty" theory, information and "know-how" are absolutely crucial for individuals to climb out of poverty. Middle-class and wealthy individuals have privately funded information at their fingertips, literally. Homeless individuals need publicly available information if they are going to have any chance in our modern economy. Oh, if only our country had public repositories of knowledge that were available to everyone, regardless of their socioeconomic status!

3. *Listen*

No one takes the time to listen to homeless individuals. If you take a few minutes to allow a homeless patron to share his hopes, fears, regrets, and triumphs, you will lift up his soul in ways you will never understand. Human beings crave to be heard. Human beings need to share their stories, and therein imbue them with meaning.

There is a side benefit. You will hear things that are completely outside of your world. I have heard stories from Vietnam. I have had people tell me how they got trapped in prostitution. I have learned about loves lost and businesses that crashed. People have told me about the best day of their lives and their worst. I have met people whose life stories couldn't be made into a movie because no one would believe it! And besides being really interesting, I am a fuller human being because of these stories.

4. *The Five Essential Elements*

   According to the ancient Greeks, there were five essential elements: earth, water, air, fire, and aether. The ancient Greeks were never homeless, though. Modern homeless individuals have a different five essential elements:

   Heat—I am certain that there are people who did not freeze to death because of their local library.

   Cold—Similarly, a sweltering summer can be miserable without air conditioning.

   Electricity—Where would you charge your cell phone if you had no home?

   Plumbing—Most communities have no other public restrooms except at the library.

   Wi-Fi—While not as important as the first four, Wi-Fi is increasingly important for staying connected with the world.

   Many people get frustrated with homeless individuals who aren't "using a library for what it was intended for." I think this frustration is a little misguided. Is helping a middle-aged lawyer get a free copy of the latest Grisham novel really a more important public purpose than helping someone avoid frostbite? Can't you do both?

5. *Help with Employment and E-Mail*

   There are two specific areas where libraries can be of particular help to homeless individuals: employment and e-mail. The vast majority of homeless individuals do not have a computer (for obvious reasons). Unfortunately, it is really hard to get a job without computer access. You can only apply for many minimum-wage jobs online. Furthermore, you have to have an e-mail address (that you check regularly) in order to find out if you have an interview. Libraries—and their computers—are an invaluable resource for the unemployed.

Unfortunately, many homeless individuals simply don't have the experience with using computers to do so effectively. Your assistance can be the difference between getting a job or not (and thus getting out of homelessness or not).

6. *Specialized Programming*

Many libraries around the world are starting to add specialized programming specifically for homeless patrons. Sometimes these programs happen in the library and sometimes the library comes to the shelter (or street). For a lengthy list of examples from other libraries to inspire you, see www.homelesslibrary.com/inspiration. Here are a few generic pieces of advice, though:

- You don't have to design programs specifically for homeless patrons. Go out of your way to include them in your "normal" programs.

- Make sure that homeless patrons know that a program is for them. They are so used to being unwelcome that they tend to assume it. Our local library recently added a "movie day" that was designed to start after our soup kitchen ended. I announced it, but it wasn't until I said, "The library added this specifically for residents of Hesed House" that people were excited to go.

- Don't bother advertising a program far in advance. It is only the advertising you do in the last 24–48 hours that matters. The lives of homeless individuals are far too chaotic for them to routinely plan much further than that. Remember from chapter 2 the discussion about homeless individuals having a shortened time horizon.

- Make sure programs are "self-contained." If a program continues over multiple weeks or days, a person should be able to start and stop anywhere in the process. Homeless individuals' lives are too chaotic to reliably do a multi-week program. Also, people are entering and leaving homelessness constantly.

- Have food, if you can. More people will come. This is true with homeless patrons, college students, and pretty much everybody else, too.

- If a program is going to be after 6:00 p.m., coordinate with the local shelter. Homeless individuals simply don't have the luxury of an evening program if it means when the program ends, it will be too late for them to get into the shelter. Similarly, don't schedule a program at lunchtime unless you are going to feed participants. Homeless patrons won't come. The best time to schedule a program is first thing in the morning (most shelters close at 7:00 a.m.) or in the late afternoon (most shelters open at 7:00 p.m.).

- Experiment. Just because your first few programs bomb doesn't mean that homeless people aren't interested. You may just not have hit on the right topic (or you might have offered it at a bad time).

7. *Advocacy and Awareness*

Your library can put on programs to educate the community and push for systemic change. The Poudre River Library District (Fort Collins, Colorado) ran a photo exhibit of homeless individuals. The Free Library of Philadelphia ran an exhibit of art and stories featuring homeless individuals. The Berkeley Public Library (which has a "Homeless Task Force") has done panel discussions.

For a list of examples from other libraries to inspire you, see www.homelesslibrary.com/inspiration.

8. *Referrals to Local Resources*

Have you ever had a patron ask about where to go for food, shelter, or counseling?

Some libraries have created a quick flier (or card) to hand out that provides information on local resources. For example, Baltimore County partnered with the Baltimore Coalition for the Homeless to produce "street cards" that can be handed out at library branches.

Here is my advice:

- Ask for help. A local shelter or other social service agency will be able to assemble the information faster (and with more accuracy).

- Don't get hung up on every single possible service available. It is better to get the basics than to spend years in development.

- Don't forget services for non-homeless people. In reality, homeless individuals have better access to information than their "merely poor" counterparts because homeless people share information among themselves. The non-homeless patrons need resource guides more.

For a template and examples, go to www.homesslibrary.com/card.

Predicament: You Want to Hire a Social Worker

It is your favorite time of year! No, not Christmas. It is your state's library association conference. You get to hang out with "your people" and talk libraries for days at a time.

After a particularly titillating discussion of "festschrifts," you grab a coffee with some colleagues. The conversation shifts to homeless patrons:

Librarian Sally: Our social worker just quit. I hope we get a new one quickly.

Librarian Steve: Oh, that is horrible! I can't even imagine functioning without a social worker!

You: You have a social worker at your library?

Sally: Of course! Don't you?

Steve: Yeah, all the cool libraries are doing it!

You: Ummmm...no...

Sally: Come on, Steve, let's go find somewhere else to sit.

You are now a pariah shunned by your peers because your library does not have a social worker.

What do you do?

Empathy-Driven Enforcement Method

One of the biggest trends in libraryland in the last decade has been hiring social workers. *I would recommend against it.*

It's not that libraries shouldn't have social workers. There is a better way, though.

A social worker in isolation at a library will not be as effective as a social worker connected to another organization. If I ran a library and I had enough money to hire a social worker, I would contract with a local homeless shelter (or other social service agency) to provide a social worker for my library. Here's why:

Question: How do I ask someone if he or she is homeless?

Answer: You don't need to ask. If they need help related to housing, they will tell you. If they don't ask for help, then their homelessness isn't relevant. Think of it this way: if a heavyset man came into your library, would you ask him if he had diabetes?

- The other agency knows what credentials to look for when hiring a social worker. You probably do not.
- A social worker who is part of a team of other social workers can tap into the expertise of peers (even if those peers are in a different location). A social worker in isolation will be less effective.
- The other agency will know if the social worker is doing a bad job, violating ethics rules, or possibly even breaking the law. You may not.
- The other agency will care about what happens at the library more if they have staff with you. Partnerships create allies.

You don't necessarily need to spend money, though, to have services at your library. Consider partnering with other organizations to provide periodic programming in your library. Consider the following examples:

- The Anchorage Public Library partners with a local social work school to have a social work intern at the library.
- The Cincinnati Public Library has invited social workers to set up an office on-site, providing counseling that targets individuals struggling with addiction.
- San Jose hosts "lawyers in the library" nights where individuals can get free 20-minute legal consultations.
- Salt Lake City has used full-time outreach workers from Volunteers of America.

For a fuller list of examples to inspire you, see www.homelesslibraries.com/inspiration.

Additional Effective Tools for This Predicament
- The Amigo (page 184)
- The Anti-Procrastinator (page 174)

Conclusion

Serving homeless patrons can be some of the most gratifying work you do as a librarian. Because their needs are so much greater than the average patron, the opportunities to change a life are proportionately greater too. The trick is in your orientation to miracles. Do not expect them, but always work towards them. In such humble ways, the world has been changed.

Note
1. Brandon Mull, *A World Without Heroes* (New York: Aladdin, 2012).

Conclusion

The End of Homelessness

We have the librarians on our side. We have justice on our side.
—Polly Shulman, *The Wells Bequest*

I haul my body up onto the roof of Hesed House. It was much easier to get up on the roof when I was twenty-one years old. Before we took it over, the building was an old, massive city incinerator. The flat roof is covered in gravel and makes a satisfying crunching sound as I walk across it. There are several soccer balls up here (no surprise) and a pink teddy bear with matted fur (a bit of a surprise). I walk carefully up to the edge of the roof and look down at the yard below.

It is a beautiful June day. The grass is recently cut (I love that smell). Two dozen children run around with their parents in bathing suits, playing with kiddie pools and slip-and-slides. A half-dozen staff mill about, pulling up swim trunks that are too large and handing out bubble wands. A boy of about twelve complains that the younger kids dumped their bubbles in the pool. To make his point, he purses his lips and blows a bubble. It floats away, much to the astonishment of staff.

The children are genuinely happy. They smile and laugh and play, just as all kids do. Some of them are too young to realize they are homeless. The older ones seem to have forgotten for the afternoon. The parents—faces weary—have genuine smiles too. Suddenly, a toddler manages to wriggle out of his swim diaper and is evading his mother by darting around erratically. The older kids giggle and point. The adults chuckle.

Seeing homeless children playing always fills me with conflicting emotions. I am glad that these children are safe and happy (the wonderful staff and volunteers at Hesed House make sure of that). But "homeless" and "child" are two words that should never go together.

Actually, "homeless" is a word that shouldn't even exist.

Hesed House gets a new homeless individual showing up at our doors every 8.5 hours (on average). This means that we have to help someone get out of homelessness every 8.5 hours, just to keep our numbers constant. Some days it feels like running up a down escalator.

But there is progress. I can feel it and the nightly count confirms my intuition. There are less homeless individuals in our community this year than last year. And last year was better than the year before. In fact, we have been steadily reducing the number of homeless individuals in our community for the last decade or so. By my rough calculations, if we can keep this up, we will completely end homelessness in our community about the time I'm too old to work. I hope I get the opportunity to turn out the lights for the last time when we shut down the organization.

I can picture a day when I'm sitting on my rocking chair with my great-grandson on my lap. He'll ask me, "Papa, tell me about Hesed House." I'll say, "There used to be these places called 'homeless shelters' where people would go if they had no home and no food. But that was a long time ago, before you were born…"

• • •

I have one final homelessness myth for you:

Myth: Homelessness Is Unsolvable

Don't believe the cynics. We can end homelessness in our country.

Homelessness is not inevitable. It did not always exist. The current phenomenon of homelessness, as we understand it today, did not exist until about forty years ago. Don't believe me? Very few shelters existed before 1980; now they're everywhere. Homelessness is a very modern invention, and is the confluence of bad policies and shifting societal attitudes about family responsibility. If we can create homelessness in a matter of decades, is it really absurd to think that we can't end it in the same amount of time?

The End of This Book

My greatest hope for this book is that it will be rendered irrelevant by the absence of homeless individuals left to go to libraries (just as my greatest hope for Hesed House is to shut down). Until that day, though, keep being a superhero for your homeless patrons. Keep believing that everyone deserves dignity. Keep believing that a better world is possible. And when your heart grows weary, find strength in some ancient Jewish wisdom that helps me get through the dark nights of my soul:

"Do not be daunted by the enormity of the world's grief.
Do justly now.
Love mercy now.
Walk humbly now.
You are not obligated to complete the work,
but neither are you free to abandon it."

Peace,
Ryan Dowd
Aurora, Illinois (June 2017)

Appendix

Key Phrases

It is helpful to have specific phrases you can use whenever a situation arises. If you use the same phrase every time, you won't mess up when you are tired or stressed. I offer these as examples, but feel free to develop your own.

1. You want to ask someone to speak more quietly:

   "Would you mind turning down the volume a notch or two?" (while turning an imaginary dial in the air).

   "Would you mind speaking more quietly? My ears are very sensitive."

2. You want to ask someone's name without being pushy:

   "Hi. I'm Ryan. I didn't catch your name."

   "Hi. My name is Ryan. What is yours?"

3. You want to use someone's name without them thinking you are Big Brother:

   "Good afternoon. It's 'Bob,' right?"

   "Good morning. Wait. Don't tell me. You are 'Susan,' right?"

4. You want to tell someone they are breaking a rule without making them defensive:

   "You probably didn't realize we have a rule about this, but…"

   "I'm sure you didn't know, but…"

5. You want to do the Bad Cop (page 128):

   "I would let you do that, but the boss would probably fire me."

   "I would let you do that, but the Board of Directors is really picky about that rule."

"I would let you do that, but the bosses are really cracking down on that one."

6. You want to do the Mirror (page 117) for active listening:

"I think what I heard you say, was ..."

"If I'm understanding you correctly ..."

"Now, correct me if I'm wrong, but I think you feel that ..."

"Let me be sure that I understand you. ..."

7. You want to do the Jerry Seinfeld (page 100) to escape a close talker:

"I'm going to take a step back. I forgot deodorant today."

"Do you mind if we talk from a little farther back? I had a lot of garlic for lunch."

8. You want to do the Sad Librarian (page 129) to show that you do not enjoy using your authority on homeless individuals.

"I don't like enforcing the rules, but I have to."

"If you don't stop that, I'll have to ask you to leave and I don't want to do that because you are a fellow Stephen King fan."

9. Someone asks you why you don't allow sleeping in the library.

"We have had people with medical conditions, so we ask everyone to stay awake so we know they are okay."

"We have had people snore really badly, which disturbs other patrons, so we ask everyone to stay awake."

10. Someone asks you why you don't allow multiple large bags in the library.

"We have limited space, so the board passed a rule to make sure that everyone has space."

"The lawyers are really worried about people are tripping over bags. We always listen to the lawyers."

11. Someone brought in a pet and you want to verify if it is a service animal.

"Is your dog required because of a disability?"

"What work or task has the dog been trained to do?"

There are no other legal questions!

12. A non-homeless patron is complaining.

    "We take the needs of all of our patrons seriously, regardless of their socioeconomic status."

    "Thank you for your concern. We have the situation under control."

    "Thank you for your concern. We are keeping an eye on the situation."

13. A non-homeless patron is being nosy.

    "It would really not be appropriate for me to talk about other patrons."

Index